World Cinema On Demand

World Cinema On Demand

Global Film Cultures in the Era of Online Distribution

Edited by
Stefano Baschiera and Alexander Fisher

BLOOMSBURY ACADEMIC
NEW YORK • LONDON • OXFORD • NEW DELHI • SYDNEY

BLOOMSBURY ACADEMIC
Bloomsbury Publishing Inc
1385 Broadway, New York, NY 10018, USA
50 Bedford Square, London, WC1B 3DP, UK
29 Earlsfort Terrace, Dublin 2, Ireland

BLOOMSBURY, BLOOMSBURY ACADEMIC and the Diana logo are trademarks of Bloomsbury Publishing Plc

First published in the United States of America 2022
Paperback edition published 2023

Volume Editor's Part of the Work © Stefano Baschiera and Alexander Fisher
Each chapter © of Contributors

For legal purposes the Acknowledgements on p. xii constitute an extension of this copyright page.

Cover image © Paul Vensth / Unsplash.com

All rights reserved. No part of this publication may be reproduced or transmitted in any form or by any means, electronic or mechanical, including photocopying, recording, or any information storage or retrieval system, without prior permission in writing from the publishers.

Bloomsbury Publishing Inc does not have any control over, or responsibility for, any third-party websites referred to or in this book. All internet addresses given in this book were correct at the time of going to press. The author and publisher regret any inconvenience caused if addresses have changed or sites have ceased to exist, but can accept no responsibility for any such changes.

Library of Congress Cataloging-in-Publication Data
Names: Baschiera, Stefano, 1977– editor. | Fisher, Alexander (Lecturer in film studies), editor.
Title: World cinema on demand : global film cultures in the eras of online distribution / edited by Stefano Baschiera and Alexander Fisher.
Description: New York : Bloomsbury Academic, 2022. | Includes bibliographical references and index. |
Identifiers: LCCN 2021052338 (print) | LCCN 2021052339 (ebook) | ISBN 9781501348594 (hardback) | ISBN 9781501392399 (paperback) | ISBN 9781501348600 (epub) | ISBN 9781501348617 (pdf) | ISBN 9781501348624
Subjects: LCSH: Motion pictures–Distribution–Case studies. | Video-on-demand–Case studies. | Streaming video–Case studies. | Television broadcasting–Case studies. | International broadcasting–Case studies.
Classification: LCC PN1995.9.D57 W67 2022 (print) | LCC PN1995.9.D57 (ebook) | DDC 384/.809051–dc23/eng/20220224
LC record available at https://lccn.loc.gov/2021052338
LC ebook record available at https://lccn.loc.gov/2021052339

ISBN: HB: 978-1-5013-4859-4
PB: 978-1-5013-9239-9
ePDF: 978-1-5013-4861-7
eBook: 978-1-5013-4860-0

Typeset by Newgen KnowledgeWorks Pvt. Ltd., Chennai, India

To find out more about our authors and books visit www.bloomsbury.com and sign up for our newsletters.

Contents

List of figures   vii
List of contributors   viii
Acknowledgements   xii

Introduction   1
   Stefano Baschiera and Alexander Fisher

Part 1   The limits of disintermediation: Problems of gatekeeping

1   Shifting gatekeepers: Power and influence in informal online film distribution   15
   Virginia Crisp
2   Cinephile file-sharing: Informal distribution, plural canons and digital film archives   31
   Angela Meili
3   Bridges, streams and dams: The multiple negotiated strategies of distribution and access in Latin American cinema   47
   Niamh Thornton

Part 2   Streaming in national and transnational contexts

4   Netflix in Europe: The national in global subscription video on demand (SVOD) services   69
   Stefano Baschiera and Valentina Re
5   Danmaku commenting: A new interaction experience on China's streaming platforms   89
   Yuanyuan Chen and Rebecca Crawford
6   Turkish online film distribution: Fighting for Indie filmmaking in a neoliberal and censored context   109
   Murat Akser

7 India's online streaming revolution: Global over-the-top (OTT) platforms, film spectatorship and the ecosystem of Indian cinemas   125
Nandana Bose

Part 3   Global transformations – Case study: Africa

8 Curating Africa online: The impact of digital technology on the consumption of African audiovisual content   151
Justine Atkinson and Lizelle Bisschoff

9 Reset mode: African digital video films as expanded cinema   171
Sheila Petty

10 Netflix and Africa: Streaming, branding and tastemaking in non-domestic African film markets   189
Alexander Fisher

Index   205

Figures

5.1 Commenters confess and use danmaku to make colourful shooting stars in honour of the meteor in the film *Your Name* 102
5.2 Chuuya's (中也) name fills the screen in *Bungo Stray Dogs Dead Apple* 103
5.3 Inverted cross symbol 104
5.4 Inverted cross danmaku in *Bungo Stray Dogs Dead Apple* 104
7.1 Netflix's first original series, *Sacred Games*, on a billboard 138

Contributors

Murat Akser is Lecturer and Course Director in Cinematic Arts at the University of Ulster, UK. Previously he served as a Professor of Cinema and Media Studies, the chair of the New Media Department and the founding director of the Cinema and Television MA programme at Kadir Has University, Istanbul, Turkey. He received his MA degree in Cinema and Media Studies and his PhD in Communication and Culture from York University, Canada. His research focuses on the history and aesthetics of Turkish cinema, film genres and transnational cinemas. His most recent book is *Alternative Media in Contemporary Turkey* (2019).

Justine Atkinson is a PhD candidate at the University of Glasgow. She is the founder and director of Aya Films, an international distribution company with a focus on African cinema. She worked as the Festival Producer of the Africa in Motion Film Festival between 2013 and 2019. Her PhD research focuses on collaborative film curation.

Stefano Baschiera is Senior Lecturer in Film Studies at Queen's University Belfast. His work on European cinema, material culture and film industries has been published in a variety of edited collections and journals including *Film International*, *Bianco e Nero*, *New Review of Film and Television Studies* and *NECSUS: European Journal of Media Studies*. He is the co-editor of *Italian Horror Cinema* (with Rus Hunter) and of *Cinema and Domestic Space* (with Miriam De Rosa).

Lizelle Bisschoff is Senior Lecturer in Film and Television Studies at the University of Glasgow, UK. She is a researcher and curator of African film, and founder of the Africa in Motion (AiM) Film Festival, an annual African film festival taking place in Scotland, inaugurated in 2006. She holds a PhD in African cinema from the University of Stirling in Scotland, in which she researched the role of women in African film. She has published widely on sub-Saharan African cinema and regularly attends African film festivals worldwide as speaker and jury member. In her current role at Glasgow, she teaches African cinema and continues her research on classic and contemporary African film.

Nandana Bose is an independent scholar, educator and author of the BFI Film Stars series monograph *Madhuri Dixit* (2019). A former British Chevening scholar at the University of Leeds, she holds a PhD degree in Film Studies from the University of Nottingham, UK, and is a former associate professor at the Department of Film Studies, University of North Carolina Wilmington, USA. She has published on Indian stardom, gender and censorship in such journals as *Cinema Journal, Feminist Media Studies, Velvet Light Trap* and *Celebrity Studies*, and in anthologies such as *Indian Film Stars: New Critical Perspectives* (2020), *Figurations in Indian Film* (2013) and *Silencing Cinema: Film Censorship around the World* (2013).

Yuanyuan Chen is Lecturer in History and Theory of Animation at the University of Ulster, UK. Her research focuses on contemporary Chinese animation, with particular interest in the influence of modernism and postmodernism on Chinese animation after the 1980s. Her broader research interests span animation theory, Asian animation, experimental animation, modernism and postmodernism, and non-fiction animation. Her articles have been published in edited books and international peer-reviewed journals, such as *Snow White and the Seven Dwarfs: New Perspectives on Production, Reception, Legacy, Modernism/Modernity, Journal of Chinese Cinemas, Alphaville: Journal of Film and Screen Media* and so on.

Rebecca Crawford is a practice-based PhD candidate in the Faculty of Arts, Humanities and Social Sciences at the University of Ulster, UK. Her interests include Japanese studies, anime, manga, Japanese video games (such as Japanese Role-Playing Games (JRPGs)), digital books, branching path and non-linear narratives, children's media and visual novels. Her publications include contributions to *Mechademia, IEEE* and *Intersections*.

Virginia Crisp is Senior Lecturer in Culture, Media and Creative Industries at King's College London. Her most recent work is the co-edited collection *Practices of Projection: Histories and Technologies* (2020). She is the author of *Film Distribution in the Digital Age: Pirates and Professionals* (2015) as well as numerous articles and book chapters on formal and informal media circulation. She is also the co-founder and director (with Gabriel Menotti Gonring) of the Besides the Screen Network (www.besidesthescreen.com) and the co-editor of *Besides the Screen: Moving Images through Promotion, Distribution and Curation* (2015).

Alexander Fisher is Senior Lecturer in Film Studies at Queen's University Belfast, where he teaches courses on world cinema and film music. His research examines the aesthetic, cultural and political aspects of international film cultures, with a particular focus on African film, alongside his work on recent transformations in international film distribution and culture. He has written extensively on African cinema, his work appearing in journals including in *Visual Anthropology*, *The Journal of African Media Studies*, *The Journal of African Cinemas*, *Music and Moving Image* and *Music, Sound, and the Moving Image*.

Angela Meili is lecturer in linguistics and Portuguese language at the State University of Paraná, Brazil. Her field of research focuses on areas related to media, technology, culture and language, in particular the uses and appropriation of communication and information tools for democratization and cultural access, including independent media, cyberactivism, cultural activism and affirmation of minority groups. She completed her PhD in social communication, in 2015, at the Pontifical Catholic University of Rio Grande do Sul, Brazil, with a thesis on circulation of cinema in BitTorrent networks, discussing piracy and cinephilia. During her PhD studies, in 2013, she worked as a visiting scholar, in Film Studies, at the University College of Cork, Ireland.

Sheila Petty is Professor of Media Studies at the University of Regina, Canada. She has written extensively on issues of cultural representation, identity and nation in African and African diasporic screen media, and has curated film, television and digital media exhibitions for galleries across Canada. She is the author of *Contact Zones: Memory, Origin and Discourses in Black Diasporic Cinema* (2008), editor of *A Call to Action: The Films of Ousmane Sembene* (1996) and co-editor of *Expressions culturelles des francophonies* (2008), *Canadian Cultural Poesis* (2006) and *Directory of World Cinema: Africa* (2015). Her current research focuses on Amazigh and North African cinemas, and issues of citizenship and immigration in French cinemas. She is currently writing a book on the Algerian feminist filmmaker, Habiba Djahnine.

Valentina Re is Full Professor of Film and Media Studies at Link Campus University, Italy. Her main research areas include film, media and literary theory; media production, distribution and consumption; film analysis and television studies. Among her publications are the books *Le belle donne ci piacciono. E come! Cinema nuovo, cultura comunista e modelli di mascolinità (1952–1958)* (2021, co-authored with E. Mandelli); *Streaming media. Distribuzione, circolazione, accesso* (2017); *Game of Thrones. Una mappa per immaginare mondi* (2017, co-edited with S. Martin); *L'innesto. Realtà e finzioni da Matrix a 1Q84* (2014, co-authored with A. Cinquegrani) and *Cominciare dalla fine. Studi su Genette e il cinema* (2012).

Niamh Thornton is Reader in Latin American Studies at the University of Liverpool, UK. She is a specialist in Mexican Film, Literature and Digital Cultures with a particular focus on War Stories, Gendered Narratives, Star

Studies, Cultures of Taste and Distributed Content. Her key research interest is in the multiple representations of conflict in literature and film. Her books include *Women and the War Story in Mexico: La novela de la Revolución* (2006) and *Revolution and Rebellion in Mexican Cinema* (2013) as well as several co-edited books, including *Revolucionarias: Gender and Revolution in Latin America* (2007), *International Perspectives on Chicana/o Studies: This World Is My Place* (2013) and *Legacies of the Past: Memory and Trauma in Mexican Visual and Screen Cultures* (2020). She recently completed a monograph on violence, curation and memorialization in Mexican film entitled *Tastemakers and Tastemaking: Mexico and Curated Screen Violence* (2020).

Acknowledgements

This edited collection is the final (and belated) outcome of the Arts and Humanities Research Council (AHRC)-funded research networking project 'World Cinema On-Demand: Film Distribution and Education in the Streaming Media Era' (March 2012–November 2013). A lot has changed since the three workshops on streaming distribution we organized in Belfast almost a decade ago, when an engagement with these matters was somehow still in its infancy, yet the principles of our inquiry remain as urgent as ever, as the internet continues to reshape the landscape of film culture.

We gratefully extend our thanks to all the participants in those events, who accepted our invitation to consider future scenarios for World Cinema as the promises of streaming technologies emerged, and who, as a result, set the premises of this volume. Among the participants were Sergio Angelini, Philippe Brodeur, Ciara Chambers, Malte Hagener, Dina Iordanova, Finola Kerrigan, Julia Knight, Paul McDonald, Lúcia Nagib, Eve Oesterlen, Alejandro Pardo, Laura Rascaroli, Karl Schoonover, Iain Robert Smith and Liam Wylie.

A sincere thanks goes to our contributors for all their hard work and enduring patience over the years. Many of them were already part of the early workshops, while others joined in the project along the way, bringing new insights and approaches as streaming distribution became an increasingly ubiquitous part of our media landscape.

Finally, a special thanks to Erin Duffy and Katie Gallof of Bloomsbury for their unfailing support as this volume reached completion.

Introduction

Stefano Baschiera and Alexander Fisher

Since the turn of the millennium, advances in online technology have transformed the circulation of film, introducing a new distribution ecology that ranges from video streaming services to informal download platforms (Lobato 2019: 7–8). Concurrently, these transformations have led to new business models, some echoing those of 'bricks-and-mortar' stores, such as the transactional video on demand (VoD) services, others offering subscription products, such as those employed by key players like Netflix, Amazon Prime Video and Mubi. In this way, the dynamic ecology of internet distribution has reshaped the circulation of feature films, bringing profound changes in the ways movies cross borders, create audiences and generate market territorialization.

In all its different shapes and forms, online distribution promises to widen the visibility, availability and, ideally, profitability of niche and marginal material, with foreign language and art-house films such as Michael Haneke's *Amour* (2012) and Alfonso Cuarón's *Roma* (2018) reaching global audiences in previously unimaginable ways, in turn promoting new kinds of archival research and cinephilia. One of the most visible examples of this may be found in the launch of The Auteurs in 2007, a global subscription video on demand (SVOD) website specializing in Art Cinema, which eventually became Mubi. Ostensibly inspired when its founder Efe Cakarel found himself unable to watch *In the Mood for Love* online at a Tokyo cafe, Mubi identified the transformative potential of streaming on the accessibility of non-mainstream movies at an early stage, particularly with regard to foreign language material and global Art Cinema. Thus, before the likes of Netflix became household names, the global spectatorship of 'World Cinema' was already firmly in the midst of its move online.

As such, these transformations were initially characterized by a kind of 'cybertopia', in which the internet offered the promise of a democratization of film circulation, where both niche and mainstream material might achieve parity of visibility and availability. Indeed, many of the early scholarly responses to these transformations underlined their disruptive role in what came to be defined as a welcomed process of disintermediation (Iordanova and Cunningham 2012; Jenkins et al. 2013). However, this emphasis on the potential disappearance of intermediaries – based on a rhetoric of unconditioned, limitless and ubiquitous content access going hand in hand with a democratization of audiovisual culture – overlooked the transformation of traditional intermediaries and the appearance of new gatekeepers. This process of reintermediation can be understood as 'a logic that involves the re-definition of market strategies, policymaking and consumption, driven by reciprocal interaction between pre-existing stakeholders (e.g. broadcasters), new players (e.g. over the top [OTT] services), supranational institutions (e.g. the EU) and end-users' (Baschiera et al. 2017: 14). It includes a wide array of business models and players, ranging from the agent aggregators to the now-dominant SVOD services, thus generating new links and connections.

The magnitude of these new intermediaries came into sharp focus in the early months of 2020, as coronavirus restrictions swept the globe, accelerating the move of cinema from traditional exhibition centres and rendering the small screen as the only available distribution outlet for new material in most parts of the world. One result of this is that the big US blockbuster releases increasingly rub shoulders with marginal and niche content, as the tech giants such as Netflix and Amazon attempt to secure the biggest releases, at the same time as lower overheads and long tail markets enable them to continually diversify their inventories. The long-term impact of these transformations on the future production and consumption of film remains to be seen, but it seems inevitable that 2020 will come to represent a transformative moment in the history of streaming distribution, rendering the last two decades as the formative era in the genesis of cinema's move online. It represents a period in which the character of online film distribution evolved from informal structures offering outlets for material that would otherwise be unable to gain a foothold in exhibition, maturing into a highly formalized, mainstream mode of film consumption in which fewer and fewer big players form the gatekeepers and beneficiaries.

However, as the case studies in this anthology demonstrate, this genesis of online distribution (as a trajectory from diverse informal practices to a monopolized, highly controlled formal structure) actually takes many different shapes and characteristics when considered at regional levels, where issues of disintermediation, gatekeeping and censorship acquire geopolitically specific characteristics that signal radically differing film cultures. Yet, the globalizing influence of online distribution provides a greater fluidity between film cultures than ever before, accelerating their cross-cultural flows. It is these specificities and interactions that form a driving factor of this anthology, bringing together diverse contributions by film and media scholars to examine World Cinema's dialogue with the transformations that have taken place over the past two decades, the contributions engaging directly with ongoing debates surrounding national cinema, transnational identity and cultural globalization, as well as ideas about genre, fandom and cinephilia. On the one hand, the contributions look at individual national patterns of online distribution, engaging with archives, SVODs and torrent communities. On the other hand, they investigate the cross-cultural presence of world cinema in non-domestic online markets (such as Europe's, for example), in particular through the streaming offerings of multinational online platforms. The chapters also aim to shed light on regionally specific issues of film circulation, consumption and preservation within a range of culturally diverse filmmaking contexts, including case studies from India, Nigeria, Ghana, Mexico and China. In this way, the collection aims to map the impact of different online distribution formats on the conceptual understanding of World Cinema, underlining the links between distribution and media provisions, as well as engaging with new forms of intermediation.

The transformative significance of streaming on film distribution has, of course, generated much scholarly interest. However, despite a rapidly building literature in the field, there remains a critical lacuna regarding the impact of streaming on the production, circulation and exhibition of World Cinema in particular, a gap which this volume seeks to address. Indeed, out of the range of recent books and edited collections that examine streaming, most are preoccupied with American and European contexts, overlooking its potentially more significant impact on the global circulation and availability of traditionally marginalized cinemas, in particular those produced in the Global South. The most recent additions to the literature include Kevin McDonald and Daniel Smith-Rowsey's volume *The Netflix Effect* (Bloomsbury, 2016), an anthology of articles examining the role of Netflix in a broad range of (principally Western) contexts, and Michael D. Smith and Rahul Telang's *Streaming, Sharing, Stealing: Big Data and the Future of Entertainment* (MIT Press, 2016), which examines how technological shifts are shaping changes in cultural production. These volumes build on a number of earlier works that lay out the foundational concepts surrounding the formative years of digital disruption, in particular notions of informal versus formal distribution, disintermediation and availability. Dina Iordanova and Stuart Cunningham's 2012 anthology *Digital Disruption: Cinema Moves On-line* (St Andrew's Film Studies, 2012) breaks some of the conceptual ground, while Ramon Lobato's *Shadow Economies of Cinema: Mapping Informal Film Distribution* (BFI, 2012) poses and develops the idea that the most accurate assessment of digital disruption's influence on film culture lies in the ways it is shaping informal practices of circulation. A growing scepticism of streaming's disintermediating potential is represented by Wheeler Winston Dixon's *Streaming: Movies, Media and Instant Access* (University Press of Kentucky, 2013), and Jon Silver and Stuart Cunningham's *Screen Distribution and the New King Kongs of the Online World* (Palgrave, 2013), which recognize the increasing power online distribution technologies have conferred on the big players in terms of determining the circulation and long-term availability of film texts.

Of the examples listed above, it is notable that only the edited collection by Iordanova and Cunningham and the volume by Lobato attempt to map – in an extensive, global way – the impact of these new technologies, while other contributions to the field tend to concentrate on the broader idea of digital disruption (especially in the US context). Much attention is given to the characteristics of different platforms, especially with regard to the dialogue between formal and informal practices. Indeed, the initial concern with informal practices has given way to an ever greater preoccupation with the roles of the new intermediaries, who take the form of the multinational tech giants, shifting the emphasis from issues of increasing diversity and visibility of texts, to concerns of expanding corporate monopoly and gatekeeping.

Another limitation in the current literature regards the focus on television and broadcast streaming, with only a few exceptions such as Lobato (2012) offering a sustained engagement with transformations in the global circulation of *film* specifically, alongside some smaller scale studies, such as those on the distribution of art film and marginal cinemas. The latter include Daniel Herbert (2011) on home viewing (of art film) generally, Anne Major (2021) on FilmStruck, Jennifer Hessler (2018) on Mubi, Alexander Fisher (2018) on M-Net's African Film Library and Moradewun Adejunmobi (2018) on the formal circulation of African film generally. Otherwise, the spotlight generally falls on the means of circulation themselves (such as YouTube, peer-to-peer (P2P) sharing, VoD platforms and the various new players such as content aggregators), rather than their impact on the cultural objects circulating. As a result, 'World Cinema' has remained largely at the periphery of these debates, despite the potential of digital disruption to transform its circulation at both regional and global levels.

Thus, our collection is unique in that it engages a range of scholars – all of whom hold significant expertise in their particular areas of World Cinema – to explore the changes to global film distribution, circulation and exhibition invoked by streaming media technologies. As demonstrated by the studies that follow, these adopt radically varying patterns within and between particular geographical regions, with the cultural impact of cinema's move online adopting very different characteristics across social, political and economic contexts. In the course of these case studies, the volume responds to a distinct lacuna surrounding the impact of multinational streaming services on the global circulation of World Cinema, complicating and amplifying issues such as transnationalism and cultural hybridity.

Indeed, positioning matters of distribution and availability at the centre of debates surrounding World Cinema aligns with some of the most crucial developments in the field, deepening our understanding of the global flow of film styles and ideas at a time when there is a growing recognition of the deficiencies inherent in the binary division of Hollywood versus 'the rest' (see Dennison and Lim 2006: 1–15; Nagib 2006: 30–7; Nagib et al. 2012: xvii–xxxii). Moreover, these new forms of distribution influence the shape and make-up of the category 'World Cinema' itself, increasing the availability of previously marginalized material at the same time as it generates new gatekeepers who, in turn, determine which texts are circulated globally (see Crisp 2018).

More specifically, the online circulation of film presents searching questions surrounding cultural specificity within the medium, such as in the ways that global SVODs can emphasize or obscure the provenance of national products. Indeed, national origin has gradually been brought to the fore, with labels such as 'Nollywood' and 'Bollywood' usurping 'World Cinema' in the categorization of content. Thus, the circulation of certain content within domestic and non-domestic markets generates tensions between the national, the transnational and the global that complicate existing notions of World Cinema as a homogenous category. This is further problematized by the expanding prominence of genres; increasingly, SVOD services have decoupled the synonymity between 'World Cinema' and 'Art Cinema', instead stressing the global presence of, for example,

'Drama', 'Action, and 'Comedy'. In organizing the seemingly endless catalogues of online platforms, genres and national labels work as metadata to feed the preference algorithms, rather than as conceptual categories for understanding cultural specificity and film flows. However, the pragmatic functions of these metadata have profound implications on the ability of certain categories of film to 'flow'; as Lobato and Ryan (2011) demonstrate with regard to Australian horror cinema, the content of the films can be dictated by its conduciveness to the systems of the key OTT players, and therefore determine its ability to travel globally.

Concurrently, this ever-increasing global flow of cinema threatens to intensify the domination of Western cultural production on global screens, as the hegemony of Hollywood is able to extend and reify its global reach, exacerbating the culturally imperialist 'one-way-flow' model of distribution. As Lobato points out regarding Netflix's catalogues at a local level, 'relatively few Netflix catalogs – especially those of small, minor-language markets – actually offer 20% local content from the country in question' (2019: 135). Yet, much of this local content is also cheap-to-license for global circulation, offering an incentive for distribution to diasporic and other niche markets beyond its countries of origin. Thus, orthodox models of flow – organized around notions of cultural imperialism – are coming under increasing pressure as they are disrupted by technological developments that generate new ways of shaping intra- and international content circulation. As Lobato goes on to argue, the algorithm filtering ability of sites such as Netflix means they possess a unique ability to combine local and global content, blurring the boundaries of 'local/global dialectics' (2019: 160).

In view of the problems outlined above, the studies in this book collectively address three main strands. Firstly, the contributions provide a historical approach to World Cinema's transformations in the face of streaming distribution, reflecting on the outcomes of these changes, as opposed to speculating on where they might lead. Secondly, many of the studies interrogate the rhetoric of disintermediation that characterized the early period of online cinema. This is a particularly pressing issue in relation to World Cinema specifically, which theoretically has much to gain from democratized film distribution structures. Thirdly, the case studies reframe what are becoming familiar debates surrounding online distribution in co-national and transnational contexts.

The chapters are presented in three main parts, the first of which interrogates the issue of disintermediation and its promise of a democratization of film culture, demonstrating some of the ways in which new gatekeepers have emerged to produce new forms of intermediation. Both Virginia Crisp and Angela Meilli address aspects of this issue in relation to the power dynamics at play in informal networks, in particular the apparently democratized, crowd-sourced world of P2P sharing. Crisp emphasizes the role of both formal and informal gatekeepers here, the business strategies of the former determining, in part, what is available in the latter. Focusing on the underground distribution community 'The Scene' as well as filesharing communities, Crisp demonstrates the influence of formal gatekeepers in determining the 'hierarchies of visibility and access' that are reproduced in the informal context, undermining the illusion of disintermediation that surrounds these channels.

Meilli's chapter focuses on 'tastemaking' and the 'cultural perception' of film through P2P's ability to imbue cinema with a greater 'heterogeneity' and 'connectivity' that operates outside of governmental or commercial power structures. Focusing on Brazilian sharing groups, the study demonstrates how these informal structures generate their own film canons around particular forms of collective cinephilia. Meilli argues that this scenario is ultimately shaped through a collaborative structure involving technology and users that creates 'a collective power over a specific cultural or social demand'. Thus, even without the influence of formal gatekeepers identified by Crisp, P2P networks generate their own forms of gatekeeping and tastemaking through their collectively generated power structures.

The issue of reintermediation is further examined by Niamh Thornton (within the context of formal distribution) through an analysis of Latin American cinema's availability in Ireland and the UK, as it begins to emerge on platforms such as Netflix and Mubi around the period of 2012–14. These platforms offer not only opportunities ('bridges') but also hindrances ('dams'), the latter often taking the forms of geo-blocking and curatorial biases. Thornton's snapshot of a particular, early point in the emergence of streaming demonstrates the tendency of 'flows and blockages' to repeat and amplify themselves in a myriad of new ways, perennially raising questions for the future of research into both World Cinema generally, as well as Latin American cinema specifically, from a non-domestic perspective.

The contributions to Part 2 examine the impact of streaming in national and transnational contexts, exploring the ways that specific political and cultural structures shape – and are shaped by – the transformative potential of digital disruption. Stefano Baschiera and Valentina Re's chapter engages with the role played by the categories of national cinema in global SVOD services, and how it impacts the understanding of European cinema. The ubiquitous presence of Netflix in the European market poses new questions pertaining to the availability and discoverability of European productions. The former leads to an understanding of the national from a production perspective, taking into account the implementation of new protectionist measures and cultural policies. The latter dictates, instead, a consumer-based approach, treating the concept of the national as metadata feeding the algorithms that underly the organization of Netflix's online catalogue. By looking at the presence of Italian cinema on Netflix's UK site, the chapter reflects on these shifting ideas of the national, and considers how the global 'Netflix-as-brand' strategy prevails over 'nation-as-brand' strategies.

Yuanyuan Chen and Rebecca Crawford's study examines issues surrounding spectator engagement in relation to 'Danmaku commenting', which facilitates the sharing of time-synchronized onscreen comments, and which has become a common and popular functionality on Chinese VoD sites. This new interaction of spectatorship blurs the line between cinema and social media, allowing users to engage in a virtual collective viewing experience, repositioning ideas about national film culture within postmodern notions of interactivity and internet culture.

The sheer complexity of streaming's disruptive elements is vividly illustrated by Nandana Bose's analysis of OTT platforms within the 'Indian cinema ecosystem', whose exponential rise in demand is rapidly forming a bubble. Yet, the big players have struggled to establish a 'membership mind-set' in the country, maintaining a uniquely heterogeneous (though congested) OTT market that has thus far resisted the monopolizing influence of the likes of Netflix and Amazon.

In stark contrast to the neoliberal system of film culture invoked by streaming in India, Murat Akser examines its impact on Turkish Indie productions in the context of governmental control and censorship, which is exercised over both formal and informal channels in the region. Whereas India has witnessed a rapid expansion of its OTT market, Turkish online distribution has emerged at a considerably slower pace, utilizing technologies to maintain an orthodox gatekeeping structure through which the transformative potential of online cinema has only gradually emerged.

The remaining chapters, which form Part 3, are all devoted to aspects of African cinemas in both domestic and non-domestic contexts. The emphasis on this continent's cinemas is born out of the fact that African filmmakers have typically had to be more creative when finding ways of distributing their work (as well as producing it). Indeed, as several scholars have pointed out, domestic industries such as Nollywood were disintermediated even before the arrival of streaming, with distribution occurring through informal circulation (Bisschoff 2017: 262; Lobato 2010: 338). Thus, the contributions to this final section map a particularly complex set of distribution practices and their cultural effects.

The section opens with Justine Atkinson and Lizelle Bisschoff's overview of streaming's impact on the domestic consumption of African films, revealing a complex interplay between formal and informal practices that has vastly extended the proliferation of domestic African cinemas beyond the oft-cited example of Nollywood, at the same time as the 'prosumption' culture generated by sites such as YouTube (which enable users to act as both producers and consumers of content) promises to challenge the traditional divide between filmmaking and spectatorship. Yet, as the authors point out, the 'digital divide' across the continent means that the online model is yet to become as prolific as it has elsewhere, and a continual emphasis on Nollywood production among formal platforms means that the transformative effects promised by streaming remain to be seen.

In Sheila Petty's study, the Nigerian industry is compared to those in Ghana and Burkina Faso, examining the cultural specificity that has developed in these regions' productions, as technological developments enable their industries' growth. Despite the lesser-known industries' deployments of Nollywood's commercial model, their outputs exhibit local narrative characteristics that demand a nuanced understanding of their functions within distinct film cultures. Petty situates streaming within a set of digital disruptions which intersect with ever-increasing media convergence in these regions' productions and, just as these emerging national film cultures are examined expansively, so is the issue of streaming itself, which is situated within the internet's widening of film communities through fan sites and forums. One result of these interactions is the emergence of an 'expanded cinema' formed of independent initiatives that 'explode screens' and 'saturate social space'.

Concentrating on the international distribution of African film, Alexander Fisher's chapter closes the anthology with an analysis of Netflix's inventory of African content in the context of their two recent initiatives, 'Made in Africa' and 'Made by Africans, Watched by the World'. These ventures represent two of the most promising developments for the establishment of an internationally visible and discoverable African cinema. However, Netflix's inventory homogenizes an increasingly fragmented range of content, offering a cross-section of African and Africa-related titles produced under radically varying circumstances, some geared to domestic markets, others more internationally oriented. Paradoxically, Netflix's ongoing need to organize and categorize its ever-expanding catalogue raises the prospect of new taxonomies emerging in African cinema. Thus, the company places 'African film' at a crossroads in the cultural imaginary, offering the possibility of culturally specific understandings of the continent's output (a possibility given an added urgency by the findings in Petty's chapter) at the same time as it threatens to homogenize an increasingly fragmented range of content.

Collectively, the contributions to this anthology offer a cross-section of global developments that occurred in the decade up to 2020. The events of that year and beyond raise ever more uncertainty regarding the future directions for World Cinema's move online, and a retrospective of developments up to that point seems particularly apt at this juncture, as the world continues to assess the ramifications of Covid-19; we look back on a decade that has seen the tech giants gain an ever tighter grip over content and its circulation, eventually accelerated by unprecedented transformations in the way we live. Yet, we have also seen previously marginalized film cultures evolve in unanticipated, and often fruitful, directions, reshaping not only the way cinema is circulated and consumed but also the global landscape of cinema itself.

References

Adejunmobi, M. (2018), 'Streaming Quality, Streaming Cinema', in K. Harrow and C. Garritano (eds), *A Companion to African Cinema*, Hoboken, NJ: Wiley-Blackwell, 219–43.

Baschiera, S., F. Di Chiara and V. Re (2017), 'The Logics of Re-Intermediation', *Cinéma & Cie*, 17 (29): 9–18.

Bisschoff, L. (2017), 'The Future Is Digital: An Introduction to African Digital Arts', *Critical African Studies*, 9 (3): 261–7.

Crisp, V. (2018), 'Access and Power: Film Distribution, Re-intermediation and Piracy', in R. Stone, P. Cooke, S. Dennison and A. Marlow-Mann (eds), *Routledge Companion to World Cinema*, London: Routledge, 445–54.

Dennison, S., and S. H. Lim (2006), 'Situating World Cinema as a Theoretical Problem', in S. Dennison and S. H. Lim (eds), *Remapping World Cinema: Identity, Culture and Politics in Film*, London: Wallflower, 1–15.

Dixon, W. W. (2013), *Streaming: Movies, Media and Instant Access*, Lexington: University Press of Kentucky.

Fisher, A. (2018), 'African Cinema on Demand? The Politics of Online Distribution and the Case of the African Film Library', *Journal of African Media Studies*, 10 (3): 239–50.

Herbert, D. (2011), 'From Art House to Your House: The Distribution of Quality Cinema on Home Video', *Canadian Journal of Film Studies*, 20 (2): 2–18.

Hessler, J. (2018), 'Quality You Can't Touch: Mubi Social, Platform Politics, and the Online Distribution of Art Cinema', *Velvet Light Trap*, 82 (October 2018): 3–17.

Iordanova, D. and S. Cunningham, eds (2012), *Digital Disruption: Cinema Moves On Line*. St Andrews: St Andrews Film Studies.

Jenkins, H., S. Ford and J. Green (2013), *Spreadable Media: Creating Value and Meaning in a Networked Culture*, New York: New York University Press.

Lobato, R. (2010), 'Creative Industries and Informal Economies: Lesson from Nollywood', *International Journal of Cultural Studies*, 13 (4): 337–54.

Lobato, R. (2012), *Shadow Economies of Cinema: Mapping Informal Film Distribution*, London: BFI.

Lobato, R. (2019), *Netflix Nations: The Geography of Digital Distribution*, New York: New York University Press.

Lobato, R., and M. D. Ryan (2011), 'Rethinking Genre Studies through Distribution Analysis: Issues in International Horror Movie Circuits', *New Review of Film and Television Studies*, 9 (2): 188–203.

Major, A. (2021), 'Not Streaming Near You: FilmStruck's Failure and the Demise of the Cinema-specific Model', *Popular Communication*, 12 May. Available online: https://doi.org/10.1080/15405702.2021.1919679 (accessed 17 August 2021).

McDonald, K., and D. Smith-Rowsey, eds (2016), *The Netflix Effect*, New York: Bloomsbury.

Nagib, L. (2006), 'Towards a Positive Definition of World Cinema', in S. Dennison and S. H. Lim (eds), *Remapping World Cinema: Identity, Culture and Politics in Film*, London: Wallflower Press, 30–7.

Nagib, L., C. Perriam and R. Dudrah (2012), 'Introduction', in L. Nagib, C. Perriam and R. Dudrah (eds), *Theorizing World Cinema*, London: I.B. Tauris, xvii–xxxii.

Silver, J., and S. Cunningham, eds (2013), *Screen Distribution and the New King Kongs of the Online World*, Basingstoke: Palgrave Macmillan.

Smith, M. D., and R. Telang (2016), *Streaming, Sharing, Stealing: Big Data and the Future of Entertainment*, Cambridge, MA: MIT Press.

Part 1

The limits of disintermediation: Problems of gatekeeping

1

Shifting gatekeepers: Power and influence in informal online film distribution

Virginia Crisp

Introduction

This chapter concerns informal online film distribution, what might be colloquially referred to as 'piracy', and the ways in which both formal and informal gatekeepers can influence the accessibility of films within complex and often interlocking online informal distribution nodes and networks. This chapter uses Ramon Lobato's (2012) concepts of formal/informal distribution to refer to distribution personnel, practices and processes that are formal, that is, sanctioned by the industry (distribution companies, sales agents, film festivals, etc.), and informal (online filesharing, DVD markets, etc.).

The ideas presented here should be read as a synthesis of a number of previous works concerning both formal and informal distribution (in particular, Crisp 2015, 2017b, 2017a, 2018) that, in examining these aspects of formal/informal film distribution together, enable a more holistic understanding of how various gatekeepers operate and influence circulation within informal distribution contexts.

It is first imperative to mention that to a large extent the formal film industry will always dictate what circulates within informal networks simply because the industry decides which films are made in the first place. Thus, in this respect, traditional formal gatekeepers inevitably exert considerable control over what films circulate online. This aspect of the influence of formal gatekeepers within informal networks will be examined in the first part of this chapter alongside how formal marketing and distribution processes also influence which films are available within informal contexts. The second part of this chapter will then explore how informal circulation has its own gatekeepers, in part due to some specific characteristics of film filesharing that cause only a few key groups/ individuals to operate as 'distributors' and thus dictate what circulates more widely online.

The wider context for this discussion concerns the changes taking place within film distribution (and indeed the cultural industries in general) where content is increasingly being distributed, exhibited and consumed online. This has led some scholars to suggest that the disruption of traditional distribution methods is characterized by a process of disintermediation, that is, the 'process whereby direct access to content makes the intermediary in a supply chain obsolete' (Iordanova and Cunningham 2012: 4). The intermediary, in this case, is the 'traditional' film distributor and sales agents, and thus Iordanova and Cunningham suggest that online forms of distribution (whether they be legal or not) are challenging the power of these traditional intermediaries.

However, while it is clear that traditional modes of distribution are still being disrupted, it has also become clear that the traditional distributor has not become entirely obsolete. Indeed, power may be shifting within the film industry, but I would contest that it is shifting *between* intermediaries rather than *away* from them. Thus, in the formal sector, the disintermediation that some have proposed appears to be more a matter or reintermediation, that is, 'the introduction of new intermediaries, often from outside the current established value chain' (Davies and Sigthorsson 2013: 166). Thus, the challenge to the incumbent powers within the film industry comes from new intermediaries like Netflix, Apple, Amazon and so on and not from the complete removal of intermediaries altogether.

However, one might argue that while there are clearly new intermediaries within the formal sector, the growth of informal mechanisms of distribution is potentially affected by disintermediation to a much greater extent. Informal online circulation (e.g. via filesharing forums, BitTorrent linking sites, streaming websites, cyberlockers, etc.) allows the audience direct access to media content that is not filtered by corporate algorithms or curated subject to commercial concerns. Thus, such informal distribution mechanisms would seem to enable the audience direct access to media content without the guiding hand of intermediaries, old or new.

However, this chapter proposes that while informal online distribution might have made access to a greater range of media options theoretically possible, it does not follow that what is available online is completely unfiltered and that consumption choices are not guided and limited in multiple ways. While in many cases the development of the internet has allowed unprecedented numbers of people to source an amazing array of films, games, TV programmes, books and comics through less than legal means, there are nonetheless some barriers still in place. Certainly, for the technically literate, who can afford the equipment, know where to go and, perhaps most significantly, know *what* they are looking for, it is possible to find (with a modicum of effort) many of the things they want. However, despite this increased availability there are still multiple mechanisms that limit our consumption choices, stemming from, firstly, the structures within the formal sector which determine which films are made, exhibited and marketed in the first place and, secondly, the gatekeepers that operate within informal networks of distribution that through their own distribution practices have a significant impact of what circulates widely within such networks.

The spectre of piracy

Somewhat unsurprisingly, public discourse surrounding piracy tends to emphasize the negative economic effects that such practices can have on the creative industries. Those working within the formal industry are frequently vocal about the damage that piracy is doing to the industry and the threat it poses. For instance, in an article in *Newsweek*, independent producer Cassian Elwes accused Google of implementing insufficient copyright protection, enabling piracy to threaten the continued existence of the independent film sector in the United States (2018), whereas in Australia, the director of cinema chain Village Roadshow, Graham Burke, has called pirates 'Leeches [and] thieves' (Wigney 2016).

Indeed, we are all familiar with the varying statistics that are frequently cited to illustrate the devastating effect that digital piracy is having on the cultural industries. For instance, a joint study from Ipsos and Oxford Economics on behalf of Australian Federation Against Copyright Theft (AFACT) claimed that direct consumer spending losses to the economy in the twelve months up to Q3 in 2010 amounted to A$575m (AFACT 2011). However, this chapter contests that the picture of the effects of piracy is more complex than a simple loss of economic profits to the industry for a number of reasons.

Firstly, the statistics used to support anti-piracy arguments have been criticized by a number of academic studies (Quiring et al. 2008; Yar 2008) alongside claims that the discourse surrounding piracy constructs it as a deviant act and thus 'reveals the idiosyncrasies of elites promoting their own interests'

(Denegri-Knott 2004: 4) while also demonstrating an 'undue rhetorical certainty about the property conceptions underlying copyright' (Kretschmer et al. 2001: 434). Overall, it benefits the owners of copyright (typically companies and not artists or content creators) to propagate and maintain the perception that piracy hurts artists so that they can protect not primarily the artists but their revenues.

Secondly, there is by no means consensus regarding the economic consequences of piracy. Studies such as that by McKenzie and Walls on the effects of piracy on Australian box office revenue have suggested that sales displacements while 'statistically significant' are also 'relatively small' (2015: 52). Danaher and Waldfogel, in their 2012 study of the effect of online film piracy on international box office since the introduction of BitTorrent in 2003, suggest that 'empirical studies as yet have not reached a consensus on whether piracy depresses movie revenue' (2012: 20) but that the possible effects of piracy in international markets can be mitigated by minimizing release windows. Thus, if there is so much disagreement about the existence of sales displacement due to piracy, then this again points to a much more complex picture of how informal distribution influences the formal industry.

Thirdly, we might temporarily disregard the economic consequences of informal distribution and consider the role that it has in enabling access to scarce, banned or politically sensitive content. Indeed, Tristan Mattelart makes the observation that 'the merchants of the informal sector are able to adapt themselves more efficiently to the specific needs of their customers' (2012: 740). This would seem to suggest that these methods of informal distribution enable the circulation of content that might be overlooked within a formal system because of its limited potential to generate revenue for distributors.

Furthermore, there are claims that some forms of informal online distribution represent a challenge to existing power structures present within content distribution (Vandresen 2012) and/or may be a subversive practice as it enables circulation that goes against state regulation and censorship (Li 2012). However, while praising the subversive potential of informal distribution, scholars such as Meng note that those challenging existing power structures do not do so 'on an equal footing' (Meng 2012: 473) within their formal counterparts.

Furthermore, some theorists have argued that piracy actually 'primes a proto-licit market for Hollywood [and] … arguably, is in Hollywood's longer-term interest' (Cunningham 2012: 417). Mattelart suggests that piracy increases the presence of Hollywood's products in markets they would otherwise not dominate and as such could be seen as 'preparing ... the ground for future legal exports' (Mattelart 2012: 747).

In such a context, without ignoring the very real concerns of people working within the formal industry (especially in the independent sector), we can see that there is much more to any analysis of informal distribution than simply straightforward economic losses. Indeed, rather than trying to ascertain the influence that informal distribution has on the formal industry, the following discussion will explore the opposite relationship, that is, the way that formal aspects of the global film business may be reproduced within informal networks rather than challenged.

Formal influence in informal contexts

It seems an obvious point, but it must be acknowledged that the only films that are available to circulate within informal networks are the ones that have been made in the first place. This is because, relative to the costs associated with recording a song or writing a book, getting a film made is almost always a costly endeavour. While *IndieWire* (2011) provides tips on how to make your first feature for a modest $5,000, a report from the European parliament (2014) notes that

> the average EU production budget ranges from some €11 million in the UK, €5 million in Germany and France to €300 000 in Hungary and Estonia, [whereas] the average budget for US-produced films amounts to €12 million and exceeds €85 million for films produced by majors and their affiliates.

That said, the picture of average film budgets in the UK is actually more complex as the BFI Statistical Yearbook (2020a) notes that the median budget for a domestic UK feature in 2019 was actually £750,000,[1] whereas inward investment features[2] had a much higher median budget of '£7.7 million, down from £10.4 million in 2018'. Thus, the existence of external film productions in the UK serves to artificially inflate the reported average cost of film production. This median production cost of £350,000 fits under the BFI's definition of a low-budget film

---

[1] The median budget for domestic UK productions overall has shown a significant increase over the period, rising by a factor of four, from £130,000 in 2010 to £750,000 in 2019 (2020a: 11).
[2] According to the BFI Statistical Yearbook, 'An inward investment film is one which is substantially financed and controlled from outside the UK and which is attracted to the UK by script requirements, eg locations, and/or the UK's filmmaking infrastructure and/or UK film tax relief' (2020b: 5).

(£250,00–£1 million), as opposed to micro- (£50,000–£250,000) and 'no'-budget films (£0–£50,000) (BFI 2008: 9).

While self-financing a film on a low/micro-budget is theoretically possible, Elliot Grove of Raindance Film Festival suggests that film finance typically comes from a few specific sources: housekeeping or development deals from production/distribution companies, distribution deals, government funding (in certain countries) and private investment from investors or talent (2014). The last BFI report on low- and micro-budget film financing (2008) outlined that this production model was on the rise in 2008, but that distribution was a significant issue for such films, with only 18 per cent of low-/micro-/no-budget films released theatrically in the UK and only 16 per cent internationally. Again, only films that are officially released and distributed are likely to end up on informal circuits and, as the BFI report hints, many more films are made each year than are actually released.

Furthermore, distribution is dominated by a few key players, and this skews which films are more likely to end up circulating within informal networks. For instance, the top 10 distributors of films in the UK had a 95 per cent share of the market in 2019 and 'distributors outside the top 10 handled a total of 671 titles (73% of all films on release) but generated only 5% of the total box office' (BFI 2020b: 4). According to the BFI (2020a: 6), 185 films[3] were produced (in whole or in part) in the UK in 2019, including 93 domestic UK features (177 in 2018; 174 in 2017) (42 of those with a budget less than £500,000), 23 co-productions (21 in 2018; 18 in 2017) and 69 inward investment features (59 in 2018; 73 in 2017). It is significant to note that 'The volume of domestic UK productions has declined every year since 2012, driven principally by a fall in the number of productions with budgets of less than £500,000' (BFI 2020a: 6).

The same Statistical Yearbook also shows that 168 independent UK films were distributed by 75 distributors in 2019, but these releases are unlikely to correspond to the same productions from 2019 due to the delay between production and exhibition. Furthermore, 96 per cent of the total box office for independent films was made by the 49 independent films that were released by the top 10 distributors, including *Downton Abbey*, *Yesterday* and *Mary Queen of Scots* (BFI 2020b: 7). As such, it is clear that the same skew towards a few

---

[3] 'There is often a delay in acquiring full data on production activity in the UK, so the number for 2019 is likely to be revised upwards' (BFI 2020a: 6).

high-budget/high-grossing releases is present within independent films as well as within studio-produced films.

Another issue that reduces the likelihood of low-/micro-/no-budget films being circulated within both formal and informal networks is the lack of visibility that can be achieved, due to the fact that such films frequently have trouble securing sales agents as well as distributors (Smits 2019). In the BFI's (2008) survey, only 45 per cent of films had a sales agent attached and while a similar percentage 'were represented by organisations that could be classified as having a significant presence in the business ... Many, however, appeared to be transient or ad hoc in nature and their effectiveness as routes to the current global market for filmed entertainment appeared to be limited' (2008: 20). As sales agents and distributors do more than secure the official release of the film in specific territories, they also work to create the value of the films through release strategies (Smits 2019), this his lack of effective representation is a significant barrier to the circulation of low- and micro-budget films.

While an independent filmmaker may choose/wish/try to self-distribute her film after efforts of financing, hard work and heartache, the self-distribution route is arduous and involves pitching your film directly to cinemas, producing 'your own film materials (DCPs), marketing materials (posters, trailers etc.) and book[ing] and pay[ing] for your own advertising ... [as well as hiring] a specialist PR company' (ICO n.d.). Another option is to pitch your film directly to festivals and/or appropriate distributors or go by the traditional route and approach the festival circuit and distributors through a sales agent (ICO n.d.). It is important to note that while self-distribution as a concept may be gaining traction, it is not via a route completely outside of the traditional sphere. Furthermore, each film, through whichever mechanism it is released, will be vying for attention in the same marketplace, and the level of visibility it achieves ultimately dictates to what extent it ends up circulating within informal online networks due to the pervasive influence of marketing within those networks.

Marketing of a film is a key factor in encouraging illegal downloads, even when a film is otherwise a commercial and/or critical failure (Bodó and Lakatos 2012). As such, 'films supported by heavy marketing investment are more likely to appear on P2P networks' (Bodó and Lakatos 2012: 435), and film marketing has a greater influence on downloading behaviour than 'word of mouth about the actual quality of the movie' (Bodó and Lakatos 2012: 423). Thus, we can see a mirroring of formal distribution patterns within informal networks (physical or virtual) which are likely to be awash with the same Hollywood films that you would see in any neighbourhood multiplex (Mattelart 2012: 740).

Furthermore, it is important to note that within Bodó and Lakatos's findings, it is specifically online distributors and site administrators who are seen to be influenced by film marketing, and it is they 'who act as filters in determining which content will be offered for users' (2012: 431). Such an observation brings us to the second examination at the heart of this chapter, the gatekeepers operating within informal online distribution networks and the ways their practices shape the content available within such networks.

Informal online gatekeepers

Firstly, it is important to indicate who might act as gatekeepers in such informal circulation contexts, and, in doing so, we must also note that informal distribution is not a homogenous practice and so a range of roles and practices might perform gatekeeping functions in these varying contexts. As I have noted elsewhere, over the last twenty or so years informal online distribution of films has been facilitated through a varied number of platforms and practices, for example, newsgroups, private filesharing communities, BitTorrent listing sites (e.g. The Pirate Bay), Direct Download Link (DDL) sites (e.g. Megaupload), streaming sites and filesharing software (e.g. Napster) (Crisp 2018: 67). Such varying methods of informal circulation have grown and declined in use and influence, but they all interconnect in what I have referred to as an 'informal distribution ecosystem'.

While varying in use and popularity over time, various content 'access points' (e.g. DDL websites, filesharing forums, etc.) are fed by a shared set of 'distributors' who themselves obtain films from a shared set of formal and informal sources (Crisp 2018: 77). It is these common 'distributors' who I will examine as gatekeepers to online content through the remainder of this chapter. It should be noted that while each access point may have its own specific gatekeepers (e.g. forum/newsgroup moderators), the remainder of this chapter will focus upon two specific examples of informal distribution (The Scene and filesharing communities) so as to examine how gatekeepers may influence the films available within informal networks and, in doing so, how they might also reproduce the hierarchies of access and visibility that exist within formal distribution channels.

At first glance, informal online circulation of media content promises the potential of a utopian exchange network. The informal online distribution ecology exists outside of the market and is therefore not tethered by the necessity of securing financial returns for films distributed through its channels. In such a context we might imagine that the criteria for selecting a film for distribution within such an informal network could (theoretically) be based on 'quality' of the film rather than factors linked to commercial constraints and, furthermore, that all films ever made might be available within this broad ecosystem of multiple access points.

However, within this context there are a relatively small number of 'distributors' who dictate what is 'released' and what is not. Furthermore, release selection criterion, while theoretically not restricted by economic considerations, can often mimic formal distribution patterns, is often influenced by the reputational concerns of release groups and is not necessarily based upon any qualitative judgement of the films themselves.

It is a specific characteristic of *film* filesharing that simply sharing a folder on your computer, or even uploading files to a specific site, does not mean you are adding to the overall number of films being shared through informal networks if those shared files were downloaded through the same networks in the first place. On the contrary, those adding to the available films within informal film distribution networks must actively source a copy of a particular film that they have selected and then convert it into a format that can be easily uploaded/downloaded otherwise they are simply circulating material that was already available. As Bodó and Lakatos have phrased it, 'Just as one can only buy a book that has been published, one can only download a film that has been transformed into a digital copy and made available to the P2P community' (2012: 430). In this respect, those who make active decisions about what films to convert and share online act as very powerful gatekeepers within informal distribution contexts. Potentially the most influential collection of such gatekeepers is made up of the release groups within The Scene.

As I have explored elsewhere (Crisp 2018) The Scene is a collective term for a selection of 'release groups' who work towards producing informal online releases for all manner of films, music, games, software and so on. They are referred to as The Scene (sometimes the Warez Scene), yet membership of such a collective is self-selecting and even members of individual release groups will not necessarily 'know' the other members of their group beyond the handle they use within each particular group.

The Scene's activities as gatekeepers who select what to release are particularly important because it has been suggested that they are responsible for removing copyright protection and 'releasing' most of the content that circulates within online informal networks (Décary-Hétu et al. 2012; Eriksson 2016; Huizing and van der Wal 2014; Rehn 2004). Scene release groups operate according to certain 'rules' that dictate the naming conventions, format and other requirements of Scene releases (see https://scenerules.org/). One aspect of the naming conventions stipulates that the release group must be mentioned in the filename for the release, and this contributes to the culture of competition that underpins Scene activities.

Participation in release groups typically brings reputational rather than monetary gains, and thus the act of releasing becomes more significant than what is actually being released (Rehn 2004). As such, release groups compete with one another to release certain content (groups tend to specialize in terms of format and genre) before other groups with the same specialism. While duplicate releases are typically 'nuked'[4] (i.e. deleted) and thus, in theory, release groups have no incentive to work on the same releases as other groups, this threat of being nuked means release groups are under internal pressure to produce releases before other groups. This then contributes to speed of releasing being particularly respected within The Scene.

Alongside speed of releasing, another way that release groups demonstrate their prowess is to release the newest content. In some cases, this is written into Scene rules, as is the case with the DVX rules which specify that only new releases should be created and distributed. The requirements clearly skew the selections of release groups towards certain types of content, in this case, newly released films rather than older ones. While this might theoretically include films newly released on physical formats or rereleased in the cinema, if the influence of the Scene on what circulates online can be believed, then such criteria will inevitably skew available content towards more recent formal theatrical releases.

This brief discussion of the Scene has been used to illustrate how a very small group of individuals may potentially have a significant influence upon the files that circulate within informal networks. While The Scene operates as a dominant supplier for multiple access points within the informal distribution ecology (Crisp 2018), specialist filesharing communities and, in particular, the

---

[4] See Nuke rules https://scenerules.org/rules.html. Scenerules.org (2018), Available from: https://scenerules.org/ (accessed 20 January 2019).

individual distributors that operate within them also have a key role to play in deciding which new films enter this ecology.

While filesharing software may be downloaded millions of times, streaming DDL and BitTorrent link sites may be visited by hundreds of thousands of users and closed forums and newsgroups may have tens of thousands of registered members; within such a complex ecosystem only a few individuals (aside from The Scene where individuals work together in release groups) actually contribute to the number of films available within the wider ecosystem. As an illustrative example from some of my previous research (Crisp 2015) that focused upon filesharing communities from 2008 to 2012, as of July 2009 the specialist East Asian film filesharing community, Chinaphiles, had 64,502 members. However, 59,175 users (91.74% of the total membership) had never posted a message to the forum and as such would be commonly termed 'lurkers'. In such a context, while the overall membership list was vast for such a specialist sharing community, the proportion of the overall forum members who actually contributed to forum discussions and/or who shared films through posting was minuscule when measured against the overall membership. Furthermore, of the 64,502 total membership only 38 forum members acted as true 'distributors' within the community, that is, those forum members actually 'released' new content into the community.

In addition, I have highlighted a distinction between distributors who share 'Scene' releases through single or multiple access points, whom I call intermediary distributors, and those who have ripped, encoded and released films themselves typically for release within a particular access point, whom I term autonomous distributors. 'Autonomous distributors', that is, those who operate as individuals and who rip, encode and share films (often within a specific community), are not generally members of larger 'release groups' who specialize in spreading copies of films through filesharing networks. 'Intermediary distributors', on the other hand, may be peripheral members of release groups or, more commonly, will simply share links to films that they have found on other forums. Importantly, intermediary distributors do not add to the overall titles available within filesharing networks but may add to the films available within a particular filesharing forum or community. However, both sets of 'distributors' may act as tastemakers within particular communities. Thus it is important to consider how these key community members choose which films to share.

In my previous work on the Chinaphiles and Eastern Legends communities (see Crisp 2015, 2017b), I explored how distributors in such settings decided what to 'release' within their community. In doing so, I found that two of the major considerations were availability and quality, but that in some respects, the selection process was at once more subjective and in many ways more practical.

Firstly, both sets of distributors paid attention to what others were releasing before choosing to distribute a particular film. As we can see from this quote from distributor Naxx, 'We are a small community ... so it really makes no sense to compete if you are going to release something with similar specifications' (Crisp 2015: 139).

Secondly, personal preference also played a strong role – as such, the gatekeeping power of these 'distributors' cannot be underestimated as both autonomous and intermediary distributors often chose to release films that they particularly enjoyed. However, availability to community members was also key, and it was not uncommon for community members to request specific films (although this factor may have had limited influence within such communities because of the aforementioned observation that the vast majority of the community are lurkers).

More commonly, a film might be released as a response to more general discussions on either forum about the lack of a 'quality' release of a certain title, or the fact that a particular distribution company was about to release a newer version. Here we can see that even when responding to the demands of the community, those demands are themselves often shaped by developments in the world of formal distribution. In particular, on the *Eastern Legends* forum, as only uncompressed DVDs and Blu-rays were allowed to be shared, all autonomous distributors needed official distributors to release new titles before they could make new releases to share with their community. Due to this reliance on official releases, and the focus on quality, arguably the professionals still existed at the dominant end of the power relationship between formal and informal distributors because they ultimately controlled the supply of official releases.

Another point worth noting is that the distributors within these specialist communities were interested in the film industry in general and (those who posted about such subjects) demonstrated utmost respect for film distribution companies. Two distributors who specialized in East Asian cinema were discussed in particular on these forums. On Chinaphiles, for instance, a range of films were available from the distributor Tartan Films, then a small London-based independent distributor[5] that became famous for its Tartan Asia Extreme

---

[5] The company went into administration in 2008 and the company's catalogue is now owned by the Palisades Media Group.

Label. Within this forum this distribution company was well known, and so certain titles were shared precisely *because* they were Tartan releases with specific extras or cuts of films that no other distribution company provided.

Another much smaller distributor, Third Window, was discussed in even more glowing terms. For example, The Third Window version of *Confessions of a Dog* came with a specific request from the uploader, Sass, to support Third Window. The request even came with a link to the Third Window website and details of special features bundled with the first thousand copies of the film. Forum members posted to the discussion thread to second Sass' request, to further suggest that UK audiences should support their small distributors, and to let other members know when they ordered/received their copy. Overall there was a sense within such discussions that Third Window really 'cared' about their customers and that they needed (and deserved) support from fans of East Asian cinema.

Such conversations suggest that within these communities, there are no attempts to subvert or challenge the current media landscape; instead, informal distributors look to their formal counterparts for a supply of quality titles with good transfers. As such, gatekeepers within such communities, while undoubtedly shaping the films available within their community and the wider informal distribution ecology, are doing so in a manner that seems to mimic activities within the formal sector rather than challenge them.

Conclusion

In conclusion, informal online distribution, while in some senses might appear (or even be) quite radical, does not necessarily represent access to a wider or more diverse range of content because of the influence of the formal sector within the informal distribution ecosystem through the actions of both formal and informal gatekeepers.

Indeed, in the community cases examined here, while total membership numbers may be vast, those who contribute to the pool of films available within informal networks are few. While community requests might be responded to, the majority of members never post and so their desires are 'unheard', and the personal preference of each distributor is a significant factor in what films are made available within the community. While the quality of a release is very important, this emphasis on 'quality' makes the informal distributors somewhat dependent upon the availability of official releases. Again, this highlights that those distributors who do exist may in turn rely on the supply of films available from third parties, whether that be The Scene or official distribution companies.

The Scene, on the other hand, is a competitive subculture all of its own that potentially privileges its own markers of respect and achievement above curatorial decisions about which films should enter the informal distribution ecology. With its emphasis on speed and newness, it is perhaps unsurprising that the informal networks are flooded with the same content that circulates through formal channels.

Furthermore, while new intermediaries are entering the formal sector in the form of Amazon, Netflix and Google, the incumbent powerhouses of the Hollywood studio–backed distributors have not yet been ousted from their dominant position within the industry. A few key distributors still dominate the market, and films still need sales agents to increase their visibility and secure a distribution deal and thus access to the marketing money and expertise that makes films 'must see' titles in both formal and informal contexts.

References

AFACT (2011), 'Economic Consequences of Movie Piracy: Australia', AFACT Website. Available online: https://www.mpa-i.org/wp-content/uploads/2014/08/IPSOS_Economic_Consequences_of_Movie_Piracy_-_Australia.pdf (accessed 20 January 2019).

BFI (2008), 'Low and Micro-Budget Film Making in the UK', British Film Institute. Available online: https://www.bfi.org.uk/sites/bfi.org.uk/files/downloads/uk-film-council-low-and-micro-budget-film-production-in-the-uk.pdf (accessed 20 January 2019).

BFI (2020a), 'BFI Statistical Yearbook 2020: Screen Sector Production', British Film Institute. Available online: https://www.bfi.org.uk/industry-data-insights/statistical-yearbook (accessed 18 May 2021).

BFI (2020b), 'BFI Statistical Yearbook 2020: Distribution', British Film Institute. Available online: https://www.bfi.org.uk/industry-data-insights/statistical-yearbook (accessed 18 May 2021).

Bodó, B., and Z. Lakatos (2012), 'Theatrical Distribution and P2P Movie Piracy: A Survey of P2P Networks in Hungary Using Transactional Data', *International Journal of Communication*, 6: 413–45.

Crisp, V. (2015), *Pirates and Professionals: Film Distribution in the Digital Age*, London: Palgrave.

Crisp, V. (2017a), 'Access and Power: Film Distribution, Re-Intermediation and Piracy', in P. Cooke, S. Dennison and A. Marlow-Mann (eds), *Routledge Companion to the Remapping World Cinema Series*, London: Routledge, 445–54.

Crisp, V. (2017b), 'Pirates and Proprietary Rights: Perceptions of "Ownership" and Media Objects within Filesharing Communities', in A. Willis and J. Wroot (eds), *Cult Media: Re-Packaged. Rereleased and Restored*, London: Palgrave, 125–41.

Crisp, V. (2018), 'Release Groups & The Scene: Re-Intermediation and Competitive Gatekeepers Online', *Cinéma&Cie: International Film Studies Journal, Special Edition – Re-intermediation: Distribution, Online Access, and Gatekeeping in the Digital European Market*, 17 (29): 67–80.

Cunningham, S. (2012), 'Emergent Innovation through the Coevolution of Informal and Formal Media Economies', *Television & New Media*, 13 (5): 415–30.

Danaher, B., and J. Waldfogel (2012), 'Reel Piracy: The Effect of Online Film Piracy on International Box Office Sales', *SSRN*, 16 January. Available online: http://dx.doi.org/10.2139/ssrn.1986299 (accessed 20 January 2019).

Davies, R., and G. Sigthorsson (2013), *Introducing the Creative Industries*, London: Sage.

Décary-Hétu, D., C. Morselli and S. Leman-Langois (2012), 'Welcome to the Scene: A Study of Social Organization and Recognition among Warez Hackers', *Journal of Research in Crime and Delinquency*, 49 (3): 359–82.

Denegri-Knott, J. (2004), 'Sinking the Online "Music Pirates": Foucault, Power and Deviance on the Web', *Journal of Computer-Mediated Communication*, 9 (4). Available online: https://academic.oup.com/jcmc/article/9/4/JCMC949/4614489 (accessed 21 January 2019).

Elwes, C. (2018), 'How Google Is Killing the Independent Movie Industry', *Newsweek*, 16 January. Available online: https://www.newsweek.com/how-google-killing-independent-movie-industry-781640 (accessed 20 January 2019).

Eriksson, M. (2016), 'A Different Kind of Story: Tracing the Histories and Cultural Marks of Pirate Copied Film', *Technoscienza: Italian Journal of Science and Technology Studies*, 7 (1): 87–108.

European Parliament (2014), 'An Overview of Europe's Film Industry'. Available online: http://www.europarl.europa.eu/RegData/etudes/BRIE/2014/545705/EPRS_BRI(2014)545705_REV1_EN.pdf (accessed 20 January 2019).

Grove, E. (2014), 'Development Finance for Films', *Raindance Website*. Available online: https://www.raindance.org/development-finance-for-films/ (accessed 20 January 2019).

Huizing, A., and J. van der Wal (2014), 'Explaining the Rise and Fall of the Warez MP3 Scene: An Empirical Account from the Inside', *First Monday*, 19 (10). Available online: https://firstmonday.org/ojs/index.php/fm/article/view/5546/4125 (accessed 11 November 2016).

Independent Cinema Office (ICO) (n.d.), 'How do I Get My Film into Distribution'. Available online: https://www.independentcinemaoffice.org.uk/advice-support/how-do-i-get-my-film-into-distribution/ (accessed 20 January 2019).

IndieWire (2011), 'How to Make Your First Feature Film for $5,000', *IndieWire*, 25 August. Available online: https://www.indiewire.com/2011/08/how-to-make-your-first-feature-film-for-5000-52636/ (accessed 20 January 2019).

Iordanova, D., and S. Cunningham (2012), *Digital Disruption: Cinema Moves Online*, St Andrews: University of St Andrews Press.

Kretschmer, M., G. M. Klimis and R. Wallis (2001), 'Music in Electronic Markets: An Empirical Study', *New Media and Society*, 3 (4): 417–41.

Li, J. (2012), 'From the D-Buffs to the D-Generation, Piracy, Cinema and an Alternative Public Sphere in Urban China', *International Journal of Communication*, 6: 542–63.

Lobato, R. (2012), *Shadow Economies of Cinema: Mapping Informal Film Distribution*, London: BFI.

Mattelart, T. (2012), 'Audiovisual Piracy, Informal Economy, and Cultural Globalization', *International Journal of Communication*, 6: 735–50.

McKenzie, J., and W. D. Walls (2015), 'File Sharing and Film Revenues: Estimates of Sales Displacements at the Box Office', *B.E. Journal of Economic Analysis & Policy*, 16 (1): 25–57.

Meng, B. (2012), 'Undetermined Globalization: Media Consumption via P2P Networks', *International Journal of Communication*, 6: 467–83.

Quiring, O., B. Von Walter and R. Atterer (2008), 'Can Filesharers Be Triggered by Economic Incentives? Results of an Experiment', *New Media and Society*, 10 (3): 434–54.

Rehn, A. (2004), 'The Politics of Contraband: The Honor Economies of the Warez Scene', *Journal of Socio-Economics*, 33 (3): 359–74.

Scenerules.org (2018), Available from: https://scenerules.org/ (accessed 20 January 2019).

Smits, R. (2019), *Gatekeeping in the Evolving Business of Independent Film Distribution*, London: Palgrave Macmillan.

Vandresen, M. (2012), 'Free Culture Lost in Translation', *International Journal of Communication*, 6: 626–42.

Wigney J. (2016), 'Village Roadshow Boss Warns Piracy Could Kill the Movie Industry: "If We Don't Solve This – It's Over"', news.com.au, 10 October. Available online: https://www.news.com.au/entertainment/movies/village-roads how-boss-warns-piracy-could-kill-the-movie-industry-if-we-dont-solve-this--its-over/news-story/cf63345de9b6b509ad0358270468a039 (accessed 20 January 2019).

Yar, M. (2008), 'The Rhetorics and Myths of Anti-Piracy Campaigns: Criminalization, Moral Pedagogy and Capitalist Property Relations in the Classroom', *New Media & Society*, 10 (4): 605–23.

2

Cinephile file-sharing: Informal distribution, plural canons and digital film archives

Angela Meili

Non-official circulation of cinema is a cultural activity that responds directly to market inefficiencies, notably in areas deprived of movie theatres and legal media distribution.[1] During the period around 2010–14, legal purchase of films was inaccessible to a large part of the global population (Almeida and Butcher 2003; Barone 2011; Bodó and Lakatos 2012; Chiang and Assane 2008). Consequently, informal sharing took on every challenge to supply cultural demands, applying its resilience to create massive distribution structures, which turned out to be powerful tools for tastemaking and cultural perception.

Informal media distribution is independent from governmental or corporate institutions. It defies the logic of established legal systems and every prohibition criterion adopted to regulate technology usage or content sharing. Informal distribution fills the void left by formal distribution and satisfies demands and interests of consumers and producers. There is a free-flowing and unstoppable collective arrangement of technical, logic and market solutions, often ignored by the official industry, a parallel distribution system, functioning as a competitive actor, since it operates with efficient strategies to deliver digital goods. Informal sharing shapes a scenario, a field of experience with films populated by *pirate audience*s, as labelled by Mendes Moreira De Sa (2013).

Historically, informal cinema circulation goes beyond digital networks and takes place at every stage of film industry development, becoming accentuated with technological progress. For instance, in the first decades of cinema, the distribution system of 16mm films was disorganized and relied on informal groups, while artistic, educational, amateur or even pornographic films

---

[1] This chapter presents results of my doctoral thesis (Meili 2015).

depended on alternative circuits. In the 1980s, the emergence of home video intensified the volume of informal circulation, albeit the low quality of video reproductions. Over time, the phenomenon became even more pervasive and massive, reaching its peak after digital technologies and the internet.

The presence of film piracy in the digital world became significant from the mid-2000s, right after overcoming technical limitations, such as low bandwidth, lack of efficient compression models (MP3, MPEG-4, DivX, etc.) and poor visual experience (screen, colours, speed, storage). There has been an intensification of domestic copies since the creation of digital media (CDs and DVDs) and home recorders, along with the development of image and audio compression technologies, followed by better internet connections, screen enhancement and the convergence between television and computer.

Informal operators quickly became drivers and feeders of complex broad-spectrum networks, growing aggregations around specific interests and originating a more voluminous distribution than the official operators, with greater agility and diversity. Since then, the digital world reproduces and amplifies the voice of the film industry (official releases, awards, festivals, exhibitions and availability in other media), but more importantly, filesharing culture covers audiovisual media with greater heterogeneity and connectivity, comprehending a series of cultural niches driven by collective intelligence.

Undoubtedly, the official scenario has a dominant impact on informal networks. On the other hand, Torrent and other peer-to-peer groups share and worship the seventh art, including titles that have never been under the spotlight of the media. Thus, along with the constant inequality of forces on the cinematographic field, there is a specific power rearrangement given by the hyper-connection that multiplies the means of content distribution.

Informal sharing is constantly investigated in terms of its structures, numbers and information systems or economic impact over industry; still it is crucial to understand its cultural motivations and expressions. If every taste is manufactured (Bourdieu [1979] 1984), then cinephile informal groups play a very specific role in public tastemaking, connecting mass culture with artistic sectors of the cinema, while the reticulation of the social network creates a cultural dynamic of both hegemonic and subterranean influences.

Focusing on the period 2010–14, there is the evident necessity, also pointed out by Bodó and Lakatos (2012: 442), to understand informal networks as distribution tools for non-mainstream films. Scholarly research, at that point, described a substantial presence of cinephile groups on informal sharing activities: Iordanova and Cunningham (2012) connected cinephile BitTorrent forums to new possibilities of cinema experience; De Kosnik (2012) presented them as the most powerful tool for archivist culture; Cardoso et al. (2012) saw them as models for distribution of non-Hollywood Cinema; Bodó (2013) described them as highly organized systems; Crisp (2012) commented on their relation to niche culture; Almeida (2011) proposed that cinephile groups popularized cinematographic knowledge, encouraging new cinephile experiences in the digital age. According to Bodó (2013), cinephile Torrent groups gave rise to a programming logic that connected popular and mainstream to fragmented niche demands within the same platform, offering users an unprecedented informational experience.

Due to its potential to become an important tool for experimentation on film distribution strategies, scholarly studies affirmed, categorically, that circulation should be seen beyond *legal vs illegal* dualism. Strictly speaking, a Manichaean perspective would leave aside complexities inherent to cultural experience in digital spaces.

Throughout the history of cinema, piracy has been seen as either an evil to be extirpated or a flag to be lifted at any cost; both are circumscribed ideological positions that encompass, but do not reduce, digital cinephile experience. Regarding the law, there is a clear inefficiency to establish rules of a game played in a deterritorialized society, since information technologies have rendered current modes of legislation obsolete (Bently et al. 2010; Oberholzer-Gee and Strumpf 2009).

Thus, studies that restrict filesharing to the scope of criminality neglect sociological aspects, since they notice how the individual stands before the law and forgets implications or interpretations of law according to the historical context. Regarding the economy, as intellectual property rights are imperative for the market, there were perspectives suggesting that more flexibility could result in more innovative markets (Anderson 2006, 2009; Lessig 2004; Mason 2009).

It is important to highlight that, during the years after 2015, there was a remarkable evolution in the surveillance tools market, digital legislation, and artificial intelligence. It allowed a greater and more efficient application of copyright law and the emergence of a whole new industry focused on these solutions. In addition, formal distribution systems (such as streaming platforms) fostered adherence to paid services, making the internet the largest market for audiovisual distribution in the early 2020s.

Distinctively, during the transitional period (2010–14), informal media sharing was driven by a profound inefficiency of centralized traditional markets, demand dissatisfaction and inequality of access to cultural goods. Cinephile groups disposed of every resource available, following and boosting technological evolution and, at the same time, re-enacting its previous cultural references and models of symbolic representation, from written text, through music, photography and the cinema itself.

Torrent group databases for media have been built by voluntary human work, including scanning, copying, selection, translation, categorization, organization and a constant process of refining technical tools. Forum interfaces and archives were fed with content acquired in official or unofficial distribution channels, from any sort of media available, and arranged as a mode of symbolic expression in itself. This ever-changing aggregation of symbolic meaning has been linked to a broader historical context, including material and technological conditions.

Phenomenologically, there are infinite possibilities of symbolic rearrangement through technology, or infinite reading paths compassed with transitory systems. Digital phenomena are discursive statements – that is, textualities performing on real conditions for production or reception and establishing dense reference networks. Symbolic production is grounded on a set of interrelated cultural features, put together by actors performing mediations or by the media themselves. Therefore, digital documents, group statements and tools become resources for purposeful human agents, affecting interactions and social organizations.

The peer-to-peer concept generates technologies that were developed for computational distributed processing, essentially enacting the principles of the World Wide Web, such as: (i) the ability to distinguish between good and bad members; (ii) regulatory mechanisms for computational resources; (iii) mechanisms for group communication; (iv) sense of community (Pouwelse et al. 2008: 705–6). Slashdot.org was the first website dedicated to disseminating and discussing the basic peer-to-peer principles; it was released in 1997 and issued daily news about technology in a pioneering way, shaped and fed by a self-regulating community of active members.

Peer-to-peer technologies evolved over time and became a faster and cheaper solution for audiovisual distribution, especially for film, as it requires large amounts of bandwidth for transferring. The technology works through mediated connection of personal computers, ordered by communication protocols, that sum processing capabilities in a common activity, such as to store data, to upload, to download and other operations. Peer-to-peer technology builds parameters for connection between computers to interchange information independently of central servers, and to establish a direct or semi-direct link between peers. Computers perform as unidentified nodes, working in a common task distributed across them. Such features provide anonymity and prevent data location, as each peer can join or leave the process at any time.

These networks perform a certain type of power, which is not only mechanical but also rooted in the idea of collaboration, individuals and machines working together to create a collective power over a specific cultural or social demand. Distributed processing multiplies computing capacity to fully aggregate resources, since the more pirates download files, the more they benefit the whole community. Ultimately, peer-to-peer networks build informational structures that are capable of making the best use of internet participatory potentialities.

Formalities of cinephile Torrent groups

At the time of writing, cinephile Torrent groups interact via web fora, their content organized hierarchically through tree-like structures of permanently registered asynchronous interactions. Every publication respects editorial guidelines, while the groups play a mediation role in the social interactions; there is a circumscribed social network built to satisfy specific needs and interests, such as the guarantee of privacy and specialized knowledge or privileged content. Their organizational schemas have a high degree of formality and strictness, involving rules for sociability, cultural or artistic values, archiving technique and interface.

As a result, cinephile Torrent groups are a cultural phenomenon with symbolic nature, represented by informational structures, archives and interactions. These systems are a collective interpretation of cinema and its cultural imagination, a formulation sustained by heterogeneous sources, their networks integrating collectors, commentators and moviegoers. Although informal groups do not sign official agreements or contracts, they follow regulation procedures and organizational systems that moderate users' participation, and control technical structures, archives and editorial projects. As a result, informality and formality coexist in a complex scenario, where huge volumes of data spread through countless ways.

Informal circulation occurs parallel to institutions, outside of bureaucratic processes and structures. Nevertheless, it occurs in a given institutionalized reality, where it is imperative to negotiate dependencies on the entertainment industry, along with market urgencies, internet service providers, software and hardware companies, and other agents. If there is a symbolic dimension to every organizational process, it is true to say that technical structures of informal networks are symbolic agreements, built to sustain communication systems; in other words, rules set guidelines for collective projects, to establish limits and offer resources for participation.

As a result, the participatory structure creates a digital ground projected into the model of an institutionalized entity; it controls behaviour, contribution, standardization, type of content, technical specificities and so on. These regulations outline the characteristics of film collections and shape the group identity, establishing the foundations of a political, technical, organizational and curatorial unity.

As an example, the Brazilian group MKO has guidelines that take as reference an implicit 'common sense' [sic], a tacit collective agreement that implies negotiation within the community. The maintenance of this collective agreement depends on a hierarchical system, where a smaller group centralizes decisions and functions, resulting in a co-dependence between administrators and users, for the purpose of mutual benefit. Some rules, for instance, guide the community to avoid competing directly with official film circuits, by discouraging: (i) films not yet released in any form of official distribution; (ii) large productions until, at least, six months after launching in the local commercial circuit; (iii) Brazilian films up to three months after the commercial launch in digital media. It reveals a strategic position in relation to the distribution market. Other MKO rules are of a technical nature and designed to guarantee content standards.

Normally, groups are concerned with the quality of their service, because they perform as distribution centres, willing to please and to serve their audience. Within this set of regulations, user behaviour is constantly monitored, which is necessary to build cohesion to deal with a context of innumerable pressures, limitations and instabilities.

Curatorial process and cyber-cinephilia

Cinephilia is both a collective and an individual experience, depending on several levels of interaction and mediation. According to Betz (2010: 131–2), cinephilia can be seen as a phenomenon of cultural, historical and geopolitical dimensions, and a form of knowledge that involves fascination, reflection and interpretation. It was conceptualized with clarity and practised with conscience from 1950/60 onward, when cinematographic art questioned its own aesthetics models through the authorial cinema.

The many forms of cinematographic content reception result in multiple experiences and definitions of the cinema object, which are even more abstract and intangible when sensory experience occurs through multiple mediations. Visiting the exhibition room is not the only possible cinematic experience for the public, because technological development of audiovisual reproduction proliferates the means of reception available, of course varying socially and historically. Therefore, cinephilia is a sort of frame through which to look at the object, to the symbolic representations that go beyond the ephemeral flow of consumption, so the understanding of cinema as an art object remains as a totally new experience.

In the context of post-internet cinephilia, art houses ceased to exist exclusively in exhibition halls of the largest cities, while populations far from central locations also wish to experience cinematic appreciation and demand for non-mainstream films. In this scenario, the public carries out distribution independently, relying on the support of a network with access to the most diverse sources and artistic microregions.

Self-perception and awareness are consequences of a hyper-connected society, taking into account that local cultures, and individuals are exposed to other local cultures and individuals, expanding their perception and curiosity about worldwide productions, since availability now has different proportions and more diverse interferences. It thus becomes possible to reassess the centrality of good taste, art or genius. Consequently, global cultural imaginaries become diversified and enriched. It is not, however, a massification of cinematographic niches but a qualitative expansion of these niches, which gain greater proportions and possibilities for cultural identification.

If Susan Sontag's (1996) statement on the death of the cinema provoked some controversy, at that time, we must not forget that the author gave a glimpse of hope, stating that the cinema could still be rescued by a new kind of cinematographic love. This is related to new forms of reception and experience, which include emotions, sensations, affective bonding, reading and knowledge. Online availability enables the engagement of film-loving communities and plays a key role in the dissemination and longevity of cinematographic works.

As an exemplary case of digital art house distribution, there is Jacques Rivette's film *Out 1: noli me tangere* (1971), which has been singled out as one of the least viewed contemporary films, since it has only been officially exhibited on a few occasions throughout its history. However, since 2009, the film has been circulating on Torrent networks; the shorter version of 253′, *Out 1: Specter* (1974), was found in MKO, and the full version of 729′ was found in the Hungarian group KG. This is an example of how digital availability perpetuates the existence of an art object in the cinephile imaginary, reaching niches and publics that are essentially unattainable by formal distribution.

Contemporary cyber-cinephilia collects rare and specialized cinema, tracing alternative paths through the cinematographic imagination and performing cultural resistance. Given the extensive amount of information available on the internet, cinephile groups act as expert knowledge groups, developing a curatorial work.

While the film industry remains profitable to some, the majority of films created in the world do not find audiences, much less make revenue. Torrent groups became fundamental actors in the transition of cinema to the digital world, helping to drive the public to watch and share films endowed with great cultural value and, therefore, to promote a cinema experience beyond entertainment through a conscious activity of film and aesthetic research.

It is worth mentioning that there is a close relationship between online communities and offline cinephilia groups, so that many active users also attend cinemas, releases, festivals and other related events. For instance, there is a direct connection between cyber-cinephilia and film clubs, with mutual feedback between the two. Relegated to marginality, both reach spectators, researchers, exhibitors, critics, collectors and archivists.

Like digital networks, film clubs have restricted-access material, either because of ideological or religious censorship or even because of trade constraints (Gonring 2014). Intersection between the two forms of cinematic experience is a natural result of digital technology's development, which has followed the historical course of previous modes of cinema experience. Technological changes have always affected film clubs and, indeed, digital technologies have helped to foster them, since they have facilitated access and display. Piracy is a quasi-essential part of film club movements, which is characterized by elements of illegality, a necessary condition for its survival due to material restrictions.

Furthermore, valuing national and author cinema is an essential feature of cinephile Torrent groups, which is an effect of cinephilia's globalized and multicultural imagination. Since the 1960s, 'national cinema' has been thought of as Hollywood's antagonist, representing the duality of culture vs commerce

(Nuñez 2013: 428). The 'national cinema' label hides a negative meaning: that is, everything that is not Hollywood. This is a clear reference to market control and an attempt to benefit local cinemas, promoting local aesthetics in resistance to the Hollywood agenda.

During postcolonial times, Hollywood ceases to be the axis of capitalist society's imagination. Although Guy Hennebelle's (1978) anti-Hollywoodian and anti-imperialist mentality persists over digital cinephile communities, the same massive informal-sharing networks reinterpret Hollywood's centrality, dissolving into fluid digital routes, with extremely dynamic connections between the public and plural cinemas (Nagib 2006: 28). The result is a deconstruction of old dichotomies: East and West, North and South, central and peripheral societies, trade and art, local and global. Geographies become more flexible, and cinema becomes transnational. In this context, cinephile Torrent groups feed transnational imagination by spreading local productions around the world. At the same time, national identities find visibility, as local audiences can access their own films, overcoming their scarcity among local suppliers.

Cinephile Torrent groups provide and select content under specific criteria, corresponding to a transnational cyber-cinephile imagination, which combines the art house, the academic canon, the underground circuit, World Cinema and mainstream and non-mainstream media (Almeida 2011; Crisp 2012; Iordanova and Cunningham 2012; Prysthon 2013). In this context, there are countless curatorial filters that create their own unstable and plural canons within group archives and forums.

MKO Curatorship

MKO's editorial line is summarized by the following slogan: 'The True Cinema'. This expression translates a specific cinephile identity, moulded by modernist canons of Authorial, Art, Experimental and World Cinema. 'The True Cinema' is not defined by the experience of visiting movie theatres or the movie circuit; rather, it is a definition developed by the group, which performs as a knowledge community, building its own perspective. Although the exhibition room is the origin, it is already distant from the digital reality of the object; in other words, the pre-digital life of a movie is not absolutely decisive, since digital circulation reinterprets that origin and reclassifies the value of the films at its own discretion.

According to its description, MKO aims to 'share rare, old, alternative, off-the-record movies and relevant documentaries'. Content niche and public evaluation are criterious, taking into account characteristics of 'taste' and 'acceptance'. In addition to satisfying particular tastes, it is also a tastemaker, as it states: 'we want to arouse in people the interest for good quality products of the cinema'.

By the time of the research covered in this chapter (2014–15), there was a constantly updated list of about 260 banned films, controlled by the admins and taken as irrevocable. Film characteristics could be quite diverse, including blockbusters or cheap productions, excluding specific actors (e.g. Steven Seagal, Sylvester Stallone, Chuck Norris, Eddie Murphy, Chevy Chase, John Candy, Arnold Schwarzenegger) or specific directors (e.g. Radley Metzger). The list also included Hollywood-branded production or commercial gender formulas, even unsuccessful or Hollywood-like productions of various national origins (e.g. Bollywood). There are no exceptions for Hollywood films of the 1980s, even with productions that came to be new classics from the 2000s onward, such as *The Goonies* (Richard Donner, 1985), *Mad Max* (George Miller, 1979), *La Bamba* (Luis Valdez, 1987) or *Back to the Future* (Robert Zemeckis, 1985).

In turn, productions of the 1970s or earlier endure a less rigorous assessment of their commercial, popular or even quality criteria, as a result of their reinterpretation as classics. Only eleven films from the 1970s were banned. The same is true for the most popular American blockbusters from the 1960s, mostly included because they achieved great success at the box office.

The judgement of the cultural or artistic value of a film is not consensual or even coherent; especially when a new release obtains increasing visibility, it is not possible to define objective standards for the exclusion criteria. For example, *The Curious Case of Benjamin Button* (David Fincher, 2008) was a topic of controversy among users, who discussed whether or not it should be in the catalogue in view of Brad Pitt's media image. By comparison, *Cidade de Deus* (Fernando Meirelles and Kátia Lund, 2002), one of the most well-known Brazilian films, was available in the catalogue, ostensibly due to its narrative and technical quality, despite its commercial success.

Definitions of 'The True Cinema' would reaffirm academic art house canons, but would include other elements like classic Hollywood, antique or vintage productions, and local productions from different countries, in various genres or styles. Through this process, MKO determines its own canon revision. The same process occurs in other environments of contemporary cinephilia; for example, Indonesian horror films and exploitation from the 1980s gain cultural status on the internet (Lobato 2012: 39–40), while Giallo films (an Italian genre of terror and exploitation, popular in the 1970s and 1980s) achieve cinematic appreciation in Torrent networks (Carter 2013). Likewise, Brazilian *pornochanchada* films, formerly undervalued by academic critics, are reinterpreted by new *cinefilias*.

Although aesthetic, artistic and intellectual evaluation is a controversial topic, it is precisely the matter that defines how cinema is experienced through cyber-cinephilia. This involves a dynamic of inclusion and exclusion of a multifaceted canon, which does not occur without conflicts, and which expresses the social dynamics of communities. Finally, online cinephilia can be summarized by the following key words and phrases: 'rarity'; 'opposition to the mainstream'; 'classics'; 'alternative'; 'independent'; 'national'; 'art'; 'good taste'; and 'experimentalism'.

Archive fever

Indexing and categorization tools are essential to information technology, as they allow users and machines to read the broad and complex universe of digital content. Cinephile Torrent groups digitalize, collect, preserve and distribute films that could be lost or forgotten, consequently accumulating knowledge about film history. There is a collective demand to retain information flows in archives, which are themselves texts to be read (Derrida [1995] 1998: 57). Although BitTorrent is not a storage technology, Torrent groups are focused on collecting, preserving, keeping alive and saving the object, as well as classifying, organizing and valuing anything that could be lost over time – that is, the rare, the ancient and the inaccessible.

Informal repositories are often broader than institutional archives that are constrained by official bureaucracy and centralized management. Informal networks overcome these limitations, by ignoring copyright restrictions and feeding databases from multiple sources to create informational redundancy through copying, in order to generate resources that effectively ensure preservation with low cost. Digital archivists or collectors, while saving films from oblivion, desacralize the rare; yet they do so through a re-sacralization that ritualizes itself in the body of the cinephile community.

The collector, archivist spirit is a phenomenon even more present in capitalist cultures, where the production of novelties is a fundamental motive. According to Sontag ([1980] 1986: 92), the present moment manufactures instant antiquities to be reread by decoders and collectors of the future. Sontag was reflecting upon the collecting passion of Walter Benjamin, who took the activity by his tactical instinct of wit, in order to find direction in the universe of symbolic objects.

One can speak of a pleasure given by the archive (Galloway et al. 2014), or even a need, an obsessive fever for it, a desire to retain information and to constantly reinterpret it as a guarantee of survival and self-knowledge (Derrida [1995] 1998: 57). In this sense, archive technical structure determines the relation between information and future times, not only recording it but also creating events and mechanisms to retain ephemerality. This is a cultural need that transcends the barriers of legal discourse or economic ethics, in the name of a collectivist, archivist and cinephile ethic, deeply concerned with the historical value of the vast and rich legacy of global cinema.

Final considerations

This investigation corroborates Mattelart's statement (2012: 747) that much of the media content that spreads through the globe does so through informal networks. Therefore, informal is not marginal in quantitative or even qualitative terms, since the volume, impact and cultural importance of these activities are central and massive.

For Bourdieu ([1979] 1984: 1–7), culture is a symbolic interaction established by power relations; in this sense, culture or cultural objects do not hold value but have their value established by social interactions and material conditions. In the digital age, technological developments altered material conditions of production and distribution for any cultural form which, in a way, altered the power balance presented by Bourdieu. Multiple voices (producers, creators, critics, curators) and channels, together with the greater mobility between continents, added to the globalization of politics and economy, resulting in even more fluid cultural references.

Aesthetic enjoyment has far more appeal than respect for copyright, so the value of cultural goods is not strictly measured by economic criteria; digital society made this evident, mainly due to the expansion of informal consumption and the consequent reorganization of economic markets. In the broad spectrum of informal exchanges, different values are given to information. Previously, the control of distribution channels governed the market value of a cultural product; in contrast, in the era of immaterial reproduction of information, informal distribution is the direct expression of cultural, artistic and symbolic value, and/

or the evaluation of what is less and less an asset of consumption, by traditional moulds.

Walter Benjamin ([1935] 1985: 165–96) questioned the ability of film to preserve art's classical function, arguing that the aura of an art object lies in its scarcity and eternity. It would be impossible for an industrial object, like cinema, to be the target of contemplation; instead, it would have a political function. After all, during the twenty-first century, the cinephilia of Torrent groups, while claiming the title of 'True Art' for the cinema, also disturbs its own auratic factors (scarcity and eternity). The exacerbated replication given by peer-to-peer interactions directly addresses the scarcity aspect, yet it triggers a new modulation for it, under the specific sense of exclusivity given by specialized and selected aggregations. It diminishes scarcity, but does so in a context of artistic appreciation for a selected audience, emulating its own aura around catalogues, and preserving artistic and aesthetic experience within a context of technical and immaterial reproducibility of the work of art.

The aura is much less a property of the object and much more a quality of the subjects who perceive it (Rodríguez-Ferrándiz 2012: 398). There is a reversal in the evaluation criteria of the artistic object, since full availability would not trivialize the film but would make the ephemeral contingency of the exhibition special and exclusive. Objects gain fluid auratic dimensions in digital media, through cults and rites, through technical entanglements and through privileged areas of exchange on underground networks.

Precisely because of the fluidity of sources on the internet, specialized mediators are increasingly required. Thus, each informational source makes their own cinematic interpretation, built with relative cohesion, and participates in a larger context of infinite sources. To conclude, one should agree with the intuition of Kenneth Goldsmith (2015: 75) that the very act of moving information from one side to another is, in itself, a cultural act of symbolic production, embodied with a dialogic context of infinite exchange universes.

References

Almeida, R. (2011), *Rasgos Culturais: consumo cinéfilo e o prazer da raridade*, Recife: Velhos Hábitos.

Almeida, P., and P. Butcher (2003), *Cinema, Desenvolvimento e Mercado*, Rio de Janeiro: Aeroplano.

Anderson, C. (2006), *The Long Tail: Why the Future of Business Is Selling Less of More*, New York: Hyperion.
Anderson, C. (2009), *Free: The Future of a Radical Price*, London: Business Books.
Barone, G. (2011), 'Assimetrias, Dilemas e Axiomas do Cinema Brasileiro nos Anos 2000', *Revista Famecos*, 18 (3): 916–32.
Benjamin, W. ([1935] 1985), 'A obra de arte na era de sua reprodutibilidade técnica', in S. P. Rouanet (trans.), *Walter Benjamin: Obras Escolhidas I: magia e técnica, arte e política*, São Paulo: Brasiliense, 165–96.
Bently, L., J. Davis and J. C. Ginsburg (2010), *Copyright and Piracy. An Interdisciplinary Critique*, New York: Cambridge University Press.
Betz, M. (2010), 'Introduction', *Cinema Journal*, 49 (2): 130–2.
Bodó, B. (2013), 'Set the Fox to Watch the Geese: Voluntary IP Regimes in Piratical File-Sharing Communities', in M. Fredriksson and J. Arvanitakis (eds), *Piracy: Leakages from Modernity*, Sacramento, CA: Litwin Books, 241–64.
Bodó, B., and Z. Lakatos (2012), 'Theatrical Distribution and P2P Movie Piracy: A Survey of P2P Networks Using Transactional Data', *International Journal of Communication*, 6 (1): 413–45.
Bourdieu, P. ([1979] 1984), *Distinction: A Social Critique of the Judgement of Taste*, R. Nice (trans.), Cambridge, MA: Harvard University Press.
Cardoso, G., M. Caetano, R. Espanha, P. Jacobetty and T. L. Quintanilha (2012), 'P2P in the Networked Future of European Cinema', *International Journal of Communication*, 6 (1): 795–821.
Carter, O. (2013), 'Sharing All'Italiana. The Reproduction and Distribution of the Giallo on Torrent File-Sharing Websites', in R. Braga and G. Caruso (eds), *Piracy Effect: norme, pratiche e studi di caso*, Milano: Mimesis Cinergie, 147–57.
Chiang, E., and D. Assane (2008), 'Music Piracy among Students on the University Campus: Do Males and Females React Differently?', *Journal of Socio-Economics*, 27 (4): 1371–80.
Crisp, V. (2012), 'Film Distribution in the Age of Internet: East Asian Cinema in the UK', PhD diss., Goldsmiths: University of London.
De Kosnik, A. T. (2012), 'The Collector Is the Pirate', *International Journal of Communication*, 6 (April 2012): 523–41.
Derrida, J. ([1995] 1998), *Archive Fever: A Freudian Impression*, E. Prenowitz (trans.), Chicago: University of Chicago Press.
Galloway, A. R., E. Thacker and M. Wark (2014), *Excommunication: Three Inquiries in Media and Mediation*, Chicago: University of Chicago Press.
Goldsmith, K. (2015), *Theory*, Paris: Jean Boîte Editions.
Gonring, G. M. (2014), 'Pirate Film Societies: Rearranging Traditional Apparatus with Inappropriate Technology', *Third Text*, 28 (2): 203–15.
Hennebelle, G. (1978), *Os Cinemas Nacionais Contra Hollywood*, São Paulo: Paz e Terra.

Iordanova, D., and S. Cunningham (2012), *Digital Disruption: Cinema Moves Online*, St. Andrews: St. Andrews Film Studies.

Lessig, L. (2004), *Free Culture: How Media Uses Technology and the Law to Lock Down Culture and Control Creativity*, New York: Penguin Press.

Lobato, R. (2012), *Shadow Economies of Cinema: Mapping Informal Film Distribution*, Basingstoke: Palgrave Macmillan.

Mason, M. (2009), *The Pirate's Dilemma: How Youth Culture Is Reinventing Capitalism*, New York: Simon and Schuster.

Mattelart, T. (2012), 'Audiovisual Piracy, Informal Economy, and Cultural Globalization', *International Journal of Communication*, 6 (April 2012): 735–50.

Meili, A. (2015), *Cinema na internet. Espaços Informais de Circulação, Pirataria e Cinefilia*, PhD Diss., Porto Alegre: PUCRS.

Mendes Moreira De Sa, V. (2013), Rethinking 'Pirate Audiences': An Investigation of TV Audiences' Informal Online Viewing and Distribution Practices in Brazil. PhD thesis. Sydney: University of Western Sydney.

Nagib, L. (2006), 'Towards a Positive Definition of World Cinema', in S. Dennison and S. H. Lim (eds), *Remapping World Cinema: Identity, Culture and Politics in Film*, London: Wallflower Press, 30–7.

Nuñez, F. (2013), 'Pensar o "Cinema Moderno Periférico": questionamentos teórico-historiográficos', *Contemporanea Comunicação e Cultura*, 11 (3): 427–45.

Oberholzer-Gee, F., and K. Strumpf (2009), *File-Sharing and Copyright*. Working Paper, Harvard Business School.

Pouwelse, J., P. Garbacki, D. H. J. Epema and H. J. Sips (2008), 'Pirates and Samaritans: A Decade of Measurement on Peer Production and Their Implications for Net Neutrality and Copyright', *Telecommunications Policy*, 32 (11): 701–12.

Prysthon, A. (2013), 'Transformações da crítica diante da cibercinefilia', *Celeuma*, 1 (1): 72–83.

Rodríguez-Ferrándiz, R. (2012), 'Benjamin, BitTorrent, Bootlegs: Auratic Piracy Cultures?', *International Journal of Communication*, 6 (April 2012): 396–412.

Sontag, S. ([1980] 1986), *Sob o signo de saturno*, A. M. Capovilla and A. Poli Jr (trans.), Porto Alegre: LP&M.

Sontag, S. (1996), 'The Decay of Cinema', *New York Times*, 25 February. Available online: https://www.nytimes.com/1996/02/25/magazine/the-decay-of-cinema.html (accessed 11 May 2021).

Bridges, streams and dams: The multiple negotiated strategies of distribution and access in Latin American cinema

Niamh Thornton

Social networking sites are a useful resource for dissemination and sharing for academics. An instance of this in 2012 led me to share a post on Twitter from a now defunct page that has a title akin to a Twitter handle, @the Library (of the University of St Andrews), offering free access to an archive of classic Mexican cinema with the view to enticing institutional subscribers to pay thousands for unlimited access (Young 2012). I blogged not only about my delight that this has been curated and is accessible but also about my reservations at the costs involved given that the same material is available for free in Mexico (Thornton 2012a). Shortly thereafter Arjan van Dijk, the acquisitions editor of Brill, the publishing company that owns this resource, emailed me to challenge my assertion that such material should be available for free. Here, I quote part of the email because it points to many of the issues that are central to my discussion:

> While I realize that scholars benefit from free access to primary sources, someone needs to pay the bill for organizing and managing a project like this, securing all permissions, selecting the material to be included (with help of a paid specialist editor), digitizing the magazines, creating metadata, building a platform, and making librarians and scholars aware of its existence through advertisements, mailings, etc. From idea to publication, this project has taken more than four years. Increasingly, governments are cutting funds for digitization projects. A commercial publisher like Brill invests in a project like this at its own risk, taking on the obligation to provide access to these rare sources for a long time to come. At the same time, I know various examples of public funded digitization projects which are no longer available online because of on going hosting costs not being budgeted. (Thornton 2012b)

Van Dijk highlights a number of concerns that have troubled archivists, scholars and the publishing industry in recent years which can be summarized as: how to pay the bills and who should pay, which also beleaguer multiple other industries faced with the new challenges of monetizing creative work and digital distribution. Access to Latin American and other non-Hollywood film is central to this current conundrum.

It was fitting that I found out about this matter through a tweet by Ernesto Priego (n.d.), a digital scholar specializing in information studies and actively engaged in debates on online publishing, in particular regarding discussions around open data research on Twitter and other public fora, because van Dijk also points to another key issue in digital access and distribution: the retreat of public funds and the increased reliance on private enterprises to fund online resources for scholars. This is taking place at a time when there is less finance available for the purchase of material and libraries are struggling to balance their budgets, which affects what researchers can access, how it is accessed and whether it can be used as teaching material. All these concerns can, in turn, influence what is researched given the pressures to publish on materials that will result in a wide readership that includes the undergraduate student body.

Given the enormity of the topics and debates that this simple two-way email correspondence conjures up – albeit via multinodal transnational encounters on Twitter, websites and blogs – I will not tackle them all in this chapter. Instead, I will consider selected case studies from the perspective of Latin American film scholarship and signal the broader debates it touches upon along the way.

Since the early 2000s Latin American film has had an increased world profile, thanks to funding, awards and showcasing initiatives by a variety of film festivals including Toronto, Sundance, Rotterdam and San Sebastian. A small group of filmmakers have been backed by well-known production companies, such as Pedro Almodovar's El Deseo with its focus on Argentina, and others have made the transition into English-language films, as has been the case with the Mexicans Alejandro González Iñarritú, Guillermo del Toro and Alfonso Cuarón (see Shaw 2013). The subsequent distribution of the films made by this select group gives the impression that Latin American films are easier to access, readily available and everywhere. Add to this picture the cybertopians who like to suggest that everything is but a click away, it would be possible to imagine that researching this geographical space has never been easier. In their optimistic reading of the potentialities of digital distribution Elizabeth Ezra and Terry Rowden write, 'Digital technology in all its aspects has enabled a growing disregard for national boundaries as ideological and aesthetic checkpoints by a range of legal and extra-legal players' (2006: 6). They were writing in 2006, prior to the wide uptake of streaming services. Where they identify national boundaries commercial interests putting up blocks and dams can be found. This chapter will consider a selection of platforms from a UK/Irish perspective (MUBI, Netflix, Curzon Home Cinema) to consider how these function as forms of bridges and dams that create flows and blockages to Latin American film. It will also take a sampling of films and reflect on their availability in two periods in 2012 and 2016 on legal platforms and consider what this means for research into Latin American film outside of the Americas.

MUBI, Curzon Home Cinema and Netflix

The two time periods for this study are February–March 2012 and January–February 2016. Only MUBI had significant content available in the first time period, which I will compare with the changes in 2016, and I am limiting myself to Netflix and Curzon Home Cinema for the second. This is because the categories for Amazon Prime were not searchable according to country, unlike the other services. I am limiting my searches to film because all three stream films, although Netflix also streams TV series.

Streaming platforms have become a popular means of viewing films and television. Netflix and its more recent direct competitor, Amazon Prime, have had the largest uptake. Both require flat subscriptions, although they do occasionally offer one-off viewings to entice new clients. Netflix launched in the UK and Ireland in 2012, but only reached wide take up in 2014. That same year Amazon Prime launched. By 2015 the market share of streaming service for Netflix was 20 per cent and Amazon Prime 9 per cent, with the spend on streaming in the UK reaching £3 billion by 2019 exceeding earlier predictions of £1 billion, while the sales of DVDs and Blu-rays are gradually falling (Savvas 2015; Sweney 2020). The content on both serves a wide audience and includes television as well as film.

MUBI and Curzon are carefully curated sites that stream content heretofore only available in art house cinemas. Both offer a flat payment subscription model or pay-per-view options with prices varying according to the film. Recent releases, in particular those with prize-winning credentials or nominated for well-known awards, are usually more expensive.

Founded in 2007 MUBI has been described as 'Netflix without the bloat', because since 2012 it only offers thirty films at a time, changing them regularly (Lyne 2015). Although all of these streaming services are carefully curated, paying attention to the perceived tastes of audiences in a given locale, MUBI foregrounds its curatorial selectivity, as evidenced in an interview with the founder Efe Çakarel: 'What we do at MUBI is much closer to that of a local cinema or a festival programmer; we search the globe for great cinema and we bring it to you – the streaming or online aspect is just the delivery method' (Li 2014). In addition, it has a social networking functioning whereby members curate lists and other users comment upon them to discuss and debate their merits or omissions. While MUBI's small number of available films is still quite bespoke, Netflix, too, has recognized that audiences prefer careful selection over quantity. In their 2014 mission statement the company stated, 'Instead of trying to have everything, we should strive to have the best in each category. As such, we are actively curating our service rather than carrying as many titles as we can' (Li 2014). This suggests that Netflix is also shedding the bloat, much like the curatorial selectivity of MUBI.

Anxiety about the screen type and size that films are watched on accompanies much of the assessment of streaming services. This is the case with Philip Maughan in the *New Statesman*, who describes Curzon Home Cinema as 'bespoke iTunes for independent cinema fans' (2013). Referencing the successful Apple-owned music streaming service indicates that Maughan, writing in 2013, expects his readers to be unfamiliar with other video streaming services. Much changed in a short few years. Curzon Home Cinema is an extension of the cinema chain's offerings to online audiences. The first Curzon cinema was opened in 1934 and in the 'About' section of the company's homepage, it describes itself as 'specializing in curated, quality international and British cinema, and hosts Q&As, events and special performances. Each cinema has its own identity and is designed with respect to the heritage of the local area' (Curzon 2016), thus emphasizing the global and local flavour of its cinemas as well as promoting the added value of events in its venues. Affiliated to Artificial Eye, a large independent distribution company, it is well placed to obtain rights for online streaming of the films shown in its twenty cinemas in the UK.

What can be shown on all of these services is determined by territorial rights. This is explained by Çakarel:

> Making a deal is a fairly straightforward process, but finding the right person takes a lot longer – rights are often passed down through generations or sold as

assets, so it's never as simple as calling up the director and signing a document. Building a global platform like MUBI, takes a lot of time ... but we've been very busy in the last seven years and now have over 4,500 films licensed globally. (Li 2014)

Licensing issues are also evident in the news stories in January 2016 about Netflix's threats 'to bring the hammer down on people who circumvent country-based content licensing restrictions using proxies or "unblockers"' (Spangler 2016). David Glance and others have suggested that this would be difficult to impose and could result in customers moving either to other platforms or to pirated content (2016). The fact that this is such a significant issue that Netflix is issuing threats to its customers suggests that it is not just scholars wishing to seek out films from across the globe in their field of expertise who are keen to watch content beyond that which the streaming services licence locally, but that there is a wider audience keen to see films heretofore not licenced in their country.

Latin American cinema

Using the blanket term 'Latin American Cinema/Film' is a contentious one, as Deborah Shaw indicates in her introduction to *Latin American Cinema Today: Breaking into the Global Market* 'in that it renders certain countries invisible, yet the term is clearly used and useful to discuss films from Latin America, not least as a marketing label' (2007: 4). As well as a category employed when marketing films from this territory and by some streaming services, there is a well-established practice of scholarly writing about Latin American film that groups a significant spread of highly differentiated countries together, although there is considerable variability in terms of production, distribution and local marketplaces. Stephanie Dennison, in the introduction to her edited collection *Contemporary Hispanic Cinema: Interrogating the Transnational in Spanish and Latin American Film*, discusses some of these, thus illuminating not only the validity of the practice but also its diversity (2013: 1–5 and 16–18). Given its prevalence, they are terms I will employ with some qualification. International co-productions funded by public finance, film festival funding and investment by private capital and television networks are but some of the means through which Latin American filmmakers have been supported, in particular the films that reach the international marketplace. As a result of the unevenness of finance models and access to distribution, the audiences they reach vary considerably. There are ebbs and flows in what is produced and where the films are seen and by whom.

There are countries with long histories of high production and international reach clearly motivated by a need to recoup on their investments, such as Mexico and Brazil, and to a lesser extent Argentina, while there are other countries that have small production outputs with little state or private infrastructure to support the industry, such as the Dominican Republic, Peru or Uruguay, for example. Some of the larger producing countries have undergone considerable changes since the 1990s seeing differential growth and some dramatic dips in production. At the same time, over the 2000s smaller producing nations have introduced new laws to encourage growth, witnessed how digital technology has changed capacity to create and distribute film, and grown unexpected diasporic markets, as is the case with the Dominican Republic. Then, there are anomalous countries, such as Cuba, who have had strong state support, less urgency to recoup the financial investment, patchy distribution and little access to new technology nor the means to distribute work globally via the internet. Given that they are at either end of this production and international distribution spectrum, Mexico and Cuba will be the focus of this study.

Mexico

The Mexican film industry grew from early newsreels of political figures and then documentation of the Mexican Revolution (1910–20) to a highly productive studio-based industrial phase from the 1930s up to the late 1950s. In order to ensure the success of the industry, the government set up a film bank as an efficient form of subsidizing production (Mora 2005: 59). During this period many of the hundreds of mostly genre films produced annually had considerable local and international audiences throughout the Spanish-speaking world. Melodramas and rural-based musicals, called *Rancheras*, were the most popular. The 1960s and 1970s saw a decline in production with the take up of television, and the 1980s was characterized by low-budget genre films (Horror, Chili Westerns and Wrestling) that often went straight to video. These had an international cult audience at a time when B-movies were flourishing globally. As a result of privatization clauses in the North American Free Trade Agreement, in the 1990s there was a considerable dip in production and two trends emerged: the growth of romantic comedies aimed at a Mexican middle-class audience that received little international distribution and a small number of high-profile international successes, the most famous of which is *Like Water for Chocolate* (Alfonso Arau, 1994) (see Mora 2005: 191; Sánchez Prado 2014). Since the mid-1990s private finance has been the primary means of economic support and the profit motive has come to predominate with an emphasis on transnational co-productions.

Like Water for Chocolate is seen as the precursor to the international success in the early 2000s of a small number of transnational filmmakers, such as the aforementioned Cuarón, González Iñarritú and del Toro who have crossed over into mainstream (Hollywood) success, another small number of internationally known filmmakers whose films get distribution via film festivals and art house cinemas, such as Amat Escalante and Carlos Reygadas, and well-known film stars, such as Salma Hayek and Gael García Bernal (Noble 2005: 2). Their output has not resulted in greater production in Mexico, nor have many local filmmakers followed the same modes and styles of filmmaking of these auteurs. However, there is a consistent output that includes comedies, historical dramas, thrillers and horror, few of which reach audiences outside of Latin America. Therefore, there is a disconnect between the high-profile Mexican cinema via a select number of auteurs and stars and the possibility of accessing a range of films that reach local audiences.

Cuba

Cuban cinema is largely defined in relation to the political regime under Fidel (and more recently Raúl) Castro that has been in place since the revolution in 1959. Prior to the revolution, in the 1940s and 1950s there were amateur filmmakers, but it wasn't until the 1950s when a select number of Cubans went to the *Centro Sperimentale della Cinematografia* in Rome to study film that filmmaking took hold on the island. Influenced by Italian neorealism and the growing revolutionary sentiment, Julio García Espinosa, aided by Tomás Gutiérrez Alea, made *The Charcoal Worker* (1954). The Argentine Fernando Birri, the founder of the Film School in Havana, sees this film as the birth of New Latin American Cinema, identified with solidarity movements and revolutionary politics, and saw filmmaking as a means of bringing about political and social change (see Chanan 1983: 2; Schroeder 2002: 9) that lasted up to the late 1980s. In 1959 filmmaking was supported through the *Instituto Cubano del Arte e Industria Cinematográficos* (ICAIC), a national organization set up as one of the first decrees of the Revolutionary Government (Chanan 1985: 19). This primarily supported documentaries; in contrast, 'the production of feature films takes on secondary importance, and then is only permitted to the extent that these films promote the creation of a monolithic democracy' (Schroeder 2002: 4). Gutiérrez Alea is one of the best-known Cuban filmmakers to sustain a career from the early 1960s up to the mid-1990s. Other notable figures whose work has attained international distribution in the 1970s are Humberto Solás and Sara Gómez. Both made films that are aesthetically and technically experimental in ways that appeal to European art house audiences.

The ICAIC long promoted 'collective creativity', and, as a result there were mutually beneficial collaborations, such as that of Juan Carlos Tabío and Gutiérrez Alea in the late 1980s and mid-1990s, in particular on *Strawberry and Chocolate* (1994) and *Guantanamera* (1995) (Chanan 1985: 138). Tabío later created a new genre, 'the sociocritical comedy' (Chanan [2004] in Stone 2007: 9) with *House for Swap* (1983), that he has followed up with subsequent successes including *The Waiting List* (2000) (see Stone 2007). Many of these films tackle the difficulties experienced by Cubans during the time of economic instability post-1989 called the Special Period, after the fall of the USSR on whom Cuba had become dependent for trade, goods and services.

Since the early 2000s there has been a growth in co-productions, particularly with the Spanish-based fund IBERMEDIA, such as *Habana Blues* (Benito Zambrano, 2005) and *Chico and Rita* (Tono Errando, Javier Mariscal and Fernando Trueba, 2010). The latter won an Oscar for Best Animated Feature Film of the Year. IBERMEDIA has been criticized as favouring Spanish talent and, consequently, being a form of neocolonialism (see Falicov 2013). Both Zambrano and Trueba are Spanish directors, and it was this association with IBERMEDIA that ensured distribution on the film festival circuit. More recent Cuban films supported by IBERMEDIA have won awards, but not had a significantly high profile or distribution beyond the festival circuit (see IBERMEDIA 2015). Cuba has a long history of a small number of films distributed internationally but can still be seen as a country that is hampered by the current distribution models that favour specific circuits or supports from large studios with easy access to global licensing.

Carefully curated content: MUBI and Curzon Home Cinema

In 2012 MUBI had 1,137 films available to view. These were filtered by a scrollable list of genres or a box that lets you type in cast or crew. There were more advanced filters that allowed searches by language, country, release date, rating and whether the films were free or had trailers. This has changed. Films are now searchable by genres, countries and years, and, then, by most popular and when the film has been streamed on the service. Therefore, it is now possible to see the titles of all of the Mexican or Cuban films ever shown on MUBI or those shown in the searchable categories: 'last week', 'last month', 'last year' or 'all time'. The problem with this is that it functions as a comprehensive list of the curatorial taste of the MUBI selectors, but these films cannot be streamed via this service if they are not part of the day's 30 choices. This goes against Çakarel's foundational narrative oft-repeated in media accounts of MUBI: that he set up the company when trying to stream *In the Mood for Love* (Wong Kar-wai, 2000) when he was on a visit to Japan (Li 2014). The current curatorial model does not provide MUBI subscribers the option to choose what to see when they want to see it. Çakarel has failed to offer what he had aspired to in his foundational narrative.

In 2012, MUBI made five Cuban films available: *Lucia* (Humberto Solás, 1968), *Memories of Underdevelopment* (Tomás Gutiérrez Alea, 1968), *Strawberry and Chocolate* (Tomás Gutiérrez Alea, 1993), *I am Cuba* (Mikhail Kalatozov, 1964) and *Between Two Hurricanes* (Enrique Colina, 2003). Until the change in curatorial policy they were possible to stream at any time. Since then, a further 149 films have been shown. The first four of these 2012 choices are predictable selections from early revolutionary Cuban filmmakers Solás and Gutiérrez Alea, and the latter's Oscar winning film (*Strawberry and Chocolate*); and a Soviet film that was rereleased in 2005 with considerable support from US independent filmmakers, Francis Ford Coppola and Martin Scorsese (*I am Cuba*). The more surprising choice is Colina's *Between Two Hurricanes*, a film that has received little attention since its release. While set and made in Cuba with Cuban crew it received much of its funding from French producers, which suggests that it was part of a package of films sold to MUBI by a European-based rights owner and not chosen because of the more typical criteria of international awards or critical praise. Therefore, the 2012 selection is a mix of canonical revolutionary films and commercial expediency.

The films shown between 2012 and 2016 include a diverse range of Cuban-made, Cuban-set, or Cuban-themed films such as: seven difficult to source films by the experimental documentary maker Nicolás Guillén Landrián, originally released between 1963 and 1972; *Havana Motor Club* (Brent-Jorgen Perlmutt, 2014), a film about underground drag-racing in Havana by a Brooklyn-based filmmaker; an adaptation of the Colombian novelist Gabriel García Marquez's eponymous short story, *A Very Old Man with Enormous Wings* (1988) by the aforementioned Birri; and *Una noche* (2012), a Havana-set film made by a New York–based filmmaker largely financed by UK producers. What this sample reveals says much about how we ascribe nationality to a film (finance, location, narrative, cast and crew) and the difficulties of curating films with this in mind.

Two further examples from MUBI's catalogue reveal how algorithms and curatorial decisions can confound traditional academic boundaries. Both are by the same director, the Chilean Patricio Guzmán, who has lived in France since leaving Chile to go into exile in 1973. His *Battle of Chile* (1975) is catalogued under 'Cuba' and *Salvador Allende* (2004) under 'Mexico'. *Battle of Chile* was shot by Guzmán and six others in Chile in the lead up to the coup by the right-wing military dictator, Augusto Pinochet. At great risk, the footage was smuggled out and, with the support of the French filmmaker, Chris Marker, and ICAIC, it was edited and released through art house and solidarity networks. Undoubtedly, the Cuban film institute was central to completing the film, but so too was Marker. But few academics would describe this as either a Cuban or French film. The political events in Chile and the crew's nationality make this definitively a Chilean film. Yet, MUBI's cataloguing system unmoors it from its sole categorization as a Chilean film.

Salvador Allende is labelled as Mexican because one of the eleven production companies is the University of Guadalajara in Mexico, another nationally funded institution, alongside public and private producers, such as the French private television cable company Canal+ and the French national film institution, the *Centre National de la Cinématographie*. This mix of financial support from national institutions and private companies muddles ownership in ways that are often too simply told when packaged for sale, read in terms of the location and narrative, or confined to scholarly framing. Both of these examples add further to the 'layered conceptions of the nation-state inevitably in tension with each other', and make space for new interventions in discussions of where the nation belongs in the consumption of transnational films (Vitali and Willemen 2006: 9). Therefore, MUBI's country labels may be read as simultaneously a miscategorization and an exciting opportunity to reread these films as other than their heretofore defining framings.

A further meta-category in MUBI points to another way of labelling low-production and/or low-distribution countries. Cuba is categorized as an 'Uncommon Country', while Mexico is a 'Common Country', referring to the numbers of films under these country labels. Under 'Mexico' in 2012, there were 27 films; by 2016 there are 1,078. As with 'Cuba', country classification must be qualified. Some of the films were shot in Mexico, were co-productions or the narrative is set there. As with 'Cuba', there is a mixture of old and new films easily categorizable as Mexican and others which have tenuous links. For example, *Jauja* (Lisandro Alonso, 2014) appears under 'Mexico' because it is one of the co-producing countries despite the fact that the film is set in Denmark and Patagonia, and there is no Mexican element to the narrative. This designation invites me as a viewer and researcher to puzzle over national labels and to follow the financing.

Another example worth pausing suggests either applied knowledge or the interesting effect of algorithms and results in an unusual presentation of Luis Buñuel's oeuvre: all that he made while living in Mexico is categorized under 'Mexico'. He did live and work for many years in Mexico and even became a citizen, but many of his films are European-based and he never renounced his Spanish citizenship. Indeed, most Buñuel scholars outside of Mexico read him entirely as a Spanish director. In his assessment of Buñuel's own attitude to this period in Mexico, Ernesto R. Acevedo-Muñoz states,

> The lack of attention [in his memoir *The Last Sigh*] given to the seventeen Mexican films [over 37 years] seems disproportional compared to the focus on briefer periods, personal pleasures, and prejudices that Buñuel thought were the highlights of his life: his student years, Paris, surrealism, a good martini. (2003: 55)

MUBI's categorization draws attention to an important facet of Buñuel's output in Mexico. This may be an accidental outcome of how the algorithms read Buñuel's work during this period, but it is one that pushes boundaries beyond how academia (beyond Mexico) reads Buñuel. Against the conventional rigidity of country categorization, MUBI's country labels have the potential to shift scholarship outside of the national and to bring new understandings of national attribution.

While nation-based understandings of film are being challenged through these categorizations, there is little challenge to other criteria of value in how MUBI has consistently allied itself to events, such as film festivals. In 2012 MUBI had collaborations with festivals around the world streaming selected content from their screenings. These ranged from the so-called 'A' list to smaller niche festivals, such as Locarno, Cannes, Mar del Plata, San Sebastian, SXSW,

Sundance, Belfast, DocsBarcelona, Outfest and so on. In recent years, it has narrower collaborations in line with its more selective approach. For example, in 2014 it streamed short films in partnership with the Cannes Film Festival's *Court Metrage* (Barraclough 2014). It also has provided sponsorship for specialist film festivals, such as the London Short Film Festival and the Sheffield Doc Fest. There is an evolution in its festival screenings with a narrower range shown, and its associated online review magazine regularly provides reviews of international film festivals. Therefore, sponsorship and reportage – rather than primarily streaming – are the current ways MUBI continues its association with international art house film culture (Sheffield Doc Fest 2016).

It has also streamed films as part of events or themes in order to help build an audience. This was the case with a Mexican film, *Revolution*, an anthology film directed by ten different directors released in 2010 to coincide with the commemoration of the centenary of the Revolution (1910–20). Produced by actor-director-producers Gael García Bernal and Diego Luna it was simultaneously released on YouTube and MUBI to avoid having to pass it by the Mexican distribution system that stalls the release of controversial films (Thornton 2013: 180–1). Given the high-profile names attached, this was a successful gambit and the film had a considerable audience in its free and pay-per-view distribution, and has subsequently been released on DVD in a special package.

Like MUBI, Curzon Home Cinema shifts clear-cut understandings of country designation. Its event presentations tend to be means of encouraging audiences to attend cinema theatres or it uses the publicity around award seasons as ways of drawing attention to their offerings rather than through exclusive screenings. The complex interplay of what country determines ownership over a given film is evident in Curzon Home Cinema's choices under 'Mexico' and 'Cuba'. On the dates I looked in 2016, there are no films under 'Cuba', with the box office hit documentary and transmedia success, *Buena Vista Social Club*, by the German filmmaker Wim Wenders standing in as the thumbnail for 'Cuba'. There is no back catalogue of films, unlike MUBI. Both the lack of films and the thumbnail signal some of the issues around distribution of Cuban (or 'Cuban') films globally. Under 'Mexico' there are seven films in the 2016 period: the transnational biopic directed by a UK filmmaker and shot in Mexico with an international cast and crew, *Frida* (Julia Taymor, 2002); two films by the award-winning director Amat Escalante – *Los Bastardos* (2008) and *Heli* (Amat Escalante, 2013), whose violent films address social issues (respectively, immigration and the drugs war); the Mexican-made and -set low-budget award-winning *Güeros* (Alonso Ruizpalacios, 2015); *Chronic* (Michel Franco, 2015), the Los Angeles-set story of an end-of-life care nurse starring British actor Tim Roth and directed by a Mexican; a documentary that shifts between two very differently motivated armed defence movements either side of the US–Mexico border directed by a US filmmaker, *Cartel Land* (Mathew Heineman, 2015); *The Golden Dream* (Diego Quemada-Díez, 2013), a film by Spanish-Mexican US-based director that follows the attempted migration by three Guatemalans across Mexico to the United States. These are all films that are relatively easy to access and, therefore, do not impel the viewer towards the seldom seen in the ways that MUBI can. That said, in the same way as MUBI's categories work, they do challenge a neat understanding of what a Mexican film is. However, what this sample of films suggests is that films set in Mexico or where the director is Mexican decides its designation for Curzon Home Cinema. This is not as fluid as either MUBI or Netflix's designations.

Algorithms and geo-blocking: Netflix

Netflix is renowned for its unusual categorization of films and 'complex ecosystem of algorithms' (Vanderbilt 2013) it refuses to fully reveal, that is part machine produced and part human built (Mittel 2016; Wu 2015). It does not follow conventional labels established by film scholarship and, instead, employs a changing set of labels designed to push audiences towards unlikely connections not unlike online shops that make recommendations based on past purchases. Some of these are categories that suggest a wide viewership: 'Popular on Netflix' and, borrowing from the social media site, Twitter's language, 'Trending Now' that is both ambiguous insofar as it is unclear where these are trending and allows for the possibility that trending can mean they are subject to online chatter and debate, and, therefore, is suggestive of popularity beyond Netflix. There is the novelty label: 'Recently added' that offers no suggestion of hierarchy and the more obviously personalized 'Top Picks for [name of subscriber]'; a series of 'Because You Watched [Name of prior viewing]' that can result in curious pairings; and 'Continue Watching for [name of subscriber]', of films or TV programmes that the subscriber began to watch but did not finish. There are other categories that are common to many subscribers: 'TV Dramas', 'Anime' and 'Children and Family Films', and then there are others that are generated as a result of personal viewing habits. For example, in 2016, the algorithms have decided on 'Drug Documentaries', 'Dark US TV Dramas', 'Witty Comedies' and 'Critically Acclaimed Independent Dramas' personalized to my viewing habits. These examples show how streaming is an individuated geographically bounded experience determined by consumption patterns and prompts.

As well as these suggestions, there is a browse function on the site where, under the 'International Movies' category, there is another searchable 'Subgenre' field with 'Latin American Films' as a subcategory. In the Irish and UK site there are only eighteen 'Latin American films', of which only four are Mexican and none are Cuban. The four Mexican films are: *Days of Grace* (Everardo Valerio Grout, 2011), a fiction film about three violent kidnappings during pivotal football World Cup games; a story of a beauty pageant winner caught up in drug violence, *Miss Bala* (Gerardo Naranjo, 2011); a horror, *Here Comes the Devil* (Adrián García Bogliano, 2012); and *Instructions Not Included* (Eugenio Derbez, 2013), a comedy that had the biggest box office earnings in Mexico to date and is currently the highest grossing foreign language film in the United States (Cervantes 2013). *Miss Bala* is the only one that got festival and art house distribution, and has received academic attention. The others have gotten little distribution or academic attention, as with many genre films from Mexico. This has much to do with the hierarchical nature of knowledge consumption and the tendency by academics to write about films that appear on curricula, few of which are conventional or high-grossing genre films.

Netflix takes a more conventional approach to country ascription to that of MUBI and Curzon Home Cinema. The broader hemispheric Latin America label goes some way to explaining this. But, it does offer a (very small) selection of films that go beyond the typical art house offering with an emphasis on genre films, in particular, horror, action, war and comedy. There are also exclusions from this Latin American category. For example, *Babel* (2006) by the Mexican director Alejandro González Iñárritu is not included, even though one of its four narratives is set in Mexico. Likewise, *Narco Cultura* (2013) by the Israeli documentary filmmaker, Shaul Schwarz, is not included in this category although it is specifically examining drug gangs in Mexico. These are revealed if you search 'Mexico'. Search for 'Cuba' and no Cuban film comes up, only films starring Cuba Gooding Jr.

Netflix is notoriously secretive about its algorithms, therefore it is only speculation as to why the categories are so narrow, although, no doubt, the scale of its offering or the aforementioned Netflix bloat bears an influence. These are all instances of a developing pattern Rob Stone observes as

> best illustrated by the breaking of the frame, which was not only the dissolution of the form and format of the artefact into free-forming pixels occasioned by the digital revolution, but the dismantling of the rigidity with which films were classified. (2015: 424)

Although he is not specifically referencing Netflix, but instead the evolution of Spanish film studies and his own research trajectory, his assertion that there is a growing breakdown of rigid classificatory systems in production and scholarly work can also be found in the streaming service as means of distribution and consumption. He further notes how, despite the ways in which nation-based framing is collapsing in some quarters, it is also seeing resistance because of 'rigid correlations between film and nationhood still prevailed in universities, however, where the language based curricula reinforced the frame' (Stone 2015: 424). Here, Stone is specifically referencing 'Spanish' cinema (he uses inverted commas), but it is clear from his article that it can be understood to refer to a wider challenge to national cinema studies governed by strict geopolitical boundaries. Further, for Stone, 'the limited and restricted, solipsistic and self-contained idea of the nation-state is a shonky frame that fails to contain the cultural diversity of the cinema' (2015: 428). This is an assessment that celebrates the turn to the specifics and particularities of regional, community-based and alternate cinemas, and also to the broader level of the transnational with which the national can intersect but where ownership can be more difficult to define. Stone's review and reflection usefully address the thorny question of national categorizations and suggests that the discipline is ready to confront the slippery nature of these definitional framings. Like Stone's disciplinary and personal assertions, the study of these streaming services reveals another instance of how rigid frameworks no longer work and how they are challenged in practice by both machines and humans.

Conclusion

The online streaming ecosystem has complexified and extended since my original research into this topic in 2012 and 2016. Some platforms have changed their offerings and shifted their access points and navigation experience.

Meanwhile other new services have been launched. Since 2020, the pandemic has strengthened the market share and led to the growth in subscriptions to platforms such as Netflix, examined in detail here. What this chapter addresses is a moment in time to give an entry point to understanding how these services have evolved using the lens of the distribution and consumption of Latin American cinema from the vantage point of the UK and Ireland. What is clear from this research is that we are in a moment of excess and blockage. Lev Manovich has written about the challenges of navigating an overabundance of information (2001: 35), and content online at this 'cultural period [which] is characterized by an unprecedented scale of production and circulation' (2018: 18). He explores artificial intelligence and algorithms as a possible solution with considerable limitations. What such machine learning and software can create is the opposite of excess, scarcity, which means that machines rather than cultural curators, those I propose as tastemakers (Thornton 2020), decide what and when we can consume if seen from the perspective of a particular geographic locale or set of concerns.

MUBI is a streaming service that obtains global licences for the films it shows. Curzon Home Cinema is UK-based and only concerns itself with the local marketplace. Netflix is a global brand that curates content according to its expectations of local demand and is subject to territorial licensing. Therefore, the Latin American offering on its US site is considerably higher than the UK and Ireland given hemispheric licences and the Hispanic market (162 in March 2016). On the back of the furore about proxies and Netflix's threats to block content, the Australian academic David Glance writes,

> Customers globally are increasingly expecting a single digital market where the same content is made available at the same time, worldwide. Companies that are working to this model are really the ones that will succeed on a global basis because they will be giving customers what they want. (2016)

His is a challenge to streaming companies to (re)consider geo-blocking and to build bridges to allow content to be available simultaneously globally. This is but one of the issues streaming services will have to face.

What my snapshot overview should provide the reader is an overview of how these services have evolved in this period and a reflection on the novel aspects of categorization that serve as a challenge to conventional academic nation-based framing and a contribution to Latin American cinema as a transnational field of study. The dams put up by the licensing companies are primarily in the interest of protecting financial gains. Netflix frames these as being difficult to surmount. The other blockages happen in the form of curatorial gatekeeping operated by Netflix implicitly, and by MUBI more explicitly. The curious viewer keen to see films under particular parameters beyond the curators' choices will have their options limited. In addition, this selectivity does not allow for the more ad hoc nature of academic research. In terms of access to content, at the time of writing none of these streaming services is offering anything that would fully replace the need for archival research, purchasing DVDs or even the occasional desperate foray into YouTube in search of rare oddities.

When considered with an awareness of the dramatic changes in viewing habits and consumption of film and other streaming content in 2020 and early 2021, the analysis in this chapter should be seen as a glimpse into the past and an indicator of the problems, some of which repeat themselves (such as access, geo-blocking, curatorial biases) and are ever-shifting in unexpected ways (such as the exponential and unexpected growth in the consumption of Spanish-language television in the UK). In what is a shift in patterns of viewing away from traditional synchronous television channels, the Spanish television series *Money Heist* (2017–) drew the largest audiences for any television series on the platform in 2020 (Tassi 2020). Some of this move was a consequence of the pandemic and the upswing in the range of available online platforms as well as the growth in subscriptions due to the lockdowns and stay at home orders around the world. The pattern of growth in Spanish-language content follows on from the huge success (Clark 2020) of *Narcos* (2015–17) and *Narcos: Mexico* (2018–), which has led to Netflix establishing production hubs in Mexico and Spain (Netflix 2018; Shaw 2020). This reveals the profitability of work produced from Spain and Latin America and the content available suggests that the Netflix audience is most interested in genre productions. Not that academic work should be determined by platform choices, such shifts should encourage scholars to pay greater attention to work that has heretofore been shunned or overlooked in favour of art house works. This chapter has considered access to Mexican and Cuban films, but similar studies are needed to track the evolution of this access and where new forms and genres may become available as they emerge. The ephemeral nature of much of the information means that this chapter is a snapshot of a moment in time that scholars need to track as they happen. It is also an insight into a moment in an early period of relatively modest growth that is now a larger trend towards online access and new gatekeeping whereby media companies become tastemakers impelled by market share and algorithms.

References

Acevedo-Muñoz, E. R. (2003), *Buñuel and Mexico: The Crisis of National Cinema*, Berkeley: University of California Press.

Barraclough, L. (2014), 'Cannes Fest, VOD Platform Mubi Partner to Unspool Past Titles (EXCLUSIVE)', *Variety*, 13 May. Available online: http://variety.com/2014/film/markets-festivals/cannes-fest-vod-platform-mubi-partner-to-unspool-past-titles-exclusive-1201179951/ (accessed 3 March 2016).

Cervantes, J. (2013), 'Las películas mexicanas más taquilleras de la historia', *Forbes*, 17 December. Available online: http://www.forbes.com.mx/las-peliculas-mexicanas-mas-taquilleras-de-la-historia/ (accessed 3 March 2016).

Chanan, Michael (1983), *Twenty-five Years of the New Latin American Cinema*. London: BFI Books.

Chanan, Michael (1985), *The Cuban Image*. London: BFI Pub; Bloomington: Indiana University Press.

Clark, T. (2020), 'Netflix's New Season of "Narcos: Mexico" Is Pacing to Be the Franchise's Most Popular Entry Yet', *Business Insider*, 14 February. Available online: https://www.businessinsider.com/netflixs-narcos-mexico-season-2-poised-to-be-a-hit-2020-2?r=US&IR=T (accessed 13 April 2021).

Curzon (2016), 'About Curzon'. Available online: http://corporate.curzon.com/#our-company (accessed 3 March 2016).

Dennison, S. (2013), 'National, Transnational and Post-national: Issues in Contemporary Filmmaking in the Hispanic World', in S. Dennison (ed.), *Contemporary Hispanic Cinema: Interrogating the Transnational in Spanish and Latin American Film*, Woodbridge: Tamesis, 1–24.

Ezra, E., and T. Rowden (2006), 'What Is Transnational Cinema?' in E. Ezra and T. Rowden (eds), *Transnational Cinema: The Film Reader*, London: Routledge, 1–12.

Falicov, T. L. (2013), 'Ibero-Latin American Co-Productions: Transnational Cinema, Spains Public Relations Venture or Both', in S. Dennison (ed.), *Contemporary Hispanic Cinema: Interrogating the Transnational in Spanish and Latin American Film*, Woodbridge: Tamesis, 67–88.

Glance, D. (2016), 'Even if Netflix Is Serious about Blocking VPNs, It Is Unlikely to Succeed', *The Conversation*, 15 January. Available online: https://theconversation.com/even-if-netflix-is-serious-about-blocking-vpns-it-is-unlikely-to-succeed-53246 (accessed 3 March 2016).

IBERMEDIA (2015), 'Siete películas de IBERMEDIA logran once premios'. Available online: http://www.programaibermedia.com/nuestras-noticias/siete-peliculas-de-ibermedia-logran-once-premios-el-festival-de-cine-de-la-habana/ (accessed 25 August 2020).

Li, C. (2014), 'A Close-up of MUBI and Its Plans to Take on Netflix and Amazon Prime with a Curated Cinema Platform', *Tech.eu*, 2 April. Available online: http://tech.eu/features/915/mubi/ (accessed 3 March 2016).

Lyne, C. (2015), 'Mubi, the curated online cinema club', *The Guardian*, 25 April. Available online: http://www.theguardian.com/media/2015/apr/25/mubi-online-cinema-club (accessed 3 March 2016).

Manovich, L. (2001), *The Language of New Media*, Cambridge, MA: MIT Press.

Manovich, L. (2018), *AI Aesthetics*, Moscow: Strelka Press.

Maughan, P. (2013), 'Cinema on Demand: The Top Five Places to Watch New Films Online', *New Statesman*, 26 February. Available online: http://www.newstatesman.com/culture/2013/02/cinema-demand-top-five-places-watch-new-films-online (accessed 3 March 2016).

Mittel, J. (2016), 'Why Netflix Doesn't Release Its Ratings', *The Atlantic*, 23 February. Available online: http://www.theatlantic.com/entertainment/archive/2016/02/netflix-ratings/462447/ (accessed 3 March 2016).

Mora, C. J. (2005), *Mexican Cinema: Reflections of a Society, 1896–2004*, Jefferson, NC: McFarland.

Netflix (2018), 'Netflix Establishes Its First European Production Hub in Madrid', *Netflix*, 24 July. Available online: https://about.netflix.com/en/news/netflix-establishes-its-first-european-production-hub-in-madrid (accessed 13 April 2020).

Noble, A. (2005), *Mexican National Cinema*, New York: Routledge.

Priego, E. (n.d.), 'Everything Is Connected' (blog entry). Available online: https://epriego.blog/ (accessed 13 April 2021).

Sánchez Prado, I. (2014), *Screening Neoliberalism. Mexican Cinema 1988–2012*, Nashville, TN: Vanderbilt University Press.

Savvas, A (2015), 'Video Streaming Now a Half a Billion Pound Market in the UK Says Mintel', *TechWorld*, 20 March.

Schroeder, P. A. (2002), *Tomás Gutiérrez Alea: The Dialectics of a Filmmaker*, New York: Routledge.

Shaw, D. (2007), 'Latin American Cinema Today: A Qualified Success Story', in D. Shaw (ed.), *Contemporary Latin American Cinema: Breaking into the Global Market*, New York: Rowman & Littlefield, 11–20.

Shaw, D. (2013), *The Three Amigos: The Transnational Filmmaking of Guillermo del Toro, Alejandro González Iñárritu, and Alfonso Cuarón*, Manchester: Manchester University Press.

Shaw, L. (2020), 'Netflix Moving Latin American Base to Mexico as Ambitions Grow', *Bloomberg*, 31 January. Available online: https://www.bloomberg.com/news/articles/2020-01-31/netflix-moving-latin-american-base-to-mexico-as-ambitions-grow (accessed 13 April 2021).

Sheffield Doc Fest (2016), Available online: https://sheffdocfest.com/about/partners-sponsors (accessed 3 March 2016).

Spangler, T. (2016), 'Netflix Vows to Shut Down Proxy Users Who Bypass Country Restrictions', *Variety*, 14 January. Available online: http://variety.com/2016/digital/news/netflix-shuts-down-proxy-access-1201680010/ (accessed 3 March 2016).

Stone, R. (2007), 'Killing Time in Cuba: Juan Carlos Tabío's *Lista de espera*', in D. Shaw (ed.), *Contemporary Latin American Cinema: Breaking into the Global Market*, New York: Rowman and Littlefield, 145–62.

Stone, R. (2015), 'The Disintegration of Spanish Cinema', *Bulletin of Spanish Studies*, 92 (3): 423–38.

Sweney, M. (2020), 'UK Spent a Record £3bn on Streaming Music, Films and TV in 2019', *The Guardian*, 3 January. Available online: https://www.theguardian.com/media/2020/jan/03/uk-spent-a-record-3bn-on-streaming-music-films-and-tv-in-2019 (accessed 14 April 2021).

Tassi, P. (2020), 'Netflix Reveals "Money Heist" Has Somehow Drawn More Viewers Than "Tiger King"', *Forbes*, 22 April. Available online: https://www.forbes.com/sites/paultassi/2020/04/22/netflix-reveals-money-heist-has-somehow-drawn-more-viewers-than-tiger-king/?sh=71cbb77cf5a1 (accessed 13 April 2021).

Thornton, N. (2012a), 'Private Archives/Public Good: Classic Mexican Film Online' (blog entry). Available online: http://www.niamhthornton.net/classic-mexican-film-online/ (accessed 25 August 2021).

Thornton, N. (2012b), 'Private Archives/Public Good: Classic Mexican Film on Line Part 2' (blog entry). Available online: http://www.niamhthornton.net/private-archivespublic-good-classic-mexican-film-on-line-part-2/ (accessed 3 March 2016).

Thornton, N. (2013), *Revolution and Rebellion in Mexican Film*, London: Bloomsbury.

Thornton, N. (2020), *Tastemakers and Tastemaking: Mexico and Curated Screen Violence*, Albany, NY: SUNY Press.

Vanderbilt, T. (2013), 'The Science Behind the Netflix Algorithms That Decide What You'll Watch Next', *Wired*, 8 July. Available online: http://www.wired.com/2013/08/qq_netflix-algorithm/ (accessed 3 March 2016).

Vitali, V., and P. Willemen (2006), 'Introduction', in V. Vitali and P. Willemen (eds), *Theorising National Cinema*, London: BFI, 1–14.

Wu, T. (2015), 'Netflix's Secret Special Algorithm Is a Human', *New Yorker*, 27 January. Available online: http://www.newyorker.com/business/currency/hollywoods-big-data-big-deal (last accessed 25 August 2021).

Young, J. (2012), 'Trial e-Resource – Classic Mexican Cinema Online', *@the library*, 30 January. Available online: http://univstandrewse-resources.blogspot.ie/2012/01/trial-e-resource-classic-mexican-cinema.html (accessed 3 March 2016).

Part 2

Streaming in national and transnational contexts

4

Netflix in Europe: The national in global subscription video on demand (SVOD) services

Stefano Baschiera and Valentina Re

Since the mid-1990s, the concept of national cinema has been at the centre of several debates within film studies, which have attempted to redefine it and reframe its use and development in a period of technological, economic and sociopolitical changes.[1] From the impact of new media[2] to the increasing transnational dimension of the screen industry,[3] the new focus on globalization and post-nationalism led to a re-evaluation of the idea of 'national' and its function within the discipline. However, as John Hill did not fail to notice, 'despite the pronouncement of the death of the "national" by a number of writers, discourses of the "national" do, nevertheless, continue to structure and inform how films of various kinds are categorised, funded, promoted and made sense of by a range of social actors ranging from politicians and civil servants to filmmakers, critics and audiences' (Hill 2016: 707).

The persistence of the national can be easily found in film policy and its definition of 'nationality' aimed to provide production support and protectionist measures.[4] Moreover, the national is still present in its 'generic function', creating sets of expectations and working within marketing strategies.

Arguably, the same definition of European cinema results from the complex relationship between national, supranational and transnational cinema, where the history of the latter that transcends that of national cinemas and that 'might

---

[1] A previous version of this chapter was published in *Comunicazioni Sociali*, 2018 (3) with the title 'National Screen Productions and Global SVOD Services: The Case of Netflix in the UK and Italy'. After working in close collaboration on all aspects of the present chapter, the two authors divided the work as follows: Stefano Baschiera wrote sections 1, 2 and 5; Valentina Re wrote sections 3 and 4.
[2] See Rosen (1996).
[3] See among others: Vitali and Willemen (2006); Hjort (2010); Higbee and Lim (2010).
[4] For the UK cultural test, please see Hill (2016); for the Italian policies, see Cucco (2017).

focus precisely on the strategies and practices by which filmic texts "travel" and become transformed according to the specific requirements of different cultural contexts and audiences' (Bergfelder 2005: 326).

By looking at national cinema from a consumption-based approach (Higson 1989), it is possible to grasp its recurrence, alongside genres, in the categorization and organization of online catalogues. We argue that an understanding of the locus of 'national' within multiterritory and transnational video platforms (see Lobato 2019) which represent the strong majority of SVOD (subscription video on demand) in Europe can help in framing the definition of European cinema in the moment of online availability and discoverability.[5]

The purpose of this chapter is therefore to analyse the role played by the category of 'nationality' in global SVOD services by looking at Netflix and its presence in the European context, with a focus on the presence of Italian cinema in a key online audiovisual market like the British one. We argue that the persistence of the concept of nationality on streaming services, albeit arguably marginal, suggests a new understanding of its function within contemporary media conglomerates and the consequent redefinition of matters of European and world cinema.

The role of Netflix in British and Italian audiovisual markets

In the VOD (Video on demand) sector, SVOD services such as Netflix represent a new disruptive force to established distribution models. Different from TVOD (transactional video on demand), which can be seen as an online substitute for physical video (rental and purchase), the SVOD model better meets the needs of a new, pervasive 'on-demand culture'. This expression was used by Chuck Tryon (2013) to define a widespread promise and expectation of 'anytime, anywhere access' or, more precisely, of new forms of immediate, personalized, ubiquitous and expanded access to films and television shows. Within the SVOD model, viewers are looking for a particular 'branded' experience, a curatorial approach and, above all, a seemingly endless catalogue accessible by paying a monthly fee.

---

[5] On Netflix as a multiterritory and transnational video platform, see Lobato (2019).

SVOD has also been considered an 'attack on ... the elements of exclusivity and timing upon which windows are constructed' (Ulin 2009: 299). Indeed, it undermines the primacy of theatrical release, bypassing it or encouraging day and date release strategies, and threatens the control exerted by traditional intermediaries, as the conflict between Cannes Film Festival and Netflix shows very well.[6]

Although SVOD revenues are still a small fraction of the pay-TV market, they represent the main growth driver of the EU audiovisual sector and in 2017 they accounted for 67 per cent of total audiovisual market revenue growth (European Audiovisual Observatory 2019). In 2020, SVOD revenues were €9.7 billion, with 103 million subscriptions and Netflix and Amazon taking the first and second place in all markets in which they operate (Grece 2021).

By 2023, SVOD services are expected to account for 25 per cent (12 billion EUR) of subscription revenues, and SVOD subscribers (127 million) for almost half of all subscription services (Grece 2019).

Additionally, SVOD services like Netflix and Amazon largely invest in original content:[7] the development of original productions allows them both to offer some easily recognizable 'branded' hits to a new customer base, and to penetrate new markets investing in local productions, problematizing once more the idea of national belonging. While in Europe such investment by global SVOD services is also increasingly embedded in policies and regulations protecting the *exception culturelle*, it presents the risk to homogenize the production across national cinemas in order to fit the services' standards and cater to a global audience.

Netflix epitomizes the SVOD model and, interesting for our argument, it features a pan-European presence; a high penetration rate and market share; and a strong reliance on the generic organization of its catalogues, making it an ideal case study. Netflix's investment plan on European productions (Garrahan 2018) not only challenged traditional broadcasters across Europe but, as we shall discuss later, contributed to ongoing debates regarding economic-driven cultural policy and production-based understanding of the concept of the national.

---

[6] Based on a sharp conflict started in 2017, the 2018 Cannes Film Festival has changed its regulation and prevented movies without a theatrical distribution to be selected for the official competition.
[7] Some studies also suggest a connection between the presence of original productions and the value of the company shares (see Kay 2017).

On this occasion, our analysis of the presence of Netflix in Europe will focus mainly on its offering in the UK of Italian products.[8] However, firstly, we need to compare the UK and Italian markets as they represent the different ends of the company's European expansion and the penetration of the SVOD model. While the UK was the first territory where Netflix launched in Europe in 2012, Italy joined at a later stage in 2015, when the presence on the continent of the SVOD service was already well established.[9] In 2017, the UK stood out with an SVOD penetration rate of 59 per cent, whereas Italy recorded only 13 per cent. In this respect, UK and Italy allow us to draw a comparison between two catalogues which significantly differ in the amount and diversity of titles, made available in two SVOD markets with a huge difference in revenues – 1092 million EUR for UK and 193 in Italy.[10]

Despite the differences between the SVOD markets, the two countries are among the traditional 'great five' of national production within the European screen industry sector. From 2011 to 2015, they represented – along with France, Germany and Spain – 65 per cent of the entire European film production volume. On average, 271 films were produced per year in the UK and 169 in Italy, making it a significant influx of national cinema into the respective local markets.

The analysis of the presence of global national productions in the British and Italian Netflix catalogues will focus on their availability and discoverability, considering in particular what features the SVOD service finds pertinent to assign a 'national' belonging, and how such a 'label' of nationality works to guide the user within the catalogue. The question of availability, therefore, frames the idea of national cinema from a production perspective by engaging with elements of cultural policy and EU protective measures. The discoverability instead dictates a pragmatic approach, encouraging an understanding of the concept of national for its function as an identifier in the labelling, tagging and categorization of online catalogues. Hence, discoverability re-establishes the importance of national cinema as a constructive taxonomic tool, just as constructive as 'authorship', 'genre' and 'period' (White 2004).

---

[8] The majority of the data research we conducted for this chapter was done in 2018, before the withdrawal of UK from the European Union.
[9] For an analysis of the introduction of Netflix in the Italian territory, see Barra (2017).
[10] For a data analysis on the European SVOD market, see Grece (2017, 2018a).

Nationality as country of origin: Availability in the European market

The availability of national screen production in a given market – namely, films or TV productions having the first (or main) country of origin corresponding to the country in which the SVOD catalogue is offered – has been at the centre of a series of specific reports.[11] Indeed, this issue has become increasingly important considering the EU DSM (Digital Single Market) policies and the revision (Autumn 2018) of the AVMS (Audiovisual Media Services) Directive (European Commission 2018) which entail cross-border portability, cross-border access and especially new programming and investment obligations for the promotion of European works (Fontaine 2019). In order to provide European citizens with richer access to online cultural goods and supporting European creative industries, these measures create a common regulatory framework for both linear and non-linear audiovisual media that fit for the digital age, thus persuading global internet companies to make a greater effort to support the audiovisual local cultures and economies in which they operate.

Under the DSM strategy and the revised Directive, VOD services need to ensure at least a 30 per cent share of European works (without further specifications about nationality) in their catalogues, while giving them good visibility (prominence). Moreover, member states will have the power to impose a financial contribution for the production of European works and to impose fees on providers of on-demand services in their territory, even if the providers are based in other member states.[12]

National laws pursue the same objectives and combine the support of European production with that of the national audiovisual industry. For instance, recent obligations in the promotion of national and European content were introduced in Italy by law no. 220/2016, which governs nowadays the entire Italian audiovisual sector, and specified in the legislative decree no. 204 dated 7 December 2017 and then slightly revised in the law no. 81

---

[11] In addition to the reports released by the European Audiovisual Observatory (Available online: https://www.obs.coe.int/en/web/observatoire/industry/home-video-and-vod, accessed 1 February 2020), see Lobato and Scarlata (2017, 2019).

[12] For a general overview of the definitions of national productions in different legal systems, see European Audiovisual Observatory (2020).

dated 8 August 2019. The ruling established specific quotas of European works – 30 per cent of the total amount of hours – and of 'audiovisual works of Italian original expression' – 15 per cent of the total amount of hours – to be included in VOD catalogues. It also specified investment commitments and the obligation to give prominence and delegated the task of preparing the implementation regulation to the Italian Communications Authority. The Regulation had a long and complex procedure. Approved on 12 December 2018 (Delibera n. 595/18/CONS), it was modified on 22 January 2019 (Delibera n. 24/19/CONS) and then submitted for a public consultation process (Delibera n. 421/19/CONS).[13] The Regulation established quotas of 30 per cent and 15 per cent for European and Italian ('of Italian original expression') titles (rather than hours) from 1 January 2020. Investment commitments for European works by independent producers accounted for an initial 12.5 per cent of the revenues in Italy (with 50 per cent of the quota reserved for works 'of Italian original expression').

It is worth noting that most of the data available about the accessibility of European works and films and TV content is based on a 'productive' definition of 'national content' (content produced in the same country in which the catalogue is offered) that may eventually not perfectly match with the 'legislative' definitions proposed by other national laws. The Italian case is a good example of this since the current notions of audiovisual/cinematic work 'of Italian original expression' do not include the country of origin as a criterion needed to be considered as Italian. For example, according to the inter-ministerial Decree dated 28 February 2013, in order to be considered a work 'of Italian original expression', a film must present 50 per cent of dialogues in Italian.[14]

Besides being relevant to national and European policies supporting the creative sector, a quantitative overview of the availability of national screen production across the continent also supplies an essential framework to address the issue of discoverability. It is, thus, important to get an estimate of how many European national and non-national items a certain catalogue offers, before analysing how these items are positioned into the catalogue through recommendation systems.

---

[13] All documents available on the AGCOM website: https://www.agcom.it/. On the implementation in Italy of the revised AVMSD see the legislative decree no. 208 dated 8 November 2021.

[14] For a general overview of the definitions of national productions in different legal systems, see European Audiovisual Observatory (2020).

The most updated and reliable data is released by the EAO, the European Audiovisual Observatory. In 2019, EU content represented only 26 per cent of the entire SVOD European market (counting films and TV titles and/or season, and not episodes), of which 78 per cent was EU non-national content.[15] Among the EU non-national productions on SVOD (therefore European films available in other nation's markets), UK accounted for 29 per cent for feature films (followed by France and Germany), while Italy accounted for only 7 per cent.[16]

According to the report prepared by Grece for the European Audiovisual Observatory (2018b) 'Netflix's 27 country catalogues had an average share of EU films comprised between 15%-16%, with EU non-national films representing the bulk of EU films with 14% and 1.5%-2% of national films' (117).

In the Italian Netflix catalogue (2,264 films), the presence of European films is about 19 per cent, while that of national productions is 5 per cent. In the UK catalogue (3,400 films), European productions have a share of 16 per cent, and national productions of 8 per cent.[17]

In addition to offering a necessary background to the qualitative analysis that follows, this brief quantitative analysis is already revealing a series of considerations of the role played by national and European productions in 2019 Netflix's catalogues and the SVOD sector. First, it shows the strength and appeal of British content, both in the internal market and abroad. Second, it demonstrates how film titles from the United States and other regions circulate better than European titles, and that EU non-national films and TV content represent the largest share of EU productions, with the EU-5 as the top five export countries, led by the UK.

However, data about the availability of European national and non-national titles in specific SVOD catalogues does not consider their discoverability. In other terms, we need more research to understand how the European and national identifiers operate in the catalogues and shape how content is searched, selected and interpreted.

---

[15] The report defines as national films those films produced in the same country of the VOD catalogue analysed, while 'EU non-national' are films that are produced in a different EU country.
[16] Data collected in June and October 2019 (see Grece and Jiménez Pumares, 2019). It must be observed that the report 'Film and TV content in VOD catalogues' 2020 edition shows a post-Brexit scenario, where 'British content moved under the Other European category, decreasing EU27 shares by 8% in average' (Grece and Jiménez Pumares 2020: 9).
[17] Data for Netflix collected in October 2017. See Grece (2018b).

The question of 'national' and SVOD catalogues: Discoverability in the European market

While availability is a quantitative notion and concerns the number of titles offered and the corresponding share, discoverability is a qualitative notion and concerns the visibility, or prominence, of specific kinds of content, that is, the multiple ways in which they are made visible in the catalogue through content structure, categories for navigation, search options and recommendation systems.

Considering the role that the concept of nationality (or origin) plays as a taxonomic tool for the organization of Netflix's catalogue is important for at least two well-defined reasons. The first, closely linked with the question of availability, is for an 'up to bottom' approach where the nationality/origin is understood based on national/transnational regulations and its presence in the catalogue is hence partially dictated by sets of policies.

As already mentioned, the revised AVMSD (EU's Audiovisual Media Services Directive, which coordinates national legislation on audiovisual media across member states) implies an obligation for VOD services to 'give prominence' to European works in their catalogues and such parameters are increasingly present also in national regulations. The main issue arising from these policies is, of course, that of a definition of 'prominence'. The 2017 report by EAO on the visibility of films and TV content defines 'visibility', as is mentioned on the home page of the service, or a promotional spot (Fontaine 2017).

For instance, the 2019 Italian Regulation about programming obligations for media services provided a list of criteria to assess the prominence given to European works by VOD services, both in their catalogues and promotional campaigns. Such criteria feature: the indication of the country of origin in the catalogue; using trailers or visuals to enhance visibility; placing in the home page a stable category or collection including all the European works; providing possibilities for searching for European works; including at least a share of 20 per cent of European works in the content suggested through recommendation systems.

The regulation of 'prominence' (at the national and supranational level) is a sensitive topic since it directly affects the branded experience and style of access that VOD services offer.

The second reason is, instead, of an 'algorithm mediated bottom up' approach, where the actual everyday use of the national taxonomy stresses the classificatory role of the streaming service and shapes the understanding of the concept of national in a moment of cross-border availability, by association with other categories, labels and genres. The national here is present in an ecosystem generating new meanings and understandings, stressing the fluidity of the concept beyond that of policymakers.

As Wade Morris and Powers point out in their argument about streaming music services, 'in an ecosystem where many of the services offer the same catalogues of content, the affective cues and features for discovering and encountering content become the main point of differentiation' (2015: 117). In addition to representing a key strategy to 'extract profit and value from the consumption process' (Wade Morris and Powers 2015: 117) interface and curatorial mechanisms create the service's identity since 'services demonstrate their quality through how they recommend and categorize content' (Wade Morris and Powers 2015: 114).

Major global SVOD services like Netflix and Amazon have been mainly associated with the idea of a new, contemporary 'data-driven algorithmic culture' (Striphas 2015: 396)[18] in which, thanks to 'application of metadata systems and filtering technologies to the process of program selection' (Uricchio 2004: 172) increasingly sophisticated recommendation systems combine popularity with personalization to produce 'a never-ending stream of custom-tailored pleasure' (Uricchio 2004: 178) or, more precisely, 'a steady stream of programming designed to stay in touch with our changing rhythms and moods, selected and accessible with no effort on our part, anticipating our every interest and nearly infinite in its capacities' (Uricchio 2004: 177).

While scholars have stressed that algorithms must be conceived as 'socio-technical assemblages' (Gillespie 2014), 'joining together the human and the nonhuman, the cultural and the computational' (Striphas 2015: 408 note 1), in the general discourses about algorithms, the fundamental human agency implied in any algorithmic system, namely the strong editorial activity that provides data to be processed, tends to be completely removed, to emphasize the efficiency and objectivity of the machine agency. Consistently with this general rhetoric about the algorithm, in the framework of its communications strategies, Netflix tends

---

[18] See also Galloway (2006). For recent overviews see Baschiera et al. (2017) and Avezzù (2017).

to remove the role of meta-data programmers, as well as the underlying tagging system[19] created by Todd Yellin, as the research done by Gomez-Uribe and Hunt on Netflix recommender system shows very well (2015).

Without any ambition to retrace Netflix's tagging practices, we aim to discuss how the idea of nationality takes shape in content organization, navigational options, and recommendation systems, by looking at the different tags and labels with which it is associated, and what categories it contributes to creating. Of course, we must assume that this discussion is inevitably affected by personalization and how the recommender system works. No 'objectives' and exhaustive outcomes are possible from a user perspective, yet we can detect some trends and recurring configurations. It is noteworthy that what makes it difficult to access reliable data about the content organization in Netflix's catalogue also raises doubts about obligations concerning prominence. Netflix's rhetoric and experience are all about choice and personalization. Therefore, it would not be acceptable that European and/or national content would be somehow 'imposed' to users who do not usually watch these kinds of products, which is the main rhetoric defence against the EU mandate to regulate the visibility and discoverability of European products in the catalogue (Lobato 2019: 150).

The Netflix homepage is organized in streams of 'personalized' content. The homepage has a key role in the Netflix experience since it is 'the main presentation of recommendations, where 2 of every 3 hours streamed on Netflix are discovered' Gomez-Uribe and Hunt 2015). First, categories in the homepage directly address the user (Because You Watched …, Continue Watching for …, Top Pics for …, Watch It Again), emphasizing both the belonging to a wider, branded community (Popular on Netflix, Trending Now) and the user's autonomy (My List), and building a relationship of mutual trust between Netflix and the viewer. Second, further categories refer to the user's previous viewings and suggest similar content, offering the impression of an infinite catalogue that takes the shape of endless, parallel flows based on the user's taste.

From this perspective, references to the country/countries can occasionally appear when they are relevant to the user's personal activity, organized in categories such as US crime, International political thriller, Foreign art house, European films and programmes, European TV War & Politics, Scandinavian Movies & TV, Romantic Latin American comedies, Italian films.

---

[19] Known as 'Netflix Quantum Theory', it provides guidelines to create almost 80,000 unique ways to describe types of video.

It is noteworthy that the use of geographical origin in the catalogue's categories is not limited to single countries, rather it can also refer to continents (Europe) or a heterogeneous set of countries – as in the case of the labels 'international' and 'foreign', intended as 'non-US'. Furthermore, the national belonging can be variously combined with elements referring to traditional genres, adjectives and other disparate descriptors.

More often, however, the national taxonomy, when present, hides in the catalogue's depth. National cinemas or TV content – produced in a different country from the one in which the catalogue is available – tends to appear as specific categories only when a user intentionally searches for them in the search engine provided by the service.

Searching for 'Italian' in the Netflix UK catalogue, the following labels become accessible: Italian Movies, Italian Movies and TV, Italian-language Movies; Audio in Italian; Italian TV Shows; Critically acclaimed Italian Films; Italian Movies based on real life.

Italian cinema, instead of being organized within genres, is rather characterized by its aesthetic qualities, stressing its cultural capital (the references to film criticism). A number of labels do not match with the productive or regulatory definitions of national cinema, suggesting instead a different thematization of nationhood.

The last issue on the presence of the concept of national within Netflix's catalogue concerns the description of the product and the users' reviews. The textual description usually lists only four genres and subgenres associated with a couple of adjectives while, in most cases, neither the origin nor the available languages for audio tracks and subtitles are mentioned. Yet, references to nationality used to recur frequently in the reviews, showing that the national belonging persists as a relevant element for consumption, interpretation and assessment. Nevertheless, in August 2018, Netflix deleted all user reviews from the website (Spangler 2018).

What Italian cinema is for Netflix UK

Looking at the national taxonomy of 'Italian' as present in the UK catalogue, we focus on the category 'Italian Films' to discuss the understanding of Italian National cinema emerging from it. While the availability of Italian TV shows is quite limited, in particular, in its variety,[20] the twenty-two texts associated with

---

[20] As of June 2018 it features fourteen titles, ten of which are children's animation like *Winx* and *Geronimo Stilton*.

'Italian films' represent a very diversified offering in terms of genre belonging, production background and ambition.[21] The list features prestigious national productions, international co-productions, TV products (some of which last one hour or less) and independent low-budget documentaries. There is quite a transversal offering of high-middle-low brow products, with films by internationally recognized directors such as Matteo Garrone, Mario Martone, Gabriele Muccino and Paolo Sorrentino. The national label also includes a good representation of awards winners, in particular of the Italian David di Donatello award, and, among the feature films, there is a predominance of films produced with the support of the Cinema division of the Italian public Broadcaster RAI, as well as, with minor impact, the *Ministero dei beni culturali*.

The generic division of the Italian film category shows a clear predominance of documentary films and drama, albeit the documentary category features a majority of low-budget non-theatrical products. According to White, a sustained and diverse tradition is a standard feature in national cinema, which needs to comprehend the following sectors: 'feature-length narrative (commercial), feature-length and short narrative (semi-commercial/independently produced), documentary (independent or government-subsidised), avant-garde (fully non-commercial), political/Third Cinema' (White 2004: 225).

With the exclusion of the last two sectors, the others are present in the selection of Italian films in Netflix UK, hence potentially showing a comprehensive picture of the national production. However, the attempt to grasp an understanding of Italian cinema in the UK by looking at Netflix is challenging.

From a production perspective, half of the films available are international co-productions, and two of those films (*The Son of the Pink Panther* and *The*

---

[21] As of June 2018 the texts labelled Italian Films are: *Bianca come il latte, rossa come il sangue* (Giacomo Campiotti, 2013); *The Comfort of Strangers* (*Cortesie per gli ospiti*, Paul Schrader, 1990); *Caffè sospeso* (*Coffee for All*, Fulvio Iannucci and Roly Santos, 2017); *Fiore* (Claudio Giovannesi, 2016); *Viaggio da sola* (*A Five Star Life*, Maria Sole Tognazzi, 2013); *Per qualche dollaro in più* (*For a Few Dollars More*, Sergio Leone, 1965); *Rimetti a noi i nostri debiti* (*Forgive Us Our Debts*, Antonio Morabito, 2018); *Franca: Chaos and Recreation* (Francesco Carrozzini, 2016); *La grande bellezza* (*The Great Beauty*, Paolo Sorrentino, 2013); *Il giovane favoloso* (*Leopardi*, Mario Martone, 2014); *Influx* (Luca Vullu, 2016); *L'estate addosso* (*Summer Time*, Gabriele Muccino, 2016); *La coppia dei campioni* (Giulio Base, 2016); *My Way* (Antongiulio Panizzi, 2016); *Numero Zero: The Roots of Italian Rap* (Enrico Bini, 2015); *Roberto Saviano: uno scrittore sotto scorta* (Pierfrancesco Diliberto, 2016); *Slam* (Andrea Molaioli, 2017); *Son of Pink Panther* (Blake Edwards, 1993); *Suburra* (Stefano Sollima, 2015); *Il racconto dei racconti* (*Tale of Tales*, Matteo Garrone, 2015); *Taratabong* (Migliazzi and Bondi, 2009); *Too Much Stress for My Heart* (Ludovica Lirosi, 2015); *Benvenuto Presidente!* (*Welcome Mr. President!*, Riccardo Milani, 2013).

Comfort of Strangers) are shot by non-Italian directors, underlying again the fluidity of the concept of national cinema in a 'transnational era'. Interestingly, even the original language available in the soundtrack does not help to clarify the Italianness of the category, with almost one-third of those films which are available on Netflix exclusively in English.

Unsurprisingly, Netflix's offering focuses on contemporaneity, with nineteen out of twenty-three films in the list produced in the past five years, making the portrayal of national cinema a contemporary and ephemeral snapshot. Such a portrayal is mainly focused on synchronicity and avoids a diachronic approach to the taxonomy, compromising in its representation questions of legacy and sustained tradition.[22]

Considering the distribution of the texts labelled as 'Italian films', we can grasp how Netflix does not seem to rely on the user's previous knowledge through the press coverage following the theatrical exhibition. Only seven of the films offered had theatrical distribution in the UK, including *For a Few Dollars More*, *The Son of the Pink Panther* and *The Comfort of Strangers*. Therefore, only four of the 2010s offering could potentially rely on the cultural capital generated by their distribution, reception and promotion in the UK market. Undoubtedly, *Suburra* and *The Great Beauty* are the films that received wide European distribution and a presence in British theatres[23] and are also the two products in the list that attracted the majority of users' reviews. In particular, national connotations emerge mainly to stress the difference of a crime film like *Suburra* in respect to Hollywood canon: 'it is not a Hollywood gore fest' or for a comparative approach concerning the genre belonging, with a user writing, 'These Italians are Scandinavia and Latin America for the gangster flicks. Original!! Political!! Real-life!! Hollywood is a joke, but that's old news'. However, on this occasion, the reviews do not present references to Italian films if not a generic 'it looks like there is a new strand of talented Italian directors'. That again raises the question of which kind of picture of Italian national cinema emerges from Netflix UK.

The SVOD service, in its attempt to personalize and categorize the catalogue, and feed the algorithms, offers also a set of metadata based on general adjectives

---

[22] After a few weeks from the initial research, *The Great Beauty* and *Tale of Tales* were pulled from Netflix catalogue.
[23] According to EAO Lumiere from 2013 to 2016 *The Great Beauty* totalled 155,732 single admissions in UK while *Suburra* is a distant second among the Italian films in June 2018 Netflix UK catalogue with 5,113 single admissions. However, *Suburra* is the only other contemporary film in the list which obtained a notable theatrical distribution in the UK.

that can be associated with a film/TV show. Looking at the products categorized as 'Italian Cinema' we have the following adjectives/labels with their recurrences in brackets. Therefore, for Netflix UK Italian cinema is: Dark (3); Wacky (3); Romantic (2); Gritty (2); Witty (2); Imaginative (2); Understated (2); Scary; Feel good; Steamy; Provocative; Emotional; Inspiring.

Despite the obvious use of national cinema as a taxonomic tool, Netflix UK does not offer an informed diachronic cultural understanding of Italian cinema based on distribution, availability and consumption history. The lack of a diachronic overview, the dominance of indie documentaries, the problematic role played by some national identifiers (languages, settings, director, production, etc.) compromise the ability of Netflix to offer a reflection on national cinema in the UK market.

Looking at the genres available is quite revealing of the disconnection between this taxonomy and the cultural capital associated with Italian cinema in different venues of film consumption and exhibition in the UK. We are thinking, for instance, the lack of Italian Horror films in the offering, which is arguably the Italian genre with the biggest subcultural capital in the UK (Baschiera 2017).

The branding of Netflix constantly overshadows other cultural signifiers. The 'Italian films' category re-establishes the branding idea, mirroring features associated with global international cinema and ignoring the peculiarities of the UK market and the cultural impact of the national cinema with its audiences. Or, more clearly, there is an attempt to frame Italian cinema in terms of continuity and a seamless flow with the rest of the catalogue. The adjectives used as labelling devices stress the universality of the film qualities (dark, whacky, etc.), instead underlying any uniqueness or distinctiveness. Italian cinema as a taxonomy overcomes the understanding based on national specificities, and it is there only to lead to something else or, better, to lead back to the wider offering of the catalogue and to Netflix's label as a global cultural signifier.

Conclusions: A question of branding

The European expansion of SVOD services allows new reflections on the role played by the concept of national production from a consumption-based approach. Interestingly, such an approach re-establishes all the complexity, fluidity and mutable persistence of the national concept in media production, circulation, and consumption. From supranational and national policies dictating national quotas – while shifting the definition of national belonging based on 'cultural tests' – to the use of national labels as taxonomic tools to manage expectations and organize the media offering, SVOD services embody some of the key debates which have surrounded the idea of national cinema in the past 40 years. Debates can eventually regroup the persistence of the 'national' within the two crucial areas for SVOD and online distribution: those of availability and discoverability. The ubiquitous presence of Netflix has offered new possibilities for a cross-border availability of European productions, inviting possible speculation of the creation of new cultural capital and understanding of national production in a given market. The idea of national has, however, played only a marginal role in the catalogue's discoverability, with the use of metadata immediately associated with broader generic labels, able to create personalized paths in Netflix's offering.

In his recent analyses of SVOD's challenge to traditional television network branding, Michael L. Wayne pointed out how 'Netflix's user interface obscured the branded origins of television content to better position themselves as the audience's primary point of identification' (Wayne 2018: 735). Netflix seems to employ a 'portal-as-brand' strategy (different from the programme-as-brand employed, for instance, by HBO), creating a brand at the expense of network brand identities and the production origin of its content. Using the label 'Netflix Originals' to market a show of which they own exclusive rights in a country is an example of Netflix's prioritization of its brand over the production (and national) origin of a text.[24] If we consider the role played by national cinema as a marketing strategy, as 'an attempt to market the diverse as ... offering a coherent and singular experience' (Higson 1989: 38), we can grasp how the concept of national can be understood as a branding practice and, as such, it is now facing the challenge of SVOD services, in a way not dissimilar to the traditional television network branding. This also applies to the concept of transnational in relation to European cinema which is both overshadowed by the transnationalism of Netflix branding, with its global reach, and made only visible as part of the recommendations dictated by an algorithm to feed the cycle of demand and supply (see also Lobato 2019: 150).

On the one hand, Netflix's offering in terms of European in its catalogues creates an endless flow of global cinema moving beyond the binary opposition

---

[24] See for instance Lotz and Havens (2016).

versus Hollywood. To some extent, such flow of films dismissing the national origin only as a secondary (and imprecise) metadata further pushes European cinema to be part of the 'more dynamic and fluid totality' of world cinema (Elsaesser 2005: 486). In such totality, we can see how Netflix could potentially contribute to the creation of what Lúcia Nagib defines as 'flexible geographies' of world cinema (Nagib 2006: 35) created by waves of films and movements and embracing the idea of polycentric multiculturalism (Shohat and Stam 2014).

Polycentrism can be present within a catalogue that is truly global (both in content and in circulation) and where genres and trends cut across film offering independently from their origins.

On the other hand, it cannot be ignored that the national is still present in Netflix, in a constant negotiation between audiovisual regulations and taxonomic tools for local markets. The idea of national emerging from the catalogue, however, aims to reinforce the global brand of Netflix rather than re-establish a national one. In this context, the global flow of films presents the risk to create a homogeneity of stories and style to be featured in Netflix catalogues, a condition that is even more established by the increased presence of Netflix as a powerhouse in the European screen production sector.

References

Avezzù, G. (2017), 'The Data Don't Speak for Themselves: The Humanity of VOD Recommender Systems', *Cinéma & Cie*, 17 (29): 51–66.

Barra, L. (2017), 'On-Demand Isn't Built in a Day: Promotional Rhetoric and the Challenges of Netflix's Arrival in Italy', *Cinéma & Cie*, 17 (29): 19–32.

Baschiera, S. (2017), 'Streaming Italian Horror Cinema in the United Kingdom: Lovefilm Instant', *Journal of Italian Cinema & Media Studies*, 5 (2): 245–60.

Baschiera, S., F. Di Chiara and V. Re (2017), 'The Logics of Re-Intermediation', *Cinéma & Cie*, 17 (29): 9–18.

Bergfelder, Tim (2005), 'National, Transnational or Supranational Cinema? Rethinking European Film Studies', *Media Culture and Society*, 27 (3): 315–31.

Cucco, M. (2017), 'L'industria e le leggi del cinema in Italia (2000–2015)', in M. Cucco and G. Manzoli (eds), *Il cinema di Stato: Finanziamento pubblico ed economia simbolica nel cinema italiano contemporaneo*, Bologna: Il Mulino, 33–83.

Elsaesser, T. (2005), *European Cinema – Face to Face with Hollywood*, Amsterdam: Amsterdam University Press.

European Audiovisual Observatory (2019), *Yearbook 2018/2019 Key Trends*, Strasbourg: European Audiovisual Observatory.

European Audiovisual Observatory (2020), *Mapping of the Regulation and Assessment of the Nationality of European Audiovisual Works*, Strasbourg: European Audiovisual Observatory. Available online: https://rm.coe.int/mapping-of-the-regulation-and-assessment-of-the-nationality-of-europea/16809ebe39 (accessed 6 September 2020).

European Commission (2018), *Revision of the Audiovisual Media Services Directive (AVMSD)*. Available online: https://digital-strategy.ec.europa.eu/en/policies/audiovisual-and-media-services (accessed 1 February 2020).

Fontaine, G. (2017), *The Visibility of Films and TV Content on VOD*, Strasbourg: European Audiovisual Observatory.

Fontaine, G., ed. (2019), *Yearbook 2018/2019 Key Trends*, Strasbourg: European Audiovisual Observatory. Available online: https://rm.coe.int/yearbook-keytrends-2018-2019-en/1680938f8e (accessed 23 June 2020).

Galloway, A. (2006), *Gaming: Essays on Algorithmic Culture*, Minneapolis: University of Minnesota Press.

Garrahan, M. (2018), 'Netflix Plots $1bn European Investment Drive', *Financial Time*. Available online: https://www.ft.com/content/952029b0-4311-11e8-93cf-67ac3a6482fd (accessed 27 July 2018).

Gillespie, T. (2014), *Algorithm (Digital Keywords)*. Available online: http://culturedigitally.org/2014/06/algorithm-draft-digitalkeyword/ (accessed 6 September 2020).

Gomez-Uribe, C., and N. Hunt (2015), 'The Netflix Recommender System: Algorithms, Business Value, and Innovation', *ACM Transactions of Management Information System*, 6 (4): 1–19.

Grece, C. (2017), *Trends in the EU SVOD Market*, Strasbourg: European Audiovisual Observatory.

Grece, C. (2018a), *Overview – The EU VOD Market. Facts & Figures*, Venice: EUROVOD. Available online: https://rm.coe.int/overview-video-on-demand-in-the-eu-facts-and-figures-eurovod-venise-4-/16808d271e (accessed September 2020).

Grece, C. (2018b), *Film on VOD Catalogues – Origin, Circulation and Age – Edition 2018*, Strasbourg: European Audiovisual Observatory.

Grece, C. (2019), *Trends in the EU VOD Market*, EUROVOD-Venice: European Audiovisual Observatory. Available online: https://rm.coe.int/presentation-eurovod-venice-2019-final-grece/168097203c (accessed September 2020).

Grece, C. (2021), *Trends in the VOD Market in EU 28*, EUROVOD-Venice: European Audiovisual Observatory. Available online: https://rm.coe.int/presentation-eurovod-venice-2019-final-grece/168097203c (accessed July 2021).

Grece, C., and M. Jiménez Pumares (2019), *Films and TV Content in VOD Catalogues – Edition 2019*, Strasbourg: European Audiovisual Observatory.

Grece, C., and M. Jiménez Pumares (2020), TV *Content in VOD Catalogues – Edition 2020*, Strasbourg: European Audiovisual Observatory.

Higbee, W., and S. H. Lim (2010), 'Concepts of Transnational Cinema: Towards a Critical Transnationalism in Film Studies', *Transnational Cinemas*, 1 (1): 7–21.

Higson, A. (1989), 'The Concept of National Cinema', *Screen*, 30 (4): 36–47.

Hill, J. (2016), 'Living with Hollywood: British Film Policy and the Definition of "Nationality"', *International Journal of Cultural Policy*, 22 (5): 706–23.

Hjort, M. (2010), 'On the Plurality of Cinematic Transnationalism', in N. Ďurovičová and K. Newman (eds), *World Cinemas, Transnational Perspectives*, New York: Routledge, 12–33.

Kay, J. (2017), 'Study Indicates a Link between Netflix Original Content and Stock Price', *Screendaily*, 31 January. Available online: https://www.screendaily.com/news/study-indicates-link-between-netflix-original-content-and-stock-price-/5114353.article (accessed June 2020).

Lobato, R. (2019), *Netflix Nations – The Geography of Digital Distribution*, New York: New York University Press.

Lobato, R., and A. Scarlata (2017), *Australian Content in SVOD Catalogs: Availability and Discoverability 2017 edition*. Report, Melbourne: RMIT University.

Lobato, R., and A. Scarlata (2019), *Australian Content in SVOD Catalogs: Availability and Discoverability 2019 edition*. Report, Melbourne: RMIT University.

Lotz, A., and T. Havens (2016), 'Original or Exclusive? Shifts in Television Financing and Distribution Shift Meanings', *Antenna: Responses to Media and Culture*, 1 January. Available online: http://blog.commarts.wisc.edu/2016/01/01/original-or-exclusive-shifts-in-television-financing-and-distribution-shift-meanings/ (accessed 24 September 2018).

Nagib, L. (2006), 'Towards a Positive Definition of World Cinema', in S. Dennison and S. Lim (eds), *Remapping World Cinema: Identity, Culture and Politics in Film*, London: Wallflower Press, 30–7.

Rosen, P. (1996), 'Nation and Anti-Nation: Concepts of National Cinema in the "New" Media Era', *Diaspora: A Journal of Transnational Studies*, 5 (3): 375–402.

Shohat, E., and R. Stam (2014), *Unthinking Eurocentrism: Multiculturalism and the Media*, United Kingdom: Taylor & Francis.

Spangler, T. (2018), 'Netflix Has Deleted All User Reviews from Its Website', *Variety*, 17 August. Available online: https://variety.com/2018/digital/news/netflix-deletes-all-user-reviews-1202908904/ (accessed 24 September 2018).

Striphas, T. (2015), 'Algorithmic Culture', *European Journal of Cultural Studies*, 4–5 (18): 396.

Tryon, C. (2013), *On-demand Culture. Digital Delivery and the Future of Movies*, Brunswick, NJ: Rutgers University Press.

Ulin, J. (2009), *The Business of Media Distribution*, New York: Focal Press, 299.

Uricchio, W. (2004), 'Television's Next Generation: Technology/Interface Culture/Flow', in L. Spigel and J. Olsson (eds), *Television after TV*, Durham, NC: Duke University Press.

Vitali, V., and P. Willemen, eds (2006), *Theorising National Cinema*, London: BFI.

Wade Morris, J., and D. Powers (2015), 'Control, Curation and Musical Experience in Streaming Music Services', *Creative Industries Journal*, 8 (2): 106–22.

Wayne, L. M. (2018), 'Netflix, Amazon, and Branded Television Content in Subscription Video-on-Demand Portals', *Media, Culture & Society*, 40 (5): 725–41.

White, J. (2004), 'National Belonging', *New Review of Film and Television Studies*, 2 (2): 211–32.

5

Danmaku commenting: A new interaction experience on China's streaming platforms

Yuanyuan Chen and Rebecca Crawford

Introduction

Danmaku, also known as bullet screen, is an emerging function on video streaming platforms that allows the audience to share time-synchronized comments across the screen as they watch videos. Originating from Japanese ACG (animation, comic and game) websites, it soon became an increasingly popular feature in most of China's video streaming platforms. An effective way to engage audiences, danmaku transfers the traditional experience of watching film alone into virtual socialization, by accommodating and encouraging interactions among the audience. This chapter will firstly look at the development of Chinese streaming platforms and the popularization of danmaku usage in China, before it will move on to investigate danmaku users, their motivations and how danmaku distorts normal perceptions of time and space. The final section of the chapter will explore how danmaku accommodates and celebrates postmodern and internet culture.

Video streaming platforms and danmaku in China

Digitization has radically shifted the film industry in China from production to distribution in the past twenty years. This transformation has also reshaped the viewing habits of the contemporary Chinese audience, from watching films mainly in cinemas towards preferencing online streaming platforms for their main source of entertainment. In the first quarter of 2019, there was a 14.5 per cent decline of cinema audiences in China, while the number of online streaming audiences on iQiyi (iQ.com 爱奇艺), one of the largest Chinese video streaming platforms, increased by 68 per cent. By June 2019, the number of active members of iQiyi was over 100 million (Ye 2019), while the number of paid memberships of Chinese streaming sites had reached over 300 million (Zhao 2019: 5).

LETV (le.com 乐视网), founded in 2004, was the first Chinese site providing video streaming services, which soon became a booming industry in China. Following LETV, many streaming platforms emerged in China between 2005 and 2007, such as Tudou (tudou.com 土豆), 56.com (56网), Youku (youku.com 优酷), AcFun (acfun.cn), PPStream (PPS影音), PPTV (pptv.com PP视频), Ku6 (ku6.com 酷6网) and 6 (6.cn 六间房). From 2008 to 2010, video streaming services in China went through a few rectifications and reformations led by the State Administration for Radio, Film and Television, mainly focusing on issues such as non-compliant registration, inappropriate content and copyright infringement. As a result, over 300 video streaming platforms were shut down. Since 2010, the industry of video streaming in China has become better restructured and has matured as a business, thanks to a series of mergers, acquisitions and IPO activities by the major Chinese commercial streaming websites, such as Youku and iQiyi.[1]

Danmaku is 'a real-time commentary system that displays user-generated comments specific to the current playback time of the video' (Chen et al. 2015: 153) which 'allows online video viewers to input "live" comments in a way that is directly overlaid onto the video' (Yang 2019: 2) to create 'a co-viewing experience' (Chen et al. 2017: 33, 731). It originated on Niconico, a Japanese video streaming website that focuses on animations, comics and games. It was introduced into China by AcFun in 2008 and was later borrowed and further promoted by Bilibili (bilibili.com 哔哩哔哩). Just like Niconico, both AcFun and Bilibili are themed around ACG, while their users are mainly ACG fans. Danmaku comments had been highly associated with otaku and ACG culture during its infancy in China, until 2012 when Tudou introduced its own danmaku product named 'doupao (豆泡)' which brought danmaku to a wider audience. Following Tudou, other mainstream video streaming platforms, such as LETV, Youku, iQiyi and Tencent Video (腾讯视频), soon began to embed danmaku in their own platforms.

---

[1] Youku was listed at the New York Stock Exchange in 2010 and merged with its competitor Tudou in 2012. iQiyi founded in 2010 by Baidu merged with PPStream in 2013 and issued its IPO in the United States in 2018.

The increasing popularity of animation in China, especially anime, has likely been aided by danmaku which – combined with streaming services – supplies a space for fans to legally gather to watch animations and discuss interests. Historically, many Asian countries banned or heavily regulated anime following the Second World War, leading to a reliance on illegal means of distribution up until recently (Garvizu 2017). While piracy of this media is still common across China (Katsumata 2012: 133–60), streaming websites like Youku, iQiyi and Bilibili supply a legal alternative to watch animations (including anime) on the same platforms. Thanks to the development of those streaming platforms, distributors and studios can benefit via membership and advertising revenue on streamed videos, while the audiences can easily and legally gain access to the content they desire.

Developments in the potential of danmaku for non-streaming uses are also increasing all the time. Danmaku was introduced into cinemas in China for the first time in 2014. Provided with internet access during the film's viewing, audiences were able to send comments simultaneously as the film was playing in the cinema, which appeared on the screen or on the wall besides the screen. The 3D animated film *The Legend of Qin* (2014), released in Hangzhou Saga Luxury Cinema (杭州传奇奢华影城) in July 2014, was the first to embrace danmaku comments during the film. Afterwards, *Tiny Times 3* (2014) in Beijing's Jackie Chan Cinema and *Brotherhood of Blades* (2014) in Beijing UME Cinema also provided the audience with danmaku options during their film viewing. It is likely, in the future, that other cinemas in China may adopt this process.

A virtual interactive viewing environment

While young people often feel the most powerless in society (Flanagan 2013), through danmaku Chinese youths may regain some of the power which they feel is silenced elsewhere in their lives. Many commenters are young; of its 100 million users, approximately 67 per cent on Bilibili are under twenty-five, with youths from the 1990s and 2000s most likely to engage in danmaku (Utalk 2016). In fact, compared to their parents, Generation Y[2] seems to be

---

[2] Generation Y is 'the new generation after generation X that can be classified as a person who was born between 1980's and 1990's'. See Fitri Mansor Mohd, 'a study on generation Y behavior at workplace', *International Conference on Business Innovation, Entrepreneurship and Engineering*, December 2013, 549.

more enthusiastic about danmaku (Djamasbi et al. 2016: 648). These users actively engage with online communities and are highly familiar with popular Chinese internet culture, memes and slang. For this generation of digital natives, danmaku offers an effective way for communication and social interaction. This is because danmaku 'combines two of Generation Y's favourite technology-based activities: texting and watching online videos' (Djamasbi et al. 2016: 648). Another study on danmaku found 44 per cent of commenters watched ACG videos, the most popular genre in the study (Ma and Cao 2017: 770–82). Therefore, it is unsurprising to note that one of the key groups who use danmaku are ACG fans and Otaku. These individuals share common interests and passions for anime, comics and games, differentiating themselves from mainstream culture through these niche interests. Danmaku creates connections between these ACG fans, as they use comments to discuss, debate and exchange ideas about the films they watch together online.

One reason people use danmaku is for exchanging information, thanks to its ability to 'provide a desired co-viewing experience' (Chen et al. 2017: 33, 740). Users watch these videos feeling like they are surrounded by others, with whom they can discuss the film as it plays, as opposed to turning to a forum to discuss it afterwards. Through danmaku the users can closely study details which might normally get overlooked – details spotted by other especially savvy viewers – and through this close analysis users gain an ostensibly better understanding of the film than viewers without danmaku. Viewers' various backgrounds, interests and educations also contribute to the pool of knowledge shared via danmaku. It is very common to find some brief but accurate explanations on screen following requests that seek for specialized knowledge relevant to the film, such as 'information about BGM (background music) please' or 'any ideas about the style of the setting?' However, at the same time, this type of danmaku arguably becomes a spoiler that robs the viewer of the enjoyment of the film, especially for viewers who would prefer to uncover this information for themselves.

Danmaku may also provide a sense of company and community as they are 'rich in emotions and together create an immersive, engaging illusion of group viewing' (Ma and Cao 2017: 780). Comments like 'you are not alone', or those that ask whether anyone watching the film comes from the same place (e.g. 'Is anybody from Shanghai?') suggest a sense of community among users. When users find something funny, they use comments such as 'hahaha' or laugh emoticons to share their feelings with other viewers. Through these interactions, danmaku users feel a sense of belonging among their like-minded companions, minimizing the loneliness felt when they watch films alone. This is because some 'viewers who watch TV shows or online videos in physical solitude are seeking synchronous co-viewing experience by sharing their feelings and opinions through various technology-enabled backchannels' (Chen et al. 2017: 33, 731). In fact, thanks to the features of the streaming platforms that integrate danmaku onto their videos, viewers may even feel like they are communicating with users instantly, adding to the 'illusion of live communication [which] is supported by the overall layout of the video player' (Yang 2019: 8).

Many danmaku comments focus on creating humorous and ironic effects to amuse other members of the video's audience. Some viewers also use danmaku for the discussion of other topics not directly related to the film they are watching, such as making satirical comments on current trends and news. Over half of danmaku users mentioned that being able to read the funny comments from one another is the main reason that they keep the danmaku on during their film viewing (Liu 2018: 30). Commenters often creatively make fun of the film or actors through playful intertextuality, parody or pastiche. Psychologist Saito Tamaki (2007: 225–38) pointed out that many consider otaku immature. Certainly, it appears that through danmaku, otaku create an eternally young-at-heart community where they can experience a shared, virtual form of Peter Pan syndrome.[3] Through these immature jokes and playful comments, danmaku allows youths of various ages to act as immaturely as they like, despite the stresses of exams, school and the adult world.

Danmaku creates a virtual interactive viewing environment, in which the audience comes together across time and space. One of the things that makes danmaku different from other comment systems is where the comments are displayed. Traditionally, in video streaming platforms such as YouTube, the comment area is usually located below the playing window, so the viewers cannot read the comments at the same time as they are watching the film. However, danmaku is located within the playing window, and appears at the same time as the film is playing, overlapping the media onscreen. This feature

---

[3] Peter Pan syndrome is a quasi-psychological syndrome explored by psycho-analyst Dr Dan Kiley which explains the refusal of some individuals to mature and suggests a possible reason behind how some adults maintain a childish sense of responsibility into adulthood. Danmaku supplies a space where behaving in childish ways and finding childish things funny is normalized and acceptable for users, but only in the digital space, as opposed to in the real world. Thus, commenters may say things or make jokes in a childish way online that they may not do with real-world peers. See Dan Kiley (1983), *The Peter Pan Syndrome: Men Who Have Never Grown Up*, New York: Dodd, Mead.

makes them a unique way to view comments. Moreover, unlike other comments systems that may appear in order of popularity based on likes or chronology, danmaku appears linked to time stamps in the film, and stays on screen for a short time thanks to their 'fleeting, ephemeral nature' (Yang 2019: 9). This is because danmaku comments are stored in the online video player and displayed simultaneously as the film plays, so the viewers can add their comments at any point during the viewing, which makes the comments more relevant to the scene. For example, comments often form around the discussion about a certain topic, such as the specific dialogues or performances at that exact time in the film.

Danmaku defies traditional understandings of linear chronology because 'the interface displays not just the live comments of co-viewers, but all past comments made by previous viewers, so as to create and reinforce an experience of co-viewing and live communication' (Yang 2019: 8). Therefore, because all the danmaku comments are stored and are constantly being updated on the online video player in real time, they can also be collected and displayed simultaneously on the film in real time. Thanks to this, every time a viewer watches the film, they will see all the comments left by others at each specific point in the film's timeline, which creates an illusion that many people are watching the film together at the same time, an effect not unlike viewers in a public theatre whispering to one another during interesting parts of a play. However, the reality is that these danmaku comments might be left a few months or even years ago by other viewers, some of whom may even be thousands of miles away, and that these comments are constantly changing as more and more are added every day. Through this time distortion, danmaku creates a virtual community across time and space, where every participant contributes to the conversation from a different non-linear point in time. Offering interaction among the audience is the core purpose of danmaku and, because of this, 'users may exploit this channel to "talk" to people who will never read their message' (Ma and Cao 2017: 780).

Danmaku: A celebration of postmodern and internet culture

Danmaku commenting provides a way for users to communicate anonymously and express themselves creatively in a virtual shared viewing environment. This section will investigate how danmaku commenting accommodates and celebrates postmodern and internet culture through the following: internet slang, carnivalesque experience, youth subculture, and the deconstruction and recreation of meanings.

Internet slang

Danmaku commenters are 'digital natives'[4] making their comments distinct from other comment types online. The language of danmaku is highly associated with internet slang such as Martian language, abbreviations and emoticons. A study on ten videos containing danmaku found '17% of the danmaku comments contain onomatopoeia such as laughter and cry and 18% come with punctuations such as "!!!" and "…"' while '5% have some emoji/emoticon'.[5] Reasons behind the use of slang and emoticons may be because danmaku 'feels more like instant messaging or online chat' (Ma and Cao 2017: 775). Gretchen McCulloch (2019: 61) explains that 'Internet writing is a distinct genre with its own goals, and to accomplish those goals successfully requires subtly turned awareness of the full spectrum of the language.' The mixed use of different linguistic styles in danmaku comments is sometimes due to the limited space, or because of the popularity of current memes. Sometimes these are in order to demonstrate personality/culture differences, or sometimes they have the aim of effectively representing emotions.

For example, it is common to see danmaku commenters using numeronyms for communicating, such as '6666' and '233'. The former is used to compliment someone, which came from a similar pronunciation of 'awesome' in Chinese, and the latter means 'laugh out loud', which derived from the no. 233 animated emoji provided by MOP,[6] a famous video game forum in China. For instance, after a commenter explains the joke about pronouns in the animated film *Your Name* (2016), another commenter replies '6666' (0:22:01) to admire his/her

---

[4] A digital native is 'a person who is very familiar with digital technology, computers, etc. because they have grown up with them' (Cambridge Dictionary 2019).
[5] Both Western emoticons and Asian emoticons (kaomoji) are used by danmaku commenters. Kaomoji are emoticons that first appeared in Japan. They typically use more characters to create faces, including non-Western characters such as the Greek and Russian alphabet. As an example, ☺ and (°▽°)/ are both emoticons used to express happiness. The first is Western, the second Asian. See Ma and Nan (2017), 'Video-based Evanescent, Anonymous, Asynchronous Social Interaction' (775).
[6] MOP (mop.com), created in 1997, was originally built for the discussion of video games. It is one of the most well-known Chinese forums for creating a number of influential internet slang.

good command of Japanese.⁷ '+1' is also a popular expression used by danmaku commenters to show that they agree with something or share the same feelings. These short abbreviation styles work better to fit the limited space of the screen and to synchronize the comments with the film, while also drawing a boundary between danmaku commenters and conventional viewers, who are unlikely to have a comprehensive knowledge of internet and ACG slang. For instance, during the animated film *Bungo Stray Dogs Dead Apple* (2018), commenters use slang to communicate something that only ACG fans will understand. When the character Dazai first appears (0:09:59) one commenter says 'mamo awsl'. 'Awsl' is short for 'ah, wǒ sǐ le' (啊，我死了), which means something like 'Ah! I'm going to die!' in English. Mamoru Miyano is the Japanese voice actor for Dazai and is often called Mamo by ACG fans. Here the danmaku commenter is expressing that she/he could die of happiness at the sound of Mamo's voice, an expression that might be incomprehensible for those unfamiliar with the fandom's slang.

Some phrases are exclusively trendy and require the viewers to have up-to-date knowledge of popular culture and current meme trends. For example, 'please accept my knee' (请收下我的膝盖) is derived from dialogue in the video game *The Elder Scrolls V: Skyrim* and is frequently used by danmaku commenters to express their admiration for the filmmakers.⁸ Similarly, 'one more drumstick' (加鸡腿) is another popular danmaku comment used to compliment the cinematographer. For aspects of the film they do not like, danmaku commenters sometimes use memes, such as 'five pence visual effects' (五毛钱特效) to criticize the poor quality of the film production, or 'collect your boxed meal' (领盒饭) to mock the actor's clumsy performance and imply that she/he should quit acting.⁹

7   Animated film *Your Name*'s central plot involves body swapping between two high school students of different genders in Japan. At one point, when the female character is 'inside' the body of the male, she accidentally uses a more female pronoun in Japanese when talking about herself ('*watashi*' instead of '*ore*'). The male characters she is talking to look confused and surprised as she struggles to find the right pronoun to use, adding to the humour. Commenters explain this gendered pronoun issue in the comments and are complimented by other commenters for their concise explanation of the Japanese language.
8   The meme originated from a dialogue of the town guard (NPCs) in the video game *The Elder Scrolls V: Skyrim*, who speaks the line 'I used to be an adventurer like you, and then I took an arrow in the knee.' It was soon developed into the snowclone 'I used to X, then I took an arrow to the knee' to express one's admiration, and soon became popular among Chinese netizens. 'Please accept my knee' expresses the same meaning in a shorter phrase. This meme has its own variation with English language netizens on the other side of the world, using a similar formula.
9   Using 'five pence' to ridicule the poor quality of the visual effects first appeared in the Chinese television series *The Journey of Flower* (2015), and later became a popular internet slang. Danmaku

Carnivalesque experience

As others have noted for subtitling (Díaz-Cintas 2018: 127–49), danmaku participants can enjoy an experience resembling that suggested by Mikhail Bakhtin's theory of 'carnival' (1984a), which considers writing that counters the typical power structure as 'carnivalesque'. Nowadays, masked balls have moved from the real to the digital world, and danmaku supplies a space for people who would normally self-censor to joke about inappropriate things, fantasize and make comments that they may be unable to utter in their real lives, thanks to the function's anonymity.

Over 60 per cent of danmaku commenters admitted that they would not normally discuss the same topics or use the same language as they would in danmaku, due to their social roles and status, which demonstrates the importance of anonymity to users (Liu 2018: 32). Thus, danmaku commenting provides users with 'a second world and a second life outside officialdom' (Bakhtin 1984b: 6) in which everyone is equal without hierarchy and free to make comments which might be forbidden by conventional social norms and values. Just as anime can be used as a tool for 'escapism' (Izawa 2000: 140), danmaku also allows escapism through exploring humour that the commenter may not otherwise mention to their peers. For example, during the climax of the film *Bungo Stray Dogs Dead Apple*, Dazai is trying to protect Chuuya from a dangerous fog by pushing his head underneath it – it just so happens that this 'safe' area is near his crotch. During this scene (1:10:11), many female fans of BL (Boy's Love)[10] take the time to comment 'I don't have the hobby of a man', joking

---

commenters regularly use it to express their disappointment at the unprofessional visual effects during their film viewing. Contrary to the comment of 'one more drumstick', which is considered as a reward to the filmmakers, 'collect your boxed meal' is often applied to suggest that the film character should be dead, and its actor should terminate their job in the film. It came from the ACG industry where, when the animated character dies, its voice actor usually collects the boxed meal before she/he leaves the crew.

[10] BL is 'the homoerotic attraction the male heroes in a genre of Japanese women's manga (comics) feel for each other'. Female fans are known as *fujoshi* while male fans are known as *fudanshi* in and outside Japan, translating to something like 'rotten girl' and 'rotten boy' in English. These fans may take male characters in non-BL manga, anime and games and match them together romantically, especially if the duo have an antagonistic or close relationship. Fans usually debate their favourite pairings as well as who is the *uke/seme* (dominant or submissive character in the homosexual relationship). Fans receive amusement and sexual gratification from certain scenes in ACG, or via imagining sexual acts or romantic scenes between their favourite characters. See Mark McLelland (2003), 'No Climax, No Point, No Meaning? Japanese Women's Boy-Love Sites on the Internet', *Journal of Communication Inquiry*, 24 (3): 274.

that they are not enjoying this scene sexually, while others claim to have enjoyed this scene 'more than 100 million times' (1:10:03), jokingly suggesting they do use it as a masturbation aid.

Humour is key to Bakhtin's theory of carnival, and he described this laughter as 'ambivalent' and 'gay, triumphant, and at the same time mocking, deriding. It asserts and denies, it buries and revives' (1984b: 11). Recalling Bakhtin's carnivalesque, a large number of danmaku comments contain a sense of duality in their use of humour. To use Bakhtin's words, 'the dual image combining praise and abuse seeks to grasp the very moment of this change, the transfer from the old to the new, from death to life' (1984b: 165). For example, in the animated film *Your Name* commenters use danmaku to transfer the mood of this sombre film into something more positive. At one point (1:21:13) during the scene where the female protagonist Mitsuha disappears from existence, viewers and the male protagonist Taki are left alone and depressed. In order to transfer this serious/sad mood, commenters make jokes such as '(the female host is) unable to connect to the network, please click Reconnect' and five seconds later another danmaku comment continues the joke with 'the female host has broken the net, it is estimated that she will be online in 10 minutes'. These comments transfer the sadness to laugher by suggesting that Mitsuha has just disconnected from the server instead of disappearing from reality, the sort of thing that often happens in an online gaming session when a friend's character disappears from the match due to the loss of a local internet connection. Once again, the playfulness of the viewer is enacted here, where a serious scene is turned comedic; only laughter is permitted by the attendees of the carnival of danmaku.

Otaku subculture and nationalism

According to Toru Honda (2005), male otaku who feel they are treated unfairly by society retreat to fantasy relationships. Thanks to this mindset, danmaku allows for gatherings to occur where viewers become surrounded by the voices of other otaku and develop a confirmation bias about the normalization of their desires. In animated film *Your Name* commenters mentioning how high schooler Mitsuha's 'pink panties look good' (0:05:16) or that they 'want to see through the white panties' (01:46:37) are free to do so without being called perverted. This tolerance towards perversity and real-world identity is mainly because 'the comment itself, or what you say, is given prominence over the (online) identity of user' (Yang 2019: 7).

Otakus desire the possession of their favourite characters (Tamaki 2007: 225–38). One way for BL fans to possess a fictional character(s) is to confess their so-called love for that character, or openly declare their love for their favourite pairings. Such expressions of sexual desire are not easy to do openly in China, and expressing interests in BL would be difficult for some as 'mainstream media reports on BL fandom and BL fan girls in China have never been favourable; this subculture and the fans within it are constantly represented in a negative and biased light' (Yi 2013). Danmaku comments allow BL fans a place to freely and anonymously voice their sexual interests for characters and BL pairings without the fear of censorship or judgement, and these fans appear to be the core audience of these films such as *Bungo Stray Dogs Dead Apple*. At the start of the film (0:00:25), commenters use 'my' to deliver a sense of ownership of the characters (e.g. 'my Akutagawa', 'my Chuuya'). There is also evidence of BL fans watching the film, with users also commenting 'Soukoku' (the name for the popular BL pairing of Dazai and Chuuya), while later, others feel the need to gloat about their favourite character as if they were dating (0:04:50), such as when Dazai appears on screen and a commenter adds, 'my man is handsome'.

Nationalism and racism can also creep into danmaku. Using the 'Keyki incident'[11] as a case study, Xiyuan Chen examined the nationalist and populist tendencies in otaku subculture groups on Bilibili, claiming that although danmaku strengthens the cohesiveness of otaku subcultures, it has also increased negativity due to its anonymity (Chen 2014: 4667–721). There has also been some degree of nationalist sentiment linked to underlying tensions between Japan, Korea and China from time to time. Hence, it is not uncommon to see danmaku used to express xenophobic sentiment by normally polite people in their daily life, though how often this occurs potentially depends on how multicultural the commenter base is. For example, as with the 'Keyki incident' mentioned by Chen, the *utaite*[12] (such as Mafumafu on Niconico in the songs 'Ghost

---

[11] Chinese singer Keyki Wu released her first album *The First Princess in the World* (2014). Many believed the music was stolen from the works of Japanese Vocaloid singer Hatsune Miku (a virtual 16-year-old girl designed in an anime style). Vocaloid is a virtual singer software (known as V-singer in China) that uses synthetized voices to sing songs. Because of it, Keyki was soon attacked by ACG lovers and Hatsune's fans in a variety of social media, and at the same time, a debate about whether Keyki should apologize for her plagiarism stirred up hatred between some Japanese and Chinese nationalists.

[12] These are Japanese singers who cover songs on Niconico, usually originally sung by Vocaloid singers. Vocaloid or V-singer is known best for the voice and character design of the virtual singer Hatsune Miku.

Rule' and 'Hated by Life Itself') feature several anti-Chinese or anti-Korean comments in a variety of languages. Compared to Chinese video streaming platforms, Niconico has more multicultural viewers who choose to comment in their own language, and Japanese nationalist netizens respond harshly to this. However, this does not mean that nationalism cannot be found in platforms primarily aimed at and utilized by a single nationality, such as Bilibili, Youku and iQiyi, where the audiences are mainly Chinese. It is not uncommon to find some aggressive arguments over Chinese versus; Japanese dubbing abounds in danmaku comments, especially in Japanese films, which usually can be watched in either language. These disturbing comments suggest that the commenter does not care about offending any potential Japanese audiences.

On the other hand, danmaku also suggests some positive influences of foreign culture. This is especially interesting when examining Japanese animations, as historically Japan has had difficult relations with China. Yet, there are still many fans of Japanese animation, as evidenced through the success of animated films *Your Name* and *Spirited Away* (2001) in China.[13] Taking the example of *Your Name* on Youku, where most of the audience are Chinese, there are moments in the film when commenters express a favouritism for Japanese culture. For instance, during the classroom scene (0:29:02) one viewer comments 'Chinese dubbing can't stand it.' At the end of the film, one commenter is also quick to encourage tourism in Tokyo, adding that (01:40:16) 'this scene is in a real place, there is a chance to go'. The Japan Foundation has suggested that nowadays around 54 per cent of people learn Japanese due to things like anime, including a large number of Chinese students (Japan Foundation 2012: 7–20). With around a thousand round-trip flights between China and Japan every week, it is evident that tourism to this nation is booming and ACG fans may be an important reason for Japan's increasing popularity (Kyodo 2019). Hence, despite political tensions, Chinese ACG fans are still learning Japanese, preferencing Japanese dubbed anime and visiting Japan because of the positive influence of its anime.

---

[13] The success of *Your Name* in China led it to become the highest grossing animated film at the time in China and when Studio Ghibli's *Spirited Away* was finally released in Chinese theatres in 2019 it surpassed the Disney film *Toy Story 4* (2019) at the box office. See Zack Sharf (2019), 'Studio Ghibli Dominates China as First *Spirited Away* Screenings Outgross *Toy Story 4*', *IndieWire*, 24 June. Available online: https://www.indiewire.com/2019/06/spirited-away-china-box-office-dominates-toy-story-4-1202152571/ (accessed 23 December 2019).

Recreation of meanings

We live in an era where the status of the author as the authority on a text is already over, as Roland Barthes ([1967] 1990: 142–9) famously argued in the latter half of the twentieth century. Danmaku commenting provides a way for the viewers to rewrite a 'text', deconstructing or recreating new meanings for the original film. Anime typically acts as a world where fantasy romance and love are the day-to-day realities faced by characters (Izawa 2000: 138–53), and danmaku allows commenters to take some of this fantasy into the real world. In the virtual community created by danmaku, viewers are surrounded by individuals confessing, and so gain confidence and join in with the confessions alongside their lovestruck peers. The popularity of this sentiment is evident, as young viewers of *Your Name* have rewritten this romantic film about two fictional Japanese teenagers into a film where real Chinese teenagers confess.

From the very outset, especially during the first five minutes and during the climax,[14] Danmaku commenters use this film as an avenue to confess their love for real people (e.g. 'XXX, I love you very much'). This turns the film into an interesting crossover of reality and fiction. For instance, when a commenter states 'XXX, I miss you' (00:59:35), there is a sense of the passage of time existing in parallel to the events of the film – past, present and future are coexisting simultaneously – much like the non-linear experience of time depicted in *Your Name*. Therefore, while watching this film the audience is also potentially watching the start and end of relationships, as the commenters go back to the film to update about the failure of their real-world romances, which may have started while confessing while watching the film, or have been inspired by its romantic atmosphere. There is also the sense that the viewers wrote these comments in the hope that their love will somehow see them, and that it will reignite a romantic spark between them, just as – despite the passage of time – Mitzuha and Taki are reunited at the end of the film. Hence, this film is no longer just about the two

---

[14] The start of the film contains a voice-over for the characters with shots of Tokyo and the sky. In the climax of the film both Mitzuha and Taki finally meet. Mizuha, using the knowledge gained from Taki, must evacuate her hometown before it is destroyed by the meteorite impact, and must try and remember the name of the boy she loves. The film ends when, years later, they finally meet again as adults in Tokyo. Having only vague memories of what happened, the film ends with the character walking past one another on a staircase before finally turning around at the last moment and asking for one another's real name. During all these moments, and especially during the final half hour of the film, confession danmaku is very popular.

protagonists' (Taki and Mitzuha) love, but also about the hundreds of Chinese teenagers' personal romantic journeys.

Instead of simply sending comments, some commenters use danmaku in purposefully creative ways. For instance, during the climax of the film *Your Name*, commenters use danmaku to make a cluster of colourful shooting stars on the top of the screen, which enhances the romantic atmosphere of the scene and recreates the original film image of a meteorite falling through the sky, surrounded by confessions. This is a very romantic moment for both commenters and characters. Fans watching this film might feel empowered by the sacrificial love that Taki and Mitzuha have for one another. They might want their own selfless love to shoot through the sky, like the meteor in the movie, and fall towards their crush (Figure 5.1).

Animated film *Bungo Stray Dogs Dead Apple* on Bilibili is another good example of creative danmaku usage. The film includes a title song that reveals a clip of each character for a few seconds, accompanied by their names. During these moments, viewers create an impressive visual effect, making danmaku comments flood the screen during character appearances. It therefore becomes possible to detect the most popular character – with more danmaku comments appearing the more popular a character is. Moments where comments fill the screen are not seen as negative or annoying but instead are 'promoted and circulated on other social media platforms as famous scenes by the website and fan communities' (Yang

Figure 5.1 Commenters confess and use danmaku to make colourful shooting stars in honour of the meteor in the film *Your Name*.

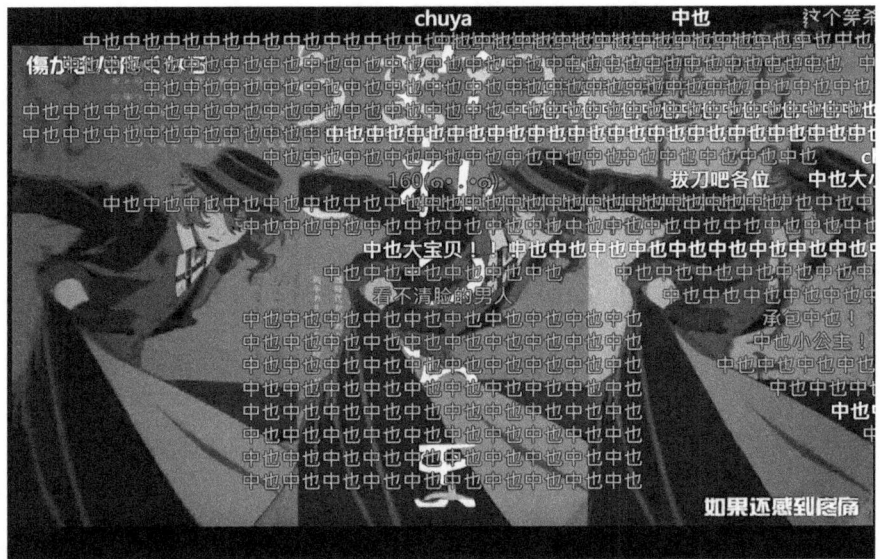

Figure 5.2 Chuuya's (中也) name fills the screen in *Bungo Stray Dogs Dead Apple*.

2019: 7). This type of danmaku reflects a collective enthusiasm by ACG fans; this is especially apparent when it comes to the character Chuuya's (中也) appearance (0:07:59), where the viewers get excited and fill the screen with the 'danmaku density' (Yang 2019: 7) of Chuuya's name (Figure 5.2).

At the opening of the film, viewers creatively apply danmaku comments to make an inverted cross out of white, red and blue phrases that combines the set-up with Soukoku (双黑, the BL pairing of Dazai and Chuuya, see Figures 5.3 and 5.4). The image of an inverted cross is popular in the gothic Lolita fashion subculture and in some gothic anime like *Black Butler* (2014) – which are both popular with many female otaku – and are not necessarily associated with Satanism in China. This image creates the same kind of gothic undertones which supplement the plot's recurring themes of death and suicide. The use of blue alongside red and white reduces associations with the Japanese flag for Chinese netizens, merely acting as a visual contrast. Using blue and red for the lower half of the cross, instead of white and red, also reduces visual associations with the American flag, disassociating the symbol with nationality and rendering it as merely an expression of the otaku's appreciation of the set-up of characters, gothic undertones and BL.

Figure 5.3 Inverted cross symbol.

Figure 5.4 Inverted cross danmaku in *Bungo Stray Dogs Dead Apple*.

Conclusion

While some argue that 'these comments can potentially increase the cognitive workload of viewers' (Ni 2017: 4) and 'distract people's attention from the original video and degrade their experience' (Ni 2017: 13), danmaku can also add to the viewing and entertainment experience of watching films for many users, as observed by some of the findings in this chapter. As discussed in the examples, otaku use danmaku to explore their desires, as seen by the danmaku on *Bungo Stray Dogs Dead Apple*. Moreover, because otaku have multiple orientations, they flick back and forth through the different layers of fiction as a 'creator and receiver' (Saitō et al. 2011: 26), so that rewriting the virtual text through danmaku forms part of the viewing experience enjoyed by fans. The use of danmaku as a means of confession in *Your Name* was both a surprising and interesting merging of reality and fiction, showing how commenters can rewrite a fictional romance into a personal story about themselves and their love. While YouTube comment systems may also evoke the playfulness of their videos' viewers, danmaku provides a combination of visuals and text where this conversation is instant and simultaneous. What stayed consistent throughout all the examples discussed in this chapter was that danmaku is often used in a creative and humorous manner, and it seems likely that it will continue to be used in increasingly more creative and humorous ways in the future.

References

Bakhtin, M. (1984a), *Problems of Dostoevsky's Poetics*, Caryl Emerson (ed.), Manchester: Manchester University Press.

Bakhtin, M. (1984b), *Rabelais and His World*, H. Iswolsky (trans.), Bloomington: Indiana University Press.

Barthes, R. ([1967] 1990), 'Death of the Author', in *Image Music Text: Essays*, London: Fontana Press, 142–9.

Chen, X. (2014), 'Study of Youth Subculture of Network Community Barrage Discourse Construction: The Bilibili Network on Keyki Incident Response as an Example', *Computer Knowledge and Technology*, 10 (20): 4667–721. (陈席元，弹幕话语构建的青年亚文化网络社群研究：以哔哩哔哩网对Keyki时间反应为例，电脑知识与技术).

Chen, Y., G. Qin and L. P. Rau, eds (2015), 'Understanding Gratifications of Watching Danmaku Video – Videos with Overlaid Comments', in P. L. Patrick Rau (ed.), *Cross-cultural Design Methods, Practice and Impact*, New York: Springer, 153–63.

Chen, Y., G. Qin and L. P. Rau, eds (2017), 'Watching a Movie Alone yet Together: Understanding Reasons for Watching', *International Journal of Human-computer Interaction*, 33 (9): 731–43.

Díaz-Cintas, J. (2018), ' "Subtitling's a Carnival": New Practices in Cyberspace', *Journal of Specialised Translation*, 30 (July): 127–49.

Cambridge Dictionary (2019), Definition of 'Digital Native', Cambridge: Cambridge University Press. Available online: https://dictionary.cambridge.org/dictionary/english/digital-native (accessed 31 December 2019).

Djamasbi, S., A. Hall-Phillips, Z. Liu and J. Bian (2016), 'Social Viewing, Bullet Screen, and User Experience: A First Look', *Proceedings of the Annual Hawaii International Conference on System Sciences*, 648–57.

Flanagan, C. A. (2013), *Teenage Citizens: The Political Theories of the Young*, Cambridge, MA: Harvard University Press.

Garvizu, N. (2017), 'Cool Japan: The Relationships between the State and the Cultural Industries', PhD diss., University of Sheffield.

Honda, T. (2005), *Moeru otoko* [The Budding Man], Tokyo: Chikuma Shobo.

Izawa, E. (2000), 'The Romantic, Passionate Japanese in Anime a Look at the Hidden Japanese Soul', in T. J. Craig (ed.), *Japan Pop Inside the World of Japanese Pop Culture*, London: M. E. Sharpe, 138–53.

Japan Foundation (2012), *Kaigai no Nihongo Kyōiku no Genjō: 2012 Nendo Nihongo Kyōiku Kikan Chōsa Yori* [Present Condition of Japanese-Language Education Abroad: Report on Japanese-Language Education Institutions Fiscal Year 2012], Tokyo: Kuroshio Shuppan.

Katsumata, H. (2012), 'Japanese Popular Culture in East Asia: A New Insight into Regional Community Building', *International Relations of the Asia-Pacific*, 12 (1): 133–60.

Kiley, D. (1983), *The Peter Pan Syndrome: Men Who Have Never Grown Up*, New York: Dodd, Mead.

Kyodo (2019), 'Number of Round-Trip Flights by Chinese Airlines Linking China and Japan Tops 1,000 per Week', *Japan Times*, 5 November. Available online: https://www.japantimes.co.jp/news/2019/11/05/national/china-japan-flights-top-1000-a-week/ (accessed 2 December 2019).

Liu, Y. (2018), 'Research on the Use of Barrage by Young Netizens Form the Perspective of Carnival', MA diss., Guangxi Teachers Education University (刘颖超，狂欢视域下青年网民弹幕使用研究，广西师范学院).

Ma, X. and N. Cao (2017), 'Video-based Evanescent, Anonymous, Asynchronous Social Interaction: Motivation and Adaption to Medium', *Proceedings of the ACM Conference on Computer Supported Cooperative Work and Social Computing*, February, 770–82.

McCulloch, G. (2019), *Because Internet: Understanding the New Rules of Language*, New York: Riverhead Books.

McLelland, M. (2000), 'No Climax, No Point, No Meaning? Japanese Women's Boy-love Sites on the Internet', *Journal of Communication Inquiry*, 24 (3): 274–91.

Mohd, F. M. (2013), 'A Study on Generation Y Behavior at Workplace', *International Conference on Business Innovation, Entrepreneurship and Engineering*, December, 549–54.

Ni, Y. (2017), 'A Study of Danmaku Video on Attention Allocation, Social Presence, Transportation to Narrative, Cognitive Workload and Enjoyment', MA diss., Syracuse University.

Saitō, T., H. Azuma, D. Lawson and K. Vincent (2011), *Beautiful Fighting Girl*, Minneapolis: University of Minnesota Press.

Sharf, Z. (2019), 'Studio Ghibli Dominates China as First Spirited Away Screenings Outgross Toy Story 4', *IndieWire*, 24 June. Available online: https://www.indiewire.com/2019/06/spirited-away-china-box-office-dominates-toy-story-4-1202152571/(accessed 23 December 2019).

Tamaki, S. (2007), 'Otaku Sexuality', in C. Bolton and Csicsery-Ronay Jr. (eds), *Robot Ghosts Wired Dreams Japanese Science Fiction from Origins to Anime*, London: University of Minnesota Press, 225–38.

Utalk (2016), 'Chen Rui, Chairman of Bilibili: Why Is Bilibili Popular with Young People?' *Weibo*, 24 September. Available online: https://www.weibo.com/ttarticle/p/show?id=2309404023202337684456 (accessed 8 December 2019) (B站董事长陈睿：B站为何如何深受年轻人喜爱？).

Yang, Y. (2019), 'The Danmaku Interface on Bilibili and the Recontextualised Translation Practice: A Semiotic Technology Perspective', *Social Semiotics*, 18 June. Available online: https://doi.org/10.1080/10350330.2019.1630962 (accessed 10 November 2019).

Ye, D. (2019), 'Cinema Audience Reduced 10.3% in the First Half of 2019 While Online Streaming and Live Entertainment Become Popular', *Xinhua Net*, 19 July. Available online: http://www.xinhuanet.com/2019-07/19/c_1124771914.htm (accessed 10 November 2019) (叶丹，上半年电影观影人次同比减少10.3% 在线视频与现场娱乐成新宠，新华网).

Yi, E. J. (2013), 'Reflection on Chinese Boys' Love Fans: An Insider's View', *Transformative Works and Cultures*, vol. 12, Available online: https://journal.transformativeworks.org/index.php/twc/article/view/424 (accessed 2 December 2019).

Zhao, A. (2019), 'Video Streaming Sites Should Aim at the Age of Big Screen', *Workers' Daily*, 17 April: 5. (赵昂，在线视频网站要瞄准大屏时代，工人日报).

6

Turkish online film distribution: Fighting for Indie filmmaking in a neoliberal and censored context

Murat Akser

Online distribution is playing an increasingly important role in Turkish Indie filmmaking practices. In the Turkish context, online distribution differs in its impact based on the format and genre of the film in question. For political/social documentaries, it is vital; for short films, it is the only source. For Indie features, it is an arena for monetization and, finally, for 'edgy' series (like *Phi-Fi*, or *Behzat Ç.*) it is an escape from the legal restraints of broadcast television, where serials can be viewed without the binds of censorship. Meanwhile, a new financial model plays a role that Indie filmmakers utilize to the fullest in Turkey, in combination with online streaming: crowdfunding. Crowdfunding helps to produce first features by women filmmakers and social documentarists who deal with sensitive issues such as LGBT and Kurdish minority rights, risking bans or censorship. Also, Turkish cinema has long been dominated by male directors, with the notable exception of Bilge Olgaç in the 1980s. There have only been nine women directors in Turkish cinema between 1914 and 1989 (Uğur Tanrıöver 2017, 326), and out of the 5,514 films made during that period, only 66 were directed by women. Moreover, the funding bodies, and selection and award juries of prominent festivals in Turkey, are also over-represented by men (Aktaş 2020: 193). In this way, crowdfunding brings a much-needed diversity in representation.

The decision by local filmmakers to seek funding through online distribution to finance their independent dream projects is hardly new, especially in a cash-strapped economy. Turkish actor/director Yılmaz Erdoğan's film and theatre company BKM recently sold the world rights to their entire film and television catalogue of twenty years to Netflix. BKM's position is that since their films reach an international audience in more than 190 countries through Netflix releases, they will improve the prospects of Turkish cinema. Erdoğan's long-standing ally and friend in business, Cem Yılmaz, also made a series of four films in *Black Mirror*'s style using a similar strategy of sponsorship. *The Comidark Films* (Karakomedi Filmler 2019, 2020) dealt with 'edgy' storylines and issues that would not have found their voice were they to have a theatrical release only. Erdoğan's BKM is just but one player that prefers to use online distribution for feature film releases. Other players in the Turkish film arena opt for alternative and local online distributors (such as BluTV and PuhuTV) that are financed through different financial structures and sponsorship, and do not charge their subscribers. Indie filmmakers use online distribution as part of the crowdfunding for their work, and to escape censorship for their socially conscious documentaries.

The transition from the old system of theatrical distribution is not without its growing pains. On 15 February 2019, after only two weeks at the box office with his film *Money Trap* (*Organize İşler 2: Sazan Sarmalı*, 2019), Yılmaz Erdoğan declared to Turkish media that he would release the film on Netflix. The decision caused fury among film producers and cinema owners in Turkey (Hurriyet Daily News 2019a). Netflix had previously been known to simultaneously release their films on both their streaming services and in cinemas, but this was the first time a commercial film production company in Turkey – that had invested heavily in the production of their film – had wanted to do the same thing. Both the Turkish producer's association and multiplex chain cinema owners protested the move, and Yılmaz Erdoğan was accused of playing it safe by making sure he recouped his investment from both ends (theatrical and online releases) and of being greedy in doubling his money by appealing to both home audiences and moviegoers. The Television and Cinema Movie Producers Association (TESİYAP) in a press release stated that 'simultaneously screening a cinema film on a digital platform would cause irreparable damage to the film industry' (Hurriyet Daily News 2019a). The Turkish Cinema Exhibitors Association (SİSAY) released a condemning statement which said that the 'sale of the film to VOD platforms for simultaneous screening, and concealing this sale from the sector, violated ethical values … it is a blow to Turkish cinema' (Hurriyet Daily News 2019a). Why Yılmaz Erdoğan chose this approach has to do with the changing technological, economic and legal structures in Turkey over the past twenty years.

A history of film industry and distribution in Turkey: From location based to online viewing

One very strong reason for the preference towards online distribution is the lack of physical capacity to screen Indie films in Turkey, and there were attempts to increase channels of alternative film distribution before online streaming came to the rescue for the Indie sector. Since 2010, there has been a significant reduction in the number of stand-alone movie theatres in major cities around Turkey, catching up with the trend elsewhere, such as in the United States/Canada and Europe. This development went hand in hand with an increase in shopping mall multiplexation in Turkish exhibition circles. Most of the golden era Turkish movie palaces of the 1950s–1970s were torn down and converted to either parking lots or shopping malls. The most notable case was the demolition of the Emek movie theatre. Emek had been the centre of Istanbul International Film Festival screenings for decades. Then the lot was sold to a government-friendly businessman, Demirören, and the decision to demolish the building was taken by the new owners. Despite protests, the demolition went ahead, and Indie filmmakers began to search for alternative venues for screenings (Ozduzen 2018).

Turkish film production peaked in the 1970s when the golden age of filmmaking called Yeşilçam (Green Pine) had its own genres, stars and audience in the millions. The audience left the scene in the 1980s and 1990s in favour of foreign films and television. They came back to Turkish cinema in the late 1990s and increased through the 2000s, reaching a peak in 2018 with 180 local films being made that realized a total of 40 million ticket sales.

There are political, social, economic reasons for this explosion of Turkish film production in the 2000s. The political reason is the support of Turkish filmmakers by left-leaning ministers of culture, who received Eurimages and government funding to make both art and commercial films. The censorship of films was lifted in 1992 by a liberal right/social democrat coalition government, which allowed Turkish filmmakers to explore 'edgy', ethnic, political and sexual content, following a combination of efforts from the leftist politicians who ran the Turkish Ministry of Culture. Socially, as the more nationalist and Middle Eastern facing AKP government of Tayyip Erdoğan – who represented a Turkish political elite – rose to power, local film production was supported by the government. Turkish television also presented domestically produced television drama that garnered a huge following. The new television drama created the necessary infrastructure and talent, which brought its own audience and demand for film production. Today, the top five grossing films in Turkey are produced and starred by actors and technical crew that honed their craft on Turkish television drama serials. Finally, the economic reason regards the rapid expansion of the Turkish economy under liberalization, globalization and the candidacy of EU membership in 2004. As a result, more money was invested in Turkish films and movie theatres than ever before.

One of the reasons why Turkish producers were investing in Turkish cinemas comes from the success of the film *Eşkıya* (*The Bandit*, 1997). Between 1989 and 1995, local film production in Turkey was very random, and there was barely an audience for it. Yet, when film school–trained commercial directors started to arrive, bringing their own studio space and camera/lighting equipment, they began investing in film production, and it paid off. Starting with the films *Vizontele* (2001) and *GORA* (2004), BKM became a big player in comedy films. Fida Film, an advertising film production company founded in 1965, branched into feature film production in 2004. Fida Film's purchase by an investor in 2007 led to its ability to self-finance feature films that had mass appeal. Fida Film further purchased the DVD production and distribution company Tiglon in 2011, which gave it massive distributor control, accounting for over 70 per cent of the whole DVD market share (Behlil 2012: 45). Fida Film's investment in local film production declined from 2013. Similarly, Özen Film began to give priority to the distribution of Turkish films instead of Hollywood, which brought the audience back. The key component was the ownership of distribution by Turkish companies that favoured Turkish filmmakers. In addition to showing Turkish films in the twenty-one movie houses it owned, Özen Film also co-produced the *Recep Ivedik* series of comedy films, which brought millions of viewers to cinemas in Turkey. With a series of economic crises in the 2010s, Özen Film withdrew from co-production and switched to distributing American films. American-owned UIP once again began to dominate film distribution when Özen Film withdrew from the scene. Another such distribution and exhibition company was Mars, which was founded in 2001 by Menderes Utku and Muzaffer Yıldırım. Mars Cinemas was sold to a South Korean company in 2017 for US$ 800 million. The company owns and operates 884 movie theatres and has virtually become a monopoly in this field, giving it access to over 120,000 cinema seats in Turkey. As a result of this foreign takeover, the global commercial competition rules came into place governing the operation of Turkish movie theatres. Many

Indie filmmakers, including Yılmaz Erdoğan and Cem Yılmaz, criticized these money-making practices (e.g. compulsory bundling of overpriced tickets and popcorn/drink in Mars operated cinemas) and declared that these decisions were made without taking the country's culture or an understanding of cinema viewing practices into account. The main complaint of the filmmakers was that the movie theatre operators gave them a low share while selling highly priced tickets alongside popcorn and beverage campaigns, exploiting both filmmakers and audiences for profits (Hurriyet Daily News 2019b).

In protest, film production companies like BKM, Çamaşırhane Film, Dijital Sanatlar, NuLook, Taff Pictures, Madd Entertainment, CMYLMZ | Fikir Sanat and Boyut Film Movie – who provide the best examples of feature filmmaking in Turkey – postponed release of their latest films indefinitely. The issue went beyond the producer–theatre owner's fight and moved into the Turkish parliament, which in turn passed the Cinema Law in an attempt to protect the interests of both parties and the audiences (Kenyon 2019).

The Mars group gave the following response to the ongoing debate in a newspaper interview through their spokesperson, Aslı Irmak Acar:

> The exhibitors can initiate certain campaigns. These are discounts in favour of the consumer. Yet producers do not want such discounts and blocking these will be at the expense of the consumer. Ticket prices rise and producers reflect the consumer as no alternative, the right to benefit from the campaign or to buy a single ticket belongs entirely to the consumer.

Referring to the lead proponent of the dispute, Cem Yılmaz, Irmak Acar made the following infuriating comment: 'It may be time to invest in new talent if they (the filmmakers) will not release the films they made. We will invest in and create new Cem Yılmazs.' Subsequently, the row moved to Twitter. Yılmaz's harsh response was not delayed: 'This lady, whom I saw for the first time in my life, says she is going to issue new Cem Yılmazs. Slow down Ma'am. Let's leave Cem Yılmaz out of this and try lowering the movie ticket prices in Turkey to 15 TL from the 40TL.' Another star actor Sahan Gokbakar humorously shared on his Instagram account: 'Newsflash. They just boarded the newly manufacture Cem Yılmaz on a plane from Korea. I loved the photo of the popcorn lady and Cengiz eating bucketful of popcorn in the empty movie theatres just by themselves, a picture they will soon have to get used to.'

This row between the filmmakers and film distributors lasted for weeks in print and online media, where the filmmakers refused to release their newly completed films and the manager of Mars Cinemas called for supporting new talent to eclipse the old guard. Irmak Acar was eventually fired (Hurriyet Daily News 2019b). The row did not change the fact that film distribution had changed hands from the major Turkish distributors like Mars to the global Korean and American distribution companies. The limited number of comedy blockbusters occupies every screen, and revenue flows to foreign investors. Following the closing of repertory cinemas like Emek and Alkazar, Indie film producers disrupted the closing of Pera cinema and took over its management to screen their films. This new initiative was called 'Başka Sinema' (other cinema) and developed as an alternative network for film distribution and exhibition (Bozdag 2016).

As a result of the *başka cinema* initiative and producers like Yılmaz Erdoğan releasing their films on Netflix, there was an increased access to both Turkish and foreign Indie films, so they reached a wider audience in this period. Meanwhile, torrented and streamed pirating of both Turkish and foreign language films were allowed by Turkish telecommunications regulators, enabling art house material to reach Turkish audiences and generate new forms of cinephilia such as binge viewing. New production companies emerged such as Erdoğan's BKM. Since 2001, Turkish cinematic output has grown every year from a handful of films to nearly two hundred features in 2018, and Erdoğan has managed to make hit films every year since 2001. Among these films, the top five box-office revenues amounted to more than half the total box office annually. The remaining 150 films accounted for the rest of the audience share, which could be as low as a few thousand viewers per film. In addition to works by Erdoğan, films of new directors like Tolga Karacelik, Berkun Oya, Onur Saylak, Serdar Akar also became available on Netflix.

Online distribution in Turkey: Why it matters

Turkish filmmakers, especially independent ones, have struggled to get proper theatrical distribution since the end of the classical Yeşilçam era. The system which was prevalent between 1950 and 1989 allowed for the production and distribution of films based on genre, regional audience tastes and star power (Behlil 2012: 42). Independent films also struggled to get distribution in the classical system. Yet they could still reach a niche audience because there were many producers, theatre owners and a large segment of the population that were ready to see any film before the coming of television and VHS in 1970s and 1980s Turkey. During these years, the exhibition of Indie films in the country was limited to private screenings at film clubs, universities and Sinematek at Istanbul. With the coming of video tape, the under-the-counter distribution of pirated copies of Indie films, especially those banned by the military government in post-1980 Turkey, became commonplace (Ogan 1988). Still, until the late 1990s, if a Turkish Indie film could not find a commercial distributor, it was destined to remain locked in the filmmakers' vaults, only occasionally surfacing for specialty screenings.

Turkish Indie filmmakers initially benefited from the emergence of 1990s private television broadcasting, due to its role as a means of alternative distribution. Throughout that decade, Indie films found new life on these channels, especially pay-per-view and, later, streaming ones. The support of liberal governments in the 1990s and subsequent support of liberal-leaning ministers of culture during the early AKP era helped the creation and distribution of Indie films in Turkey. The Turkish film industry benefited immediately following an autonomous self-liberalization of the broadcasting regime by private radio and television stations in 1992. Old Yeşilçam films were used to fill time in the ever-increasing number of private television channels. The government first banned all private broadcasting and then, bowing to pressure, made it all legal. Political strings were attached by the creation of the FCC-style Radio and Television Supreme Council (RTÜK) that would fine or even ban channels based on content. It is a state creation where the board members are representatives of political parties present in parliament. During that time – between 1992 and 2013 – topics covering the critique of forced modernization of the early Turkish republican era, such as the repression of ethnic identities, were a favoured subject by the AKP government, which led to the proliferation of films by Kurdish directors (Akser 2015). Another cohort that benefited from such support were first-time feature filmmakers, some of whom were women. All the support for Indie film production and distribution came under threat by the conservative neoliberal AKP government in the late 2010s, as the Kurdish peace process collapsed, Gezi protests were crashed and a massive political witch-hunt led to the exclusion of all politically engaged Indie filmmakers from government-funded film production and distribution grants. This new political and economic climate forced Indie filmmakers to seek alternative means of funding and distributing their films.

As with previous telecommunication technologies, internet streaming arrived in Turkey almost instantly in 1995. However, the legal framework and content provision have been continually debated among the service providers and policymakers. The tendency over the last decade was in favour of restricting internet content. The Turkish government's blocking of YouTube, Twitter and Wikipedia is notoriously well-known (Akser 2018). The streaming service Netflix quietly entered the Turkish market in December 2015, and for a long while managed to exclude itself from the content restriction of regulators. In August 2019, the RTÜK declared that all internet-based streaming films, television series and video content would be subject to scrutiny and approval of the board, which jeopardized Netflix's position against censoring any film or series content. Netflix had been a lifeline for some Turkish commercial and Indie filmmakers for its uncompromising acceptance of 'edgy' material. Meanwhile, art house film directors like Nuri Bilge Ceylan relied heavily on European funds to make films that were apolitical in content (Cerrahoğlu Ziraman 2019), while Indie filmmakers like Zeki Demirkubuz and Tolga Karaçelik, who produced socially conscious films in the past, were now excluded from Ministry of Culture film grants due to their support for Gezi Park. Both directors had to appeal to the public in 2015 regarding their projects' rejection by the Ministry, and subsequently were granted Ministry support to make their films in 2016. Karaçelik went on to win best international feature with *Butterflies* in 2018 at Sundance film festival. Both directors released their films online to reach wider audiences via Netflix, BluTV and PuhuTV.

During the period between 2015 and 2019, film distribution in Turkey experienced enormous changes, due to developments in online streaming technologies. Such changes introduced mobile viewing, time-independent streaming and a vast array of new and alternative channels of film distribution. YouTube, Vimeo, Amazon Prime and MUBI are heavily used in video sharing in Turkey. New social practices like communal binge nights emerged among young adults in upper-class neighbourhoods in Istanbul, Ankara and Izmir. Yet, the Turkish government were like a Damocles sword over online media distribution. To counteract such liberalization, particularly the circulation of 'dangerous' content, the government acted as a gatekeeper, creating a new form of intermediation. Yet pirating and illegal streaming of content through such platforms as BluTV and PuhuTV allowed material to bypass such gatekeeping at a transnational level. Indeed, there have been dozens of times when YouTube was banned in Turkey in the 2010s. It took many years for Netflix to launch its service in the country, as the government demanded that the company, along with counterparts such as YouTube and Twitter, set up corporate offices in the country so they could be taxed for revenues, be held accountable, have their content controlled and be fined for contraventions. Ironically, the problems of censorship and random removal of their films online had attracted Turkish Indie filmmakers to the newly created online distribution providers in the first place. The total control of sites such as YouTube and Vimeo, peer-to-peer communities and video on demand (VoD) platforms such as Netflix by the Turkish government puts Turkish filmmakers in an increasingly difficult position. The situation is so bad that major Turkish film producers delayed the production of their films in 2019 as the Turkish government introduced its new Cinema Law (enacted on 22 October 2019) that would allow the government to ban the distribution of any film based on its content (Kenyon 2019). Uncertain as to how the new law would operate, the producers simply did not invest in film production that year, which led to a fall in revenue and in the number of films produced. The Cinema Law also tried to prevent the simultaneous release of films in theatres and online, to protect exhibitors' interests. For the first time in theatres, commercial films are evaluated and classified for audience admission. First-run films are not allowed to be made available via paid cable, satellite, terrestrial, internet or other media within the first five months of their release (or the first six months where they are available free of charge). This makes it very difficult for independent filmmakers to monetize their films after the first few weeks of limited release.

In spite of all these restrictions. Turkish Indie filmmakers like Ali Vatansever, Emin Alper, Tolga Karaçelik and Zeki Demirkubuz still find their niche audiences through online distributors in Turkey via Netflix, BluTV and PuhuTV. Turkish creative talent – directors, producers, screenwriters and actors along with technical crew – is trained and live on the production of popular television series in the country. With online platforms increasing since 2015, the traditional time/space fixed ways of seeing films and series have changed. Now Netflix, BluTV and PuhuTV all produce Turkish language television series without the restriction on content and storyline, and have a wider reach to new audiences, with some of the content finding its way to Netflix (Lotz 2021). For example, *Phi*, an original series on BluTV, is sold to Netflix in Turkey, and later screens on the traditional private broadcaster ShowTV, which also streams the episodes for free through its website and mobile app.

From crowdfunding to online release: *Blue Wave* and *Inflame*

Crowdfunding and the use of streaming platforms by Indie filmmakers is a trademark of post-2013 Turkey. One of the leading cinephile groups is *Altyazı*, based at Bogazici University Mithat Alam Film Centre. Since the early 2000s, the young university-educated cinephiles have been able to create a tradition of film criticism that led to Indie filmmaking efforts being supported through the centre. These former film critics have now become film producers and directors. These thirty-something, educated, metropolitan, European-oriented Indie filmmakers are among the many who share their films through online streaming services, and several of those at the forefront are women directors.

The online distribution of Indie films in Turkey helped women filmmakers in particular. The commercial support for women filmmakers is totally non-existent within competitive Turkish commercial film production. The Ministry of Culture support, routinely distributed since 1992, is almost exclusively awarded to male directors. Yet, through broadcasting and film school routes, thousands of women have entered the film industry in the last decade, at both artisanal and creative levels. In the absence of financial support, women filmmakers began joining forces though film co-ops that utilized their connections and resources, such as the creation of the Flying Broom International Women's Film Festival in Ankara. Similarly, IF! Istanbul Indie Film Festival has long been run by an all-female team. Founded by Serra Ciliv and Pelin Turgut, the festival management progressively gave voice to female filmmakers over several years. Similarly, with the support of Zeynep Özbatur (the producer for award winning Turkish directors Nuri Bilge Ceylan and Kutluğ Ataman) they helped to create a producers' lab for emerging women filmmakers through the Antalya Golden Orange Film Festival. These women created seed money to make their first feature films through crowdfunding.

Crowdfunding turned out to be a viable support for women filmmakers. The whole premise of crowdfunding is 'online first', with supporters being treated to the first online screening of the film. Two such examples are Zeynep Dadak and Merve Kayan's *Blue Wave* (Mavi Dalga, 2013) and Ceylan Özçelik's *Inflame* (Kaygı, 2017). Both directors appealed to online support for the initial development grant (US$ 15,000) which led to them getting more financial support from European development and production grants. The system of crowdfunding allows for cinephiles, friends and family of the filmmakers to directly support the production of a film through small donations online. The rewards ('perks') to the financiers include visits to the set, invitations to premieres and merchandise. For example, *Blue Wave*'s perks included a signed postcard, poster, script and DVD by directors and cast; a visit to the set during shooting to meet cast and crew; an appearance in the film as an actor; a gala invitation/dinner with cast and crew; and a film credit as a co-producer. While *Blue Wave*'s producer Yamaç Okur used IndieGoGo for crowdfunding in 2013, a newly established Turkish version of the film crowdfunding portal *Fongogo* was used to sponsor Ceylan Özçelik's *Inflame* in 2016 (Güler 2016). Ozcelik gave similar perks to contributors including copies of the DVD. As with *Blue Wave*, the DVD also included access to a private Vimeo link to stream the film. In both cases, once the crowdfunding money was gathered, the directors became eligible for development and production grants, such as the Turkish minister of culture's first feature grant, Sundance Screenwriters Lab, FEST Pitching Forum and the Istanbul Film Festival's 'Meetings on the Bridge', creating a financial snowballing effect which helped the production and further distribution of the film without the risk of financial bankruptcy.

A platform for social documentaries: Crowdfunding

Many Turkish film festivals have increasingly been censoring documentaries that deal with social issues such as the repression of the Kurdish, women and LGBT identities in Turkey. Documentaries about the Gezi Park resistance and Kurdish repression in southeast Turkey are banned from film festivals in cities run by AKP mayors. Their filmmakers found that alternative exhibition outlets, such as the Ayvalik Festival, created new niche festivals with film workshops. Yet more social and political reach is desired, and their new strategy is to go crowdfunding and release through new streaming services. Koçer (2015) discusses three recent documentaries that were both financed and distributed online through crowdfunding as cases in point. All three films deal with topics that are forbidden by the film festivals and broadcasters, such as LGBT rights and Kurdish issues. *My Child* (*Benim Çocuğum*, d. Can Candan, 2013) features seven parents who have gay, lesbian and transsexual children. The parents stand by their children and form a group to support them and other LGBT people. As Koçer states, the collective financing and online distribution strategy is integral to the ways in which *My Child* has been cited within public discourse for mobilizing a liberal public around LGBT rights (Koçer 2015: 232).

Similarly, *Ecumenopolis: City without Limits* (Imre Azem, 2012) is a social documentary criticizing the rapid urbanization during the AKP era. *Ecumenopolis* reveals the link between Istanbul's deteriorating sub-urbanization as a result of AKP's neoliberal economic policies. The documentary gives voice to academics, developers, citizens and community advocacy groups. *Ecumenopolis* also *follows* a migrant family whose squatter house is demolished, highlighting their struggle to live in an urban space. Finally, this documentary gives a representative voice to urban conservationists, ecological resistance groups and activists who want to see the city as a better living environment. *Ecumenopolis's* producers used crowdsourcing and the help of friends to make the film, and also used crowdfunding for the distribution of the film. The producer Gaye Gunay launched a website and asked for donations, and over two hundred people donated around US$ 9,000 in three months, receiving perks such as signed postcards, t-shirts and film posters in return. The film's crowdfunding allowed it to be distributed to film theatres, and it was subsequently available both on DVD and online, a feat hard to achieve for an Indie social documentary in Turkey.

The third documentary example, *I Flew You Stayed* (*Ez Firiyam Tu Mayî Li Cî*, Müjde Arslan, 2012), is a road movie. Since 2007, Arslan has been practising as a film critic, academic and feature film director actively raising issues related to Kurdish identity, and she is the editor of the first scholarly film studies volume on Turkish cinema. Around 2009–10 she was briefly interned as part of the crackdown on Kurdish activists and politicians (Koçer 2016: 137). Her release from prison coincides with the drying up of Turkish Ministry of Culture grants to Kurdish filmmakers and increased blocking of Kurdish-themed films and documentaries in Turkish film festivals. As a result, Arslan resorted to crowdfunding and online distribution of a subject very dear to her heart. In the self-narrated documentary, Arslan traces her life by taking a journey into the heartland of Kurdish armed struggle to find the missing grave of her father, who died fighting against Turkish armed forced in south-eastern Turkey as a Kurdish guerrilla, alongside the forces of the Kurdistan Workers Party (PKK) (Koçer 2015: 233).

All three of these cases consist of social/political documentaries that could not be funded due to government and film festival censorship but were able to get production and distribution funds through crowdfunding initiatives. The producers used these initiatives to raise awareness and reach a larger public, alongside distribution of their films through online portals. In fact, there is a very strong interrelation between the crowdfunding model and online distribution for these groups, as not only is it the only viable option, but it also allows for certain kinds of filmmaking that are 'edgy', independent and focused on ethnic and gender-related issues. These films are counter-products that bypass restrictions of state censorship and thus reach wider audiences in their home country and abroad. This new method of funding/distribution is more inclusive, subject-specific and wide-reaching.

Conclusion

As Baschiera states (2014), online distribution of Indie films 'could potentially offer new distribution opportunities for specialised niche cinema and help a new proliferation of genres and subgenre films'. Thus, the online distribution of Indie films in Turkey can be seen not just as a kind of 'last resort' but rather as a creative starting point for women and alternative documentary filmmakers in the country. Subscription video on demand (SVOD) streaming services like Netflix and local online distributors like PuhuTV and BluTV are increasingly becoming the most important creative and viable platforms for distribution of otherwise censored content. Although online streaming was initially embraced by Turkish Indie filmmakers, the restrictive laws of the Turkish government easily project a near-future in which new laws may block creative freedom of content in the long run. One reason for the emergence of these platforms – as almost the saviour of minor cinemas in Turkey – is that Turkish Indie filmmakers faced the collapse of the physical theatrical chain system, following multiplexation and the transfer of distribution to foreign companies. It is also due to the post-2013 Gezi Park political climate in the country in which women and Kurdish documentary filmmakers found themselves increasingly relying on crowdfunding as a sponsorship model that allowed them to reach their niche audiences as patrons through online streaming. Initially, this emerged as a democratization of film circulation in which both niche and mainstream films gained visibility and availability, summarized by Iordanova and Cunningham (2012) as 'digital disruption'. However, Turkish governments started to pass laws and regulations to locally control the content of services like Netflix in Turkey. Yet, through local use of VPNs, fans and cinephiles can still access the otherwise-blocked material from the overseas versions of Netflix. Thus, despite the limitations, the future is bright for the Turkish Indie filmmakers. Censored or not, Turkish Indie filmmakers and documentary filmmakers are increasingly able to get their funding from two sources (crowdfunding and Netflix) to produce films about political and social issues that can reach global audiences, even though there may be partial restrictions on their reach to domestic audiences.

References

Akser, M. (2015), 'Turkish Independent Cinema: Between Bourgeois Auteurism and Political Radicalism', in D. Baltruschat and M. P. Erickson (eds), *Independent Filmmaking around the Globe*, Toronto: University of Toronto Press, 131–48.

Akser, M. (2018), 'News Media Consolidation and Censorship in Turkey: From Liberal Ideals to Corporatist Realities', *Mediterranean Quarterly*, 29 (3): 78–97.

Aktaş, S. (2020), 'Labelling Directors as "Women"', in S. Gulsah and D. Cetin (eds), *International Perspectives on Feminism and Sexism in the Film Industry*, Hersey, PA: IGI, 188–99.

Baschiera, S. (2014), 'Streaming World Genre Cinema'. *Frames Cinema Journal*, 6 (December 2014). Available online: https://framescinemajournal.com/article/streaming-world-genre-cinema (accessed 17 August 2021).

Behlil, M. (2012), 'Majors, Mavericks and Contenders: Financing Practices in Contemporary Turkish Cinema', *Spectator*, 32 (2): 41–9.

Bozdağ, Ç. (2016), 'Turkey: Coping with Internet Censorship', in R. Lobato and J. Meese (eds), *Geoblocking and Global Video Culture*, Amsterdam: Institute of Network Cultures, 130–8.

Cerrahoğlu Zıraman, Z. (2019), 'European Co-productions and Film Style: Nuri Bilge Ceylan', *Studies in European Cinema*, 16 (1): 73–89.

Güler, E. (2016), 'Turkish Films Turn to Crowdsourcing for Funding', *Hurriyet Daily News*, 20 June. Available online: http://www.hurriyetdailynews.com/turkish-films-turn-to-crowdsourcing-for-funding-100653 (accessed 17 August 2021).

Hurriyet Daily News (2019a), 'Netflix Release of Turkish Film in Cinemas Stirs Reactions', 18 February. Available online: https://www.hurriyetdailynews.com/netflix-release-of-turkish-film-in-cinemas-stirs-reactions-141320 (accessed 17 August 2021).

Hurriyet Daily News (2019b), 'CEO of Movie Theater Chain Fired Amid Row with Producers' 19 February. Available online: https://www.hurriyetdailynews.com/ceo-of-movie-theater-chain-fired-amid-row-with-producers-141339 (accessed 14 August 2021).

Iordanova, D. and S. Cunningham, eds (2012), *Digital Disruption: Cinema Moves On-line*, St Andrews: St Andrew's Film Studies.

Kenyon, P. (2019), 'New Law in Turkey Has People in Film, TV Industries Worried about Censorship', *NPR*, 11 March. Available online: https://www.npr.org/2019/03/11/702355704/new-law-in-turkey-has-people-in-film-tv-industries-worried-about-censorship?t=1618309609673 (accessed 17 August 2021).

Koçer, S. (2015), 'Social Business in Online Financing: Crowdfunding Narratives of Independent Documentary Producers in Turkey', *New Media & Society*, 17 (2): 231–48.

Koçer, S. (2016), 'Ez Firiyam Tu Mayî Li Cî (I Flew You Stayed/Ben Uctum Sen Kaldin): An Example of Domestic Ethnography', in S. Koçer and C. Candan (eds), *Kurdish Documentary Cinema in Turkey: The Politics and Aesthetics of Identity and Resistance*, Newcastle-Upon-Tyne: Cambridge Scholars, 131–9.

Lotz, A. (2021), 'In Between the Global and the Local: Mapping the Geographies of Netflix as a Multinational Service', *International Journal of Cultural Studies*, 24 (2): 195–215.

Ogan, C. (1988), Media Imperialism and the Videocassette Recorder: The Case of Turkey', *Journal of Communication*, 38 (2): 93–106.

Ozduzen, O. (2018), 'Cinema-going during the Gezi Protests: Claiming the Right to the Emek Movie Theatre and Gezi Park', *Social & Cultural Geography*, 19 (8): 1028–52.

Uğur Tanrıöver, H. (2017), 'Women as Film Directors in Turkish Cinema', *European Journal of Women's Studies*, 24 (4): 321–35.

7

India's online streaming revolution: Global over-the-top (OTT) platforms, film spectatorship and the ecosystem of Indian cinemas

Nandana Bose

India's millennial digital revolution has dramatically transformed its media, communications and entertainment sectors. It is one of the fastest growing and largest markets for smartphones and tablets in the world due to the rise of indigenous cellular network companies such as Reliance Industries' Jio and Bharti Airtel (the leading Indian mobile network operator), offering high-speed, affordable and reliable 4G broadband connectivity in urban and semi-developed regions with the intention of penetration and expansion of telecom services among rural populations. The conjunction of favourable economic, technological, infrastructural and demographic factors in recent years has enabled increased internet usage, affordable smartphones, cheaper data packages, faster broadband and cellular data connectivity, and improved bandwidth, resulting in one of the fastest growing and most competitive markets for online streaming and over-the-top (OTT)[1] platforms and content providers in the world. With the entry of global players Netflix and Amazon Prime, the video-on-demand (VoD) platform of the Seattle-based online retailer, adding a competitive edge, the Indian OTT ecosystem has been further energized, and is witnessing a fierce battle between home-grown platforms such as Star India's Hotstar, Viacom18's Voot, Zee's dittoTV, Balaji Telefilms'

---

[1] In broadcasting, OTT stands for 'over-the-top', a term used for the delivery of audio, video and other media content delivered over the internet without the involvement of a multiple-system operator (MSO) in the control or distribution of the content which implies that users do not require to subscribe to a traditional cable or satellite pay TV service.

ALT Balaji and Sony's SonyLIV, independent players like Spuul and the two global streaming giants.

This chapter examines the sweeping changes transforming the Indian mediascape as it grapples with the 'disruptive innovations' being introduced by the deluge of global and home-grown VoD platforms that are reportedly 'undermining cable TV' (Izardar 2019), and are anticipated to become 'as big as the Indian film industry' (Gupta 2019). It will survey the implications of the emergent online digital media platforms (OTTs) for the Indian film industry, and their immediate and long-term impact on film cultures, cinephilia and spectatorial habits of Indian film audiences. It will delve into how OTTs are affecting existing business models established in the Indian cinema ecosystem, specifically in terms of online distribution and their impact on traditional modes of theatrical exhibition; and the likely barriers and challenges to the continued expansion of OTTs in India and their future directions and prospects for growth. Furthermore, it will explore whether OTTs and web content generators can encourage 'a membership mind-set' (van Eeden and Chow 2018: 17), and develop a subscription-based, pay-on-demand model of revenue in India, which has traditionally been averse to such kinds of expenditure on entertainment, and if OTTs shall remain an urban phenomenon with primarily elitist creative content.

At the outset it should be noted that this chapter confines itself to a macro-level, generalized examination and interrogation of rapidly changing film cultures and content; and the spectatorial habits and practices of Indian viewers as a consequence of the recent entry of online streaming platforms. It is a broad overview of the ongoing disruptive trends noticeable in the Indian cinema ecosystem, and does not intend to engage in a micro-level content analysis of specific web serials (or episodes), streaming platforms, programming and curation by any OTT, or analyse a particular regional language film industry (such as Marathi, Malayalam or Bangla cinema) vis-à-vis the disruptor's impact on it, all of which represent possible areas for future academic work and enquiry.

Rise and growth of OTTs in India

According to Frank D'Souza, media and entertainment analyst with PricewaterhouseCoopers (PwC), Mumbai,

That India is poised to have one of the fastest growing Media market in the world, is well known (PwC's Global Outlook forecast for 2018-22, amply confirms that), and good enough to place it in the Top 10 media markets in the world before the end of this forecast period, what is encouraging is how non-linear mediums such as OTT, E-sports, etc. are also picking up pace. By PwC Global Outlook forecast, India will be one of the top 10 OTT markets in the world by the end of the forecast period. (D'Souza, 2018)

The rise of OTTs can be traced back to the launch of dittoTV in 2012 by one of the pioneers in satellite television, Zee Entertainment Enterprises Ltd (ZEEL), which became India's first home-grown OTT TV distribution platform (Verma 2015). In the same year, the on-demand entertainment platform Eros Now, a division of Eros International Plc, was launched, offering customers access to the world's largest collection of premium Indian entertainment, with hundreds of titles in several languages, including Hindi and Tamil.[2] It was now possible for Indian viewers to watch Bollywood and regional Indian movies, TV shows, Eros Now Video Shorts, music and music videos anytime, anywhere, on nearly any internet-connected computer or iOS or Android mobile device. With rights to over 5,000 movies and over 250,000 audio tracks from thirteen Indian music labels providing music content, the platform has grown 28.7 per cent to 13 million paid subscribers and 128 million registered users worldwide as of September 2018. By establishing partnership with iQiyi, the largest Chinese online streaming service, it has become the first South Asian OTT player to penetrate the Chinese digital space (Bestmediainfo 2018).

Prior to their advent, YouTube, the popular video-sharing website created in 2005, was the only name Indians could think of when they wanted to watch VoD online (apart from visiting Torrent sites). Launched in 2015, the next OTT proved to be the most popular till date – Hotstar, a premium streaming service owned by Novi Digital Entertainment, a subsidiary of Star India wholly owned by The Walt Disney Company. Its raison d'être was to provide the growing young adult demographic an alternative to YouTube 'by offering high-quality curated content that featured very targeted advertising', according to its CEO Sanjay Gupta (Arzoo 2015). The current market leader with over 150 million users monthly, it is available in seventeen languages, operates both a free ad–supported

---

[2] Eros International Plc (NYSE: EROS) is a leading global company in the Indian entertainment industry that acquires, co-produces and distributes Indian-language films in multiple formats, including cinema, television and digital media.

service and two subscription-based tiers in India, and secured exclusive digital rights to the global sensation *Games of Thrones* (2011–19) and the 2019 *Cricket World Cup*. Predictably, all leading broadcasters such as Star, Sony and Zee have online platforms now to protect their business and stay competitive in a cut-throat, shape-shifting market. 'The broadcasters have decided that if they are going to be cannibalised they should also utilise the opportunity. Since they have the content, it makes perfect sense to offer it beyond linear television,' says Sridhar Pai, vice-president, Asia Pacific, Dataxis, a global firm that tracks the telecom, TV and media businesses (Verma 2015).

According to a 2018 Federation of Indian Chambers of Commerce and Industry (FICCI)-Frames report, 'digital media grew 29.4% in 2017, with a 28.8% growth in advertising and 50% growth in subscription. India will be the second largest online video viewing audience in the world by 2020' (Shrivastava 2018). There are several favourable intersectional conditions and factors that are driving the exponential growth and market congestion of OTTs. The number of internet users in India has risen fivefold since 2011. The aggressive launch of telecom service provider Reliance Jio in September 2017 has shaken up the Indian telecom sector, resulting in even cheaper data prices, expanded geographic coverage and improved internet and mobile connectivity (Knowledge at Wharton 2017). As a result, the amount of time that Indians spent on video and entertainment apps rose by 85 per cent in 2017 from the year before, according to the market research group App Annie. Netflix founder and CEO, Reed Hastings, told an audience in New Delhi in February 2018 that 'even we couldn't predict the last two years of Indian internet growth … It's the most phenomenal example anywhere in the world in terms of lower data costs, more people online, expansion of 4G [mobile data]. … And we didn't see that coming' (Bengali 2018). According to PwC, 'mobile Internet TV is one of the biggest growth areas in India and a third of smartphone users are watching TV on their devices' (Verma 2015). For S. Sadagopan, professor and director of the International Institute of Information Technology (IIIT) Bangalore, factors enabling this growth are the 'near universal availability of mobile phones, millennial driving the growth [and] reduced attention span of everyone' (2018).

Another significant contributory factor is India's booming $33 billion e-commerce market (Bengali 2018) as more and more Indians venture online to purchase essential and luxury commodities and services from such e-commerce companies as Flipkart, the Bengaluru-based giant shopping portal founded in

2007 by Sachin and Binny Bansal (representing Amazon's main competitor), and its subsidiary, Myntra, a fashion e-commerce portal acquired in 2014, and Jabong.com, acquired in 2017; Snapdeal, Flipkart's domestic rival; Ola and Uber; Nykaa; Big Bazaar; Swiggy; and many more app-based services. A popular marketing strategy is for OTTs to collaborate with many of these e-commerce portals to offer deals and discounts to India's teeming online customers. However, these are still early days for the world's second most populous nation of 1.3 billion potential e-customers, and Amazon CEO, Jeff Bezos, is certainly alert to this fact as he points out that 'Amazon.in is the most visited and the fastest growing marketplace in India. It's still Day one for e-commerce in India, and I assure you that we'll keep investing in technology and infrastructure while working hard to invent on behalf of our customers and small and medium businesses in India' (Knowledge at Wharton 2017).

India's streaming wars: Arrival of Netflix and Amazon Prime Video

Amazon entered India in 2013 and introduced its popular subscription-based programme, Amazon Prime, in July 2017, a year after Netflix was launched in January 2016, at Rs. 499 per annum (approximately $8), to drive customer loyalty through features such as unlimited one-day deliveries and early access to lightning deals. At around $8 a year (far cheaper than its US rates, which range from $8.99 to $11 a month depending on the plan), it is among the cheapest internet video services in India. Gaurav Gandhi, chief operating officer of Viacom18 Digital Ventures, the digital arm of media house Viacom18 that runs the online video service Voot, describes it as a 'very disruptive price point' (Knowledge at Wharton 2017). The Amazon video service, as in the United States, is bundled with its Prime membership which offers free shipping for its e-commerce site. It launched its streaming media device, the Amazon Fire TV Stick, in the country, making India only the fifth market – after the United States, the UK, Germany and Japan – where Amazon has introduced it. To quote Nitesh Kripalani, director and country head of Amazon Video India, 'our aim is to solve the problems our customers face. With the Fire TV Stick, customers can watch our latest and exclusive movies and TV shows from the comfort of their living rooms' (Knowledge at Wharton 2017).

For Hastings, India is 'hugely important' to Netflix because 'it's one of the strongest internet markets', adding that 'India has seen the highest growth among all its Asian markets' (Knowledge at Wharton 2017), a candid statement that underscores how the American studios' global ambitions increasingly centre on India, home to half a billion internet users, and second only to China which has its own home-grown digital platforms and remains closed to American content providers. The paid services of Netflix and Amazon Prime are competing against nearly thirty Indian streaming portals, many of which give away popular sports and local language programming for free.

OTTs as disruptive innovators: Local content is king

What are the immediate and long-term ramifications of the entry of these two big global players for one of the largest entertainment industries in the world, the Indian cinema ecosystem? 'The biggest impact will be on the content market', say industry players and analysts such as Gaurav Gandhi who further elaborates,

> The bread and butter of online video in India is catch-up TV or sporting rights. While sporting rights are very expensive, 80% to 90% of the TV content is owned by six to eight players like Star TV, Sony, Viacom and Zee. Of these, most have their own streaming services; they sell only limited content. Netflix and Amazon therefore have to outbid for local content and also create from scratch. In the long term, creating original content will be more sustainable and also a strong differentiator. (Knowledge at Wharton 2017)

Thus, it is not a surprise that Amazon and Netflix are investing millions of dollars to develop Indian films and series that they hope will make this their next big growth market, with Amazon Prime Video producing more than twenty original series in India aimed squarely at the mass market, having already released its first Indian original series drama about professional cricket *Inside Edge* (2017), a workplace sitcom, a musical reality show, a dating programme and a slew of stand-up comedy specials.

Reiterating Gandhi's observation is PwC's D'Souza who points out how 'both Netflix and Amazon realize that, independent of their international library, local content is extremely important in India. They're pumping in quite a lot of money in creating that local library … and original programming is going to be important for both of them' (Bengali 2018). Kartik Hosanagar makes a similar observation: 'Both players – especially Amazon – have started investing a lot in content acquisition. They have started paying a lot of money to content producers to produce original shows for them, sometimes even in the Rs.1 crore to Rs.5 crore ($150,000 to $800,000 per episode range)' (Knowledge at Wharton 2017). Adds industry analyst Jenil Thakkar, 'The content production market in India has really perked up because of Amazon and Netflix. This will force other players to produce original content faster than they would otherwise have done' (Knowledge at Wharton 2017). This is certainly an accurate prediction as analysts point out that most home-grown players like Hotstar, Eros Now, Sony Liv and Voot have increased their content budgets significantly since the entry of Netflix and Amazon.

Despite its original premium subscription pricing which was significantly reduced in 2021, Netflix, which is aiming to produce 'at least five to six Indian originals a year' (Bhushan 2017), is betting that Indian customers will judge its 'Netflix Original' Movies and Series favourably compared to their local TV dramas, with their broad storylines, low production values and high-quality shows that will appeal to global audience, while keeping cost of production low by shooting in India, with a predominantly Indian production team and cast that, in turn, is creating many jobs in the film industry. 'I think we'll be a giant exporter of Indian stories', declares Hastings (Bengali 2018). And in order to achieve his ambitious goal, Netflix, whose entry provided Indian viewers access to the company's super-hit original shows such as *House of Cards* (2013–18) and *Narcos* (2015–17), is now offering local and regional content in India through both licensing it from local content providers and also producing it in-house as high priority. For instance, it tied up with acclaimed filmmaker Anurag Kashyap's production company Phantom Films to create an original series, based on author Vikram Chandra's critically acclaimed book *Sacred Games*, which turned out to be so popular that a second was released on India's Independence Day, 15 August 2020.

Not to be left behind, Amazon has reportedly earmarked 'an investment of Rs. 2000 crore ($310 million) for acquiring and producing content in India' (Knowledge at Wharton 2017) to add to its library of international movies and TV shows. 'To date, it has signed up with 18 original content partners for streaming their shows, with nine Indian original shows already in production, making it one of the largest Indian original line-ups on an OTT platform' (Knowledge at Wharton 2017). According to James Farrell, head of content, Asia Pacific, Amazon Prime and Amazon Studios, 'India is a focus market in terms of content creation just behind the U.S. and Japanese markets' (Knowledge at Wharton 2017) and Kripalani echoes this sentiment:

> We are committed for the long term to the Indian market and excited to be making multiple Indian original shows – many of which are in production – with top talent. Meanwhile, we have licensed top content. It's no secret that Amazon is making a big investment in India and is happy to take original content, created by Indian talent, to audiences worldwide. (Knowledge at Wharton 2017)

Reportedly, Amazon Prime Video is now looking to expand its offerings in 'vernacular languages, to have an edge over competitors. The platform already has a library of movies in five Indian languages' (Shrivastava 2018). This is a significant strategy because, as film festival programmer and critic Aseem Chhabra points out, 'Netflix had made the mistake of initially being slow to acquire content in non-Hindi language creative content' (2018). 'Our goal is to win with Indian customers first,' says Vijay Subramaniam, director of Amazon Prime Video in India. 'We're really looking to make sure that our stories and content selection are providing our customers in India with the best value at all times' (Bengali 2018).

While both Amazon and Netflix have big budgets, aggressive marketing strategies and growing libraries of Indian content, both have cleverly tapped into the massive pre-existing fan bases of the three Khan superstars who have dominated Bollywood for the past decades by securing TV rights to their films – while Amazon secured the rights to Bollywood megastar Salman Khan's movies and Aamir Khan's *Thugs of Hindustan* (2018), Netflix won global streaming rights for movies produced by another A-lister, Shah Rukh Khan (Bengali 2018).

'Amazon gives us wings': Impact on Indian mediascape, cinephilia and film spectatorship

What has the creation of local content by these global streaming giants meant for the film industries of India, and especially Bollywood? Chhabra believes that 'OTTs are *energising* the Indian film industry, taking it to an international level, and impacting in a big way. The film industry is very excited about OTTs as it gives the industry an alternative option' (2018). D'Souza points out that

> Given the regulatory arbitrage that OTT platform currently enjoy in India (for that matter even in most parts of the world), ie [*sic*] the content exhibition on OTT is not restricted by any of the programming and certification or censorship restrictions that may apply to programming that has to be viewed in movie theatres and televisions ... this arbitrage provides two unique opportunities to the ecosystem involved in creating content for OTT platforms. Firstly, it can push the boundaries of creativity, and aided by significant production budgets, up the production values; and secondly, give space to new and fresh talent, in a manner more amiable than that currently exists. As both Amazon and Netflix beef up their content production teams and get hands on, this can be viewed as the second coming of the foreign 'studios' in India. However, they need to avoid the mistakes of the past Studios [*sic*] in their earlier avatar, ie [*sic*] namely of undue reliance on few cast and crew, and unfeasible investments on key projects. (2018)

At this point in time the consensus among those this author spoke to suggests that online streaming platforms promise to liberate filmmakers and artistes in more ways than one. It could continue to usher in a refreshingly new era for filmmakers and actors who traditionally could only choose between film and television. As Sidharth Bhatia, the founder-editor of *The Wire* observes,

> The OTT platforms will offer a multitude of opportunities for Indian film makers. To begin with, some of these platforms are original content producers, who may finance films. In addition, they provide a new way to distribute, not just in the home country but all over the world. I think it will also influence content – film makers may be willing to experiment with form and theme, which the multiplex model, with the need to recover costs within the first three days, does not allow. Most of all, these OTT platforms are not 'censored' by government bodies allowing for much more freedom. (2018)

Truly it has been unprecedented for creative industries to not have any censorship restrictions or even self-imposed censorship, a common practice in film industries of India. Indian cinema has historically been subjected to the most whimsical, arbitrary and often draconian censorship rules and regulations by the State-controlled Central Board of Film Certification (CBFC) which mandates the display of its censorship certificates onscreen before films begin, and at cinema halls.[3] From doing away with the mandatory anti-smoking

---

[3] For more on censorship of Indian cinema, see Lalitha Gopalan (2002), Someshwar Bhowmik (2009) and Monika Mehta (2011).

disclaimers to the unbridled freedom to show characters cussing, kissing or killing each other in visceral ways, Netflix and Amazon had opened up a whole new world of possibilities for filmmakers and artistes.

Consequently, bold new content has been produced by Netflix, namely, *Lust Stories* (2018), an anthology film and sequel to the 2013 Bollywood anthology film *Bombay Talkies*, comprising of four separate stories, directed by four well-known filmmakers Anurag Kashyap, Zoya Akhtar, Dibakar Banerjee and Karan Johar that depict female sexuality from the perspective of four women in a graphic, direct and unapologetic manner, previously unimaginable on either the silver screen or the telly. This new-found creative licence may account for the astounding popularity of *Sacred Games* (2018) that brought to life, with gritty realism and a dark, raw edginess, the sordid diegetic world populated with inimitable characters from Mumbai's criminal underbelly. Unsurprisingly, the series became controversial for featuring high incidences of visceral violence, profane language, nudity and sexual imagery resulting in demands for OTT players to start self-regulating after a public interest litigation (PIL) was filed in the Delhi High Court for an allegedly defamatory reference to India's former prime minister Rajiv Gandhi. For Chhabra, both these Netflix Originals were 'unprecedented in terms of nudity, sex, abusive words' (2018).

Amazon Prime's *Inside Edge*, that showed the ugly nexus between underworld, politicians and cricket, featured graphic scenes that, although seemingly true to life, would have been inconceivable in a film today. The gripping web series appeared to be partially inspired by incidents surrounding the popular annual T-20 Cricket series held in India that often finds a place in newspaper reports and television news debates. The very first shot of the gripping web series featured a sexual act and was parallel cut with a cricket match; besides the expected effect to titillate, the former was included to infuse dramatic tension and more than summed up why it could never have been possible in any other medium or era (Chintamani 2017).

Overall, there has been a growth spurt in innovative, diverse content, offering a wider variety of programmes, especially during the pandemic from March 2020 onwards, that has witnessed a massive surge in OTT viewership with Bollywood blockbusters such as *Shakuntala Devi: The Human Computer* (2020), *Laxmmi Bomb* (2020) and *Gunjan Saxena: The Kargil Girl* (2020) directly released on streaming platforms due to the closure of theatrical exhibition sites. In fact, for a while a new liberating space had been created by these global players by freeing creative content generators from the age-old shackles of censorship norms and protracted power struggles with regulatory bodies, although such freedoms have been modified in recent times. This has encouraged genre experimentation, specifically, horror and the crime drama/thriller genres as gore, torture and graphic violence can now be portrayed as evident from Netflix's second original series, *Ghoul* (2018), a horror mini-series starring Radhika Apte and based on a Arab monster folklore; *Delhi Crime* (2019), based on the 2012 Nirbhaya rape case in New Delhi that had caused global outrage; Amazon Prime Video original series *Mirzapur* (2018); the wildly popular *Sacred Games*; and *Soni* (2018), a realist, slice-of-life feature-length film about the trials and tribulations of two female police officers which premiered to critical acclaim at the 2018 Mumbai International Film Festival after which it was directly released on Netflix without a theatrical release, now a viable option in terms of extended film exhibition. Apart from the crime genre, the stand-up/political satiric comedy genre is enjoying a boom period not just globally (HBO's multiple Emmy award–winning *Last Week Tonight with John Oliver* (2014–) available on Hotstar, Netflix's *Trevor Noah: Son of Patricia* (2018) and *Patriot Act* (2018–) with Hasan Minhaj are a few examples) but also in India, with Netflix streaming its first Indian comedy special *Abroad Understanding*, featuring one of the country's leading stand-up comedians, Vir Das, who says he 'love[s] working with Netflix. They are spearheading comedy across the world right now. Every major comic I love watching is innovating on their platform,' and has signed a two-programme deal (First Post 2018).

Thus far, due to the proliferation of OTTs, there is a growing audience for innovative, provocative, often expletive-ridden, graphic content on Indian screens in an unprecedented manner. For far too long Indian audiences had been infantilized by the state, the censor board and self-censoring film industries. The kind of audience that would have been considered staple for a Saif Ali Khan or an Anurag Kashyap film have happily gravitated to online streaming platforms. Besides, the upwardly mobile, young audience, accustomed to instant access and gratification, would be easier to attract online as opposed to being enticed to the cinema hall. OTTs encouraged the production of creative content for grown-ups by minimizing censorship and giving access to a wide range of audiences across different age groups (Chintamani 2017), especially catering to millennials who form a sizeable and growing demographic, India having one of the largest under-twenty-four youth populations in the world. As Pritish Nandy, chairman of Pritish Nandy Communications (PNC), points out, 'We have a new generation that already consumes entertainment differently. Hopefully, they will be the harbingers of change, offering them content they want at their convenience – anytime, anywhere and on any device of their choice' (Verma 2015). Vikram Malhotra, chief executive of Abundantia Entertainment, a content provider for Amazon Prime, speaks of 'changing tastes in entertainment in a country that has long been defined by the extravagant, genre-mashing melodramas of Bollywood cinema. The Indian audience is maturing' (Bengali 2018). However, in the aftermath of the controversy surrounding the Amazon Prime political web series *Tandaav* (2021) for allegedly hurting religious sentiments, furious national debates ensued demanding censorship of streaming content. Consequently, it will be interesting to see how OTT platforms respond to a self-regulatory body to oversee content and a three-layer oversight mechanism initiated by the government in February 2021; and whether investing an authorized officer with the power to block access to content will be problematic in terms of logistics and creative output (Farooqui 2021).

OTTs has created a much needed 'third space' or 'third screen' beyond film and television, for the reinvention of stars like Saif Ali Khan, Vivek Oberoi and Abhay Deol, giving them more options when their film careers flounder. While Saif Ali Khan's Bollywood comedy-drama film *Chef* (2017) was a miserable box-office failure, there is already talk of another Netflix release, as audiences eagerly await his return as the conflicted Inspector Sartaj Singh in *Sacred Games 2*, directed by Kashyap and Vikramaditya Motwane. They are also offering exciting opportunities for the nurturing of new acting talent such as Radhika Apte, who has become synonymous with the Netflix series; Saloni Batra and Geetika Vidya Ohlyan in *Soni*, Rasika Dugal in *Delhi Crime* and Mithila Palkar, who stars in the Netflix Original film *Chopsticks* (2019). In fact, Amazon Prime is on a mission to 'go seek talent', including actors on the edge of the Hindi film industry (Chhabra 2018).

These global OTT players provide a unique global launch pad and guarantee instantaneous visibility for new actors and creative talent in India. As Vir Das points out, '*Abroad Understanding* took me to an audience across the world' (First Post 2018). Reportedly, Netflix would like to introduce Indian actors in US productions and encourage more Indian talent to work on its US productions, citing the example of director Ritesh Batra (*The Lunchbox*) who helmed the video giant's recent original film *Our Souls at Night*, starring Robert Redford and Jane Fonda, which reunited the two actors five decades after 1967's *Barefoot in the Park*. In terms of showcasing acting talent, Netflix's *Sense8* featured Indian actress Tina Desai in a prominent role (Bhushan 2017).

Chhabra also draws attention to the important fact that marketing is taken care of by these global streaming giants, citing aggressive advertising campaigns undertaken by Netflix followed by Amazon Prime Video. Known for investing in heavy out-of-home (OHH) advertising in United States, Netflix India reportedly spent approximately Rs. 5–6 crores (or 50–60 million) on outdoor advertising to promote its first original series, *Sacred Games* (exchange4media 2018). Its spending power for authoring hype and acumen for creating 'buzz' for its original web series, including *Lust Stories*, was evident from its huge advertising billboards installed on expressways, malls and footbridges in metros (Figure 7.1).

Additionally, for Indian artists, the entry of Netflix and Amazon has opened new opportunities for storytelling as writers, historically overlooked and underpaid by film and television industries, are earning higher fees than they typically did in Bollywood where budgets are opaque and set aside mainly for directors and actors. 'These platforms provide an unparalleled opportunity for writers,' opines Datta Dave, a partner in Tulsea, India's first talent agency representing writers and directors, which has more than thirty clients working on programmes for Amazon, Netflix and other online platforms. 'Experienced feature film writers are given the opportunity to be showrunners, which essentially elevates them to a producer role … Up-and-coming writers get the chance to contribute to writers' rooms. There's a renewed respect for the profession, which is a wonderful step toward creating better content' (Bengali 2018).

Rangita Nandy, creative director at PNC, and producer of the Amazon Prime web series *Four More Shots Please!*, dubbed India's *Sex and the City*, observes that Indian dramas rarely featured such women in lead roles or dealt frankly with issues like sex and relationships. 'You've seen Indian women in villages, women who've had crimes done to them, who've been victims,' says Nandy. 'You haven't seen a group of women like this who try to do what women in the rest of the world do' (Bengali 2018). Zoya Akhtar and Reema Kagti's critically acclaimed web series *Made in Heaven*, about two wedding planners in Delhi, created by Excel Entertainment, and released in March 2019 on Amazon Prime Video, is also a case in point. It delves into sensitive societal issues from which film and the television industries have hitherto shied away, and has touched a chord with educated, financially independent, upper-middle-class female audiences, a historically overlooked demographic. In addition to having bigger budgets

Figure 7.1 Netflix's first original series, *Sacred Games*, on a billboard.

than usual for Indian TV shows, Nandy reveals that Amazon brought in a US showrunner to run a workshop for its Indian writers and directors, and as her creative team had never written for television before, it received assistance in episode structure and character development (Bengali 2018). She says, 'Amazon gives us wings. We can develop content we always wanted to do without worrying about censorship or the box office. All of us are doing pieces we've wanted to make but haven't had the platform for' (Bengali 2018).

In terms of emergent forms of cinephilia, film spectating cultures and film exhibition sites as a consequence of the rise of OTTs, there are indications of a tendency towards gentrification of the Indian entertainment sector. It is significant to note that in a country of extreme wealth disparity and uneven development, Netflix subscription starts at about $8 per month, the same as in the United States, and is the most expensive video streaming service in India. That is more than a day's wages for nearly 90 per cent of Indians, and affordable only for a small urban elite that travels abroad, is fluent in English and takes cultural cues from the West, having been brought up on Hollywood blockbusters, and habituated to binge-watching reruns of American sitcoms *Friends* (1994–2004) and *The Big Bang Theory* (2007–19) on cable television. 'Netflix's pricing makes it clear they're in it to get the really wealthy Indian population,' comments Hosanagar (Bengali 2018). Compare it with Star India's Hotstar which offers most of its content for free; its paid subscription for premium content is priced at Rs. 199 ($3) per month which might explain why it's the market leader. Hastings says premium pricing is part of Netflix's India strategy. In a recent visit to the country, he says, 'There are around 300 million smart phone users in India. But we are targeting mostly the high end – 10 or 20 million – for whom our pricing is not a problem' (Knowledge at Wharton 2017).

This gentrification can be traced to the advent of multiplexes in the late 1990s and the introduction of premium pricing of film tickets at multiplex chains, such as the upscale PVR and Inox, which are typically located inside exclusive, gated, sanitized spaces of malls, closely surveilled by security personnel who man detectors at entrances reminiscent of airports. In a country that has embraced a neoliberal capitalist, globalized economy fairly recently, access to entertainment is increasingly behind steep paywalls meant for consumption by India's privileged, urban, affluent and aspirational sections of society that remain largely beyond the means of the general populace.[4] This scenario that has been unfolding over the past two decades is a far cry from the cheap tickets, loud participatory audiences and easy access to democratic spaces of single-screen theatres that are gradually disappearing or being refurbished and converted into plush multiplexes in Tier 1 and Tier 2 cities.[5]

The gentrifying drive incorporates a growing predilection for less communal and more personalized viewing spaces that may eventually lead to the gradual demise of communal TV viewing at home. 'Increasingly, people are opting for alternate avenues to consume content, and television is no more the first screen option,' according to Shailesh Kapoor, CEO of Ormax Media, a Mumbai-based industry tracker who observes how the '"second screen" phenomenon is on the rise. ... As individual spaces are getting well-defined, personalised entertainment is becoming an every day reality.' That the subscriber can pick

---

[4] For more on the 'malltiplex' phenomenon in India, see Adrian Athique (2009).
[5] For more on film spectatorship, Indian audiences and single-screen exhibition, see Lakshmi Srinivas (2016, 2013, 2010, 2005).

and choose, pay and watch, on TV or mobile has become the key driver (Verma 2015).

Increasingly shorter theatrical runs for the average film suggest that OTTs are fast becoming viable alternatives for the continued exhibition of films that either did not fare well in cinema halls (such as *Mard Ko Dard Nahi Hota Hai*/Men Don't Feel Pain which premiered at MAMI to critical acclaim in 2018) or were unable to secure or were inappropriate choices for wide theatrical releases and saturation bookings (for instance, Sujoy Ghosh's fourteen-minute mythological Bangla thriller *Ahalya* (2015), starring Radhika Apte, was released only on YouTube). OTTs provide a much-needed platform for the distribution of 'indie' cinema. From spectators' perspective, they can now wait for films to release on streaming platforms instead of visiting cinema halls for reasons of comfort, convenience, affordability, safety or enjoyment of individualized viewing space, which has become a global spectatorial trend; or wait for DVD/Blu-ray releases.

Another favourable disruptive aspect of OTT players is the creation and curation of a digital archive of Indian language cinema accessible anytime, anywhere in excellent image quality (unlike the bootlegged, grainy, distorted versions of films that may be available on YouTube). They have made possible easy availability of regional language cinemas which are usually restricted to theatrical releases in specific geo-linguistic areas. Additionally, English subtitles make regional cinema accessible to a much wider (albeit English-educated) audience within India. For instance, *Tumbbad* (2018), a groundbreaking horror film, is made available on Amazon Prime after its theatrical run ended in the western state of Maharashtra; *Sairat* (2016), a critically acclaimed, hard-hitting Marathi film on lovers divided by caste, and the cult Malayalam films *Angamaly Dairies* (2017) and *Kumbalangi Nights* (2019) are similarly available on Netflix. More recently, the much-anticipated thriller loosely based on Macbeth, *Joji*, starring the popular Malayali actor Fahadh Faasil, was released on Amazon Prime in April 2021. However, constant, uninterrupted availability and permanent storage of these streamed films are valid concerns, especially for film scholars and educators.

Speculating about overall trends in Indian cinema that may emerge in future as a response to VoD platforms, S. Ramesh Kumar, professor of marketing at the Indian Institute of Management (IIM) Bangalore, prognosticates that 'customized content and pay as you use models are distinct possibilities. Also, diverse and fragmented market segments would emerge due to the competitive environment with foreign brands coming into India. Consequently, the film industry may start producing exclusive content for the mega brands while simultaneously engaging the mass through the conventional films' (Kumar 2018). According to Bhatia, although 'Netflix etc. are no doubt influenced by the large numbers of potential subscribers in countries like India, it is a diverse audience, divided by not just language but also class/economic status' and believes that

> for the time being most films will be urban, if not thematically, then in terms of sensibility and treatment. In recent years, dubbed and subtitled films have been successful with a wide range of audiences – for example *Bahubali* [2015, 2017] and the superhero genre of films. But these come along once in a while and are expensive to make. Plus they are best enjoyed on the big screen. Smaller intimate films on a smaller screen, the kind that OTT platforms will make and show, may not necessarily be successful across India. Which means big budgets could go to Hindi films which reach out to more people. (Bhatia 2018)

Will the OTT bubble burst? Barriers and challenges

PwC reports that in the United States there has been

> growth in streaming video-on-demand (SVOD) and OTT subscription. Whether Netflix or Amazon Prime, the NBC Sports Gold Cycling Pass or the NBA League Pass, HBO Now, Hulu or CBS All Access, SVOD and OTT subscriptions are one of the fastest-growing components of the video ecosystem. And they are primarily ad-free. With each passing month, a greater proportion of premium video viewing is taking place through subscription-supported environments, especially among affluent households. (van Eeden and Chow 2018: 16)

One of the barriers to OTTs' continued expansion and penetration beyond the Tier 1 metro cities hinges on whether the average Indian OTT customer will follow suit and be willing to switch to a new subscription-based model. Netflix and Amazon are the only major 'subscription-only' players in India. Others typically are advertisement-led and are either totally free for the viewers or have a freemium model. 'According to industry estimates, of the approximately $220 million video streaming market, only a fraction is subscription-based' (Knowledge at Wharton 2017).

According to a 2017 Wharton School report,

> Netflix and Amazon are expected to both pave the way for paid content in India and also benefit from the tailwinds that are driving the subscription model. So

far, there have been three main barriers to this. One, the mindset. At a basic monthly package of around $3, cable TV is cheaper in India than in most places around the world. The average Indian consumer doesn't like paying extra (beyond cable) for content that is delivered at home. They are willing to pay extra for content only if it is part of an experience – like an outing to a movie theatre. (Knowledge at Wharton 2017)

Thakkar reiterates, 'the Indian consumer doesn't like to pay explicitly for content. They don't mind paying implicitly. So even though the consumers pay for their OTT service by way of data charges, they believe they are paying for access rather than content. Two, high data costs. And three, limited options and low adoption of online payments' (Knowledge at Wharton 2017). Besides, piracy is a serious issue and results in massive losses in annual box-office revenues to the film industry and to DVDs and Blu-ray sales. As Chhabra observes, 'Indians are used to illegally downloading and filesharing – why would they pay for online content when they can access it for free?' (2018).

Initial subscriber figures remain low for both Netflix and Amazon, and pricing will be a key determinant for the future expansion of OTT subscriber base, especially pertaining to the prospects of Netflix, which had previously refused to discount its prices for overseas customers. Even Hotstar subscription, 'the country's biggest streaming platform … part of an Indian media conglomerate owned by 21st Century Fox with tens of millions of users – is minuscule next to the more than 2 billion movie tickets sold in this country every year, or the estimated 152 million who subscribe to pay-TV services' (Bengali 2018). For Hosanagar there is no doubt in his mind that there will not be any early returns from these investments (of Netflix and Amazon). 'It will take some time before people start switching to digital platforms en masse. So the real question then is whether they will have the patience and stay invested for the long run' (Knowledge at Wharton 2017). Certainly, sustaining continued subscription over a period of time and beyond the free trial period will be one of many foreseeable challenges, another being the tendency to share subscription accounts among extended family and friends. Taking cognizance of this fraudulent practice of rampant password sharing, Netflix has recently trialled a crackdown on ineligible users who do not live in the same household as the account owner (Godwin 2021).

Yet another challenge Netflix and Amazon need to factor in, unique to the Indian OTT market, is whether they shall be able to produce content tailor-made for the Indian cell phone viewer. Unlike the United States where internet video is watched primarily on TV screens, in India, which is largely a single TV home market (only 5 per cent are multi-TV homes) this viewing is more on mobile screens. According to the Indian Media and Entertainment Report 2017 by KPMG India and FICCI,

> Between 2016 and 2021 mobile video traffic in India is expected to grow at a compound annual growth rate of 68% and the number of video capable devices and connections is expected to grow 2.2 times, crossing 800 million in number. Video is expected to grow to 78% of the overall mobile data traffic by 2021. 'Making content for the mobile screen requires a different kind of storytelling,' says Voot's Gandhi. 'On the phone you have multiple distractions – calls, messages, social media, etc. If you want to tap into the Indian viewer who is watching content on the phone, you have to structure your content very differently. You have to make sure that the content is so compelling that the viewer doesn't get distracted.' (Knowledge at Wharton 2017)

Future prospects and directions

Much of this chapter was written in pre-pandemic times. India has witnessed the exponential growth and popularity of OTTs during the pandemic with its content reaching much wider and diverse audiences than previously envisaged. The future growth and directions that the OTT market shall take will largely be determined by how well, and within what timeframe the aforementioned barriers and challenges are overcome including specific advantages created by the ongoing pandemic. Firstly, as PwC's D'Souza points out, 'global trends indicate that though consumers want to be seen as being global, consumption patterns and tastes tend to be largely local. Given the Indian market size and competition, each player would need to determine how they interplay foreign content with creation and delivery of local content to be able to have a meaningful share of the OTT market' (Knowledge at Wharton 2017). Sadagopan reiterates thus: 'Netflix has the potential to disrupt, provided it is able to source Indian content, price it right and manage the speed of delivery. A small number would love the Netflix U.S. content, but the real disruption will need "Made in India, Made for India" content' (Knowledge at Wharton 2016).

Secondly, D'Souza asserts that based on the current industry dynamics, 'a model which can support a gradual shift from AVOD (advertisement-led video on demand) to SVOD (subscription-led) and TVOD (transaction-led) will survive in the longer run. Also, how effectively AVOD models can be put into play would depend largely on how better targeted advertising can be created by analyzing individual consumer behaviors through appropriate data mining' (Knowledge at Wharton 2017). Industry analyst Thakkar believes that video streaming cannot be profitable purely on an ad-led model because 'in the long term, you have to build a strong subscriber base' (Knowledge at Wharton 2017).

Thirdly, will India follow the United States by way of switching over to internet TV? Thakkar believes that 'unlike in the U.S. where many people have cut the cord and replaced cable television with an OTT service, in India the two will co-exist' because cable TV is very cheap. However, despite strong tailwinds for a robust video streaming industry, challenges will continue. For instance, 'customer experience is an important element of an OTT platform and can be a strong differentiator. However, that experience is largely beyond the control of an OTT player and is dependent upon the telecom ecosystem prevalent in the country' (Knowledge at Wharton 2017). For D'Souza, 'over the next two to three years how the telecom ecosystem responds to a higher number of people using high-speed bandwidth services, and what kind of collaborations emerge within the industry, will determine the rate of growth of the OTT market in India' (Knowledge at Wharton 2017).

While pointing out that the next two to three years are crucial, Hosanagar does not 'expect that the market will grow exponentially. ... The hope is that the e-commerce story – massive investments fueled by unrealistic expectations followed by tightening of the purse strings – doesn't play out here' (Knowledge at Wharton 2017). Sadagopan opines that Netflix and Amazon could have an advantage in India because of their deep pockets and global expertise. But, he adds, 'If 4G penetration to remote areas is sustained and if 5G becomes a reality in urban pockets, the barriers to entry will drop dramatically. Superior quality, local content and affordability are the three mantras for success in this market. Whoever – global or local – meets these three KPIs (key performance indicators), will be the winner' (Knowledge at Wharton 2017). These are early and exciting times for India's streaming revolution, and once the novelty and necessity fade in post-pandemic times, only time will tell if this currently congested OTT market will continue to thrive or whether consolidations, acquisitions and mergers will result in a more streamlined entertainment segment.

References

Athique, A. (2009), 'Leisure Capital in the New Economy: The Rapid Rise of the Multiplex in India', *Contemporary South Asia* 17. 123–40. 10.1080/09584930902860843.

Arzoo, D. (2015), 'With Hotstar, Star India Aims to Change the Way Content Is Consumed in India', *Live Mint*, 11 February. Available online: https://www.livemint.com/Consumer/Nfv7GOoewo9xdcGKVnOVnL/With-Hotstar-Star-India-aims-to-change-the-way-content-is-c.html (accessed 7 June 2019).

Bengali, S. (2018), 'Big-budget TV Meets Bollywood as Amazon and Netflix Do Battle in India', *Los Angeles Times*, 3 March. Available online: http://www.latimes.com/world/asia/la-fg-india-netflix-amazon-2018-story.html (accessed 28 May 2018).

Bestmediainfo.com (2018), 'Eros Now's Paid Subscribers Grow 28.7% to 13 Million in Q2FY19', *Bestmediainfo.com*, 19 November. Available online: https://bestmediainfo.com/2018/11/eros-now-spaid-subscribers-grow-28-7-to-13-million-in-q2fy19/ (accessed 9 June 2019).

Bhatia, S. (2018), Electronic communication, 17 July.

Bhowmik, S. (2009), *Cinema And Censorship: The Politics Of Control In India*, Hyderabad, India: Orient Blackswan.

Bhushan, N. (2017), 'Netflix Targets 5-6 Indian Originals a Year', *Hollywood Reporter*, 13 October. Available online: https://www.hollywoodreporter.com/news/netflix-targets-5-6-indian-originals-a-year-1048470 (accessed 28 May 2018).

Chhabra, A. (2018), Telephone interview, 10 July.

Chintamani, G. (2017), 'Sacred Games: Marriage of Online Streaming Platforms, Bollywood Will Liberate Indian Filmmakers', *First Post*, 4 November. Available online: https://www.firstpost.com/entertainment/sacred-games-marriage-of-online-streaming-platforms-bollywood-will-liberate-indian-filmmakers-4192693.html (accessed 28 May 2018).

D'Souza, F. (2018), Electronic communication. 12 July.

exchange4media (2018), 'Netflix India Creates Buzz through OOH for Sacred Games', *exchange4media*, 4 July. Available online: https://www.exchange4media.com/out-of-home-news/netflix-india-creates-buzz-through-ooh-for-sacred-games-90856.html (accessed 8 June 2019).

Farooqui, M. (2021), 'Govt Creates a 3-Layer Mechanism to Check OTT Content but No Blanket Censorship', *Moneycontrol.com*. 25 February. Available online: https://www.moneycontrol.com/news/trends/entertainment/govt-creates-a-3-layer-mechanism-to-check-ott-content-but-no-blanket-censorship-6573251.html (accessed 25 April 2021).

First Post (2018) 'Netflix to Produce Two More Live Stand-up Specials with Comedian Vir Das after Abroad Understanding', *First Post*, 22 May. Available online:

https://www.firstpost.com/entertainment/netflix-to-produce-two-more-live-stand-up-specials-with-comedian-vir-das-after-abroad-understanding-4478527.html (accessed 28 May 2018).

Godwin, C. (2021), 'Netflix Considers Crackdown on Password Sharing', *BBC News*. 12 March. Available online: https://www.bbc.com/news/technology-56368698 (accessed 26 April 2021).

Gopalan, L. (2002), *Cinema of Interruptions: Action Genres in Contemporary Indian Cinema*, London: Bloomsbury.

Gupta, A. (2019), 'OTT Players Will Be as Big as the Film Industry', *DNA India*, 13 March. Available online: https://www.dnaindia.com/analysis/column-ott-players-will-be-as-big-as-the-indian-film-industry-2729003 (accessed 8 June 2019).

Izardar, K. (2019), 'The Deluge of OTT Platforms in India Undermining Cable TV', *Financial Express*, 24 January. Available online: https://www.financialexpress.com/industry/technology/the-deluge-of-ott-platforms-in-india-undermining-cable-tv/1452887/ (accessed 8 June 2019).

Knowledge at Wharton (2016), 'Netflix in India: Will It Be a Blockbuster?', *Knowledge at Wharton*, 22 January. Philadelphia: Wharton School Press University of Pennsylvania. Available online: https://knowledge.wharton.upenn.edu/article/the-prospects-for-netflix-in-india/ (accessed 5 June 2019).

Knowledge at Wharton (2017), 'Can Netflix and Amazon Disrupt India's Streaming Video Market?', *Knowledge at Wharton*, 4 May. Philadelphia: Wharton School Press University of Pennsylvania. Available online: https://knowledge.wharton.upenn.edu/article/can-netflix-amazon-disrupt-indias-streaming-video-market/ (accessed 28 May 2018).

Kumar, R. S. (2018), Electronic communication. 30 May.

Mehta, M. (2011), *Censorship and Sexuality in Bombay Cinema*, Austin: University of Texas Press.

Sadagopan, S. (2018), Electronic communication. 30 May.

Shrivastava, A. (2018), 'Gaurav Gandhi Quits Viacom 18 Voot to Join Amazon Prime Video', *Medianama.com*, 13 March. Available online: https://www.medianama.com/2018/03/223-gaurav-gandhi-quits-viacom-18-voot-to-join-amazon-prime-video/ (accessed 28 May 2018).

Srinivas, L. (2005), 'Communicating Globalization in Bombay Cinema: Everyday life, Imagination and the Persistence of the Local', *Comparative American Studies*. 3 (3): 319–44.

Srinivas, L. (2010), 'Cinema Halls, Locality and Urban Life', *Ethnography* 11 (1): 189–205.

Srinivas, L. (2013), 'The Active Audience and the Experience of Cinema', in Moti Gokulsing et al. (eds), *Handbook of Indian Cinemas*, London: Routledge, pp. 377–90.

Srinivas, L. (2016), 'House Full: Indian Cinema and the Active Audience'. University of Chicago Press. Reviewed in: *American Journal of Sociology, Symbolic Interaction, Visual Anthropology, South Asian Ethnology, South Asia: Journal of South Asian Studies*.

van Eeden, E., and W. Chow (2018), 'Perspectives from the Global Entertainment & Media Outlook 2018–2022 Trending Now: Convergence, Connections and Trust', PricewaterhouseCoopers (PwC) report, 16–17. Available online: https://www.pwc.com/gx/en/entertainment-media/outlook/perspectives-from-the-global-entertainment-and-media-outlook-2018-2022.pdf (accessed 13 July 2018).

Verma, S. (2015), 'The Online Streaming Revolution', *The Telegraph*, 7 June. Available online: https://www.telegraphindia.com/7-days/the-online-streaming-revolution/cid/1313938 (accessed 28 May 2018).

Part 3

Global transformations – Case study: Africa

8

Curating Africa online: The impact of digital technology on the consumption of African audiovisual content

Justine Atkinson and Lizelle Bisschoff

The so-called 'digital revolution' has had a major impact on the African film industries, not only in terms of film production but also in terms of exhibition and distribution. From a techno-optimistic – some would say techno-deterministic – viewpoint, digital technology can play a democratizing role in African countries. Certainly, digital technology has been shown to contribute to empowerment and communication within African societies, with the use of social media during the 2010–12 Arab Spring a case in point, and importantly, it can transcend geographical boundaries. Digital technology has contributed immensely to the development of Africa's first economically self-sustainable popular film industries through the video film phenomenon spearheaded by Nigeria's Nollywood, a model of popular filmmaking which is now replicated all over the continent. Whereas video films were initially primarily distributed on DVD and VCD (video compact disc), improved broadband and internet streaming technology means that these films can now be downloaded or watched on multiple video on demand (VOD) platforms online, in Africa and internationally. Today online content has proliferated far beyond Nollywood films. Content has diversified and multiplied and so has the platforms for online viewing of African films which range from free and subscription-based VOD platforms; peer-to-peer (P2P) downloading and file sharing (often part of the 'grey economy' due to its lack of legal transparency); streaming on existing platforms such as YouTube, Vimeo, Google Play and Amazon; and the participatory culture of sites such as YouTube, which enable users to both consume and produce content, so-called 'prosumption'. In this chapter, we discuss some of the most important digital technological developments that have changed the consumption patterns of African cinema, particularly on the continent.

We know that African cinema is hugely marginalized worldwide, contributing less than 1 per cent of theatrical distribution internationally. From an ideological point of view, the increased access to African cinema that digital technology offers could have a profound cultural benefit in increasing access to African stories and voices, providing an access point for these films to reach audiences across the globe. Historically, access to African cinema on the continent itself has been very limited, in particular after the economic decline of the 1980s which saw cinema culture in most African countries all but disappear. The earlier political and artistic films from Francophone West Africa in particular, by directors such as Ousmane Sembene, Djibril Diop Mambety, Souleymane Cissé and their peers and protégés, were often primarily seen in European film festivals and art house cinemas in the West, with very limited distribution on the continent itself. This changed with the advent of Nollywood, which bypassed theatrical release for a straight-to-DVD strategy, and has changed further over the past decade or so with the gradual increase and resurrection of cinemas in Africa, the increase of informal viewing spaces and the proliferation of film festivals on the continent, most often prioritizing African content in their programming line-ups. However, overall access to African film – in cinemas, on DVD, at festivals – on the continent and internationally remains low, and it is here that digital technology can play a hugely significant role.

Online access to cinema can greatly bolster the transnational dimension of film, with more and more people turning to the internet for cultural consumption that transcends borders (Iordanova 2012: 7). The transnationality of African cinema is underlined by increased global migration and the formation of diaspora communities worldwide; Nigerian, Kenyan, Ghanaian and other African expat communities now have access to cultural products from 'home' through the internet. The increase of audiovisual products available online can simultaneously erase national borders and liberate film from the 'tyranny of geography' (Iordanova 2012: 23), while also strengthening imagined communities, leading to the formation of a kind of digital diaspora congregating in virtual spaces online.

Importantly, the proliferation of, and increase in access to, media streaming platforms means that African-produced content, at least in certain parts of the continent and in the diaspora, can now compete with the imported and foreign content that previously formed the main film diet of African audiences. In early 2016, US-based VOD provider Netflix announced that it is launching in 130 countries, including in all 54 countries of Africa, as part of a plan to become a global streaming TV network (Mwansa 2016). Netflix is also increasingly acquiring and producing African content, particularly in Nigeria and South Africa as two of the major industries in the African continent, as we will go on to show in the case studies below. The increase of African content on global VOD platforms such as Netflix is having a significant impact on increasing the visibility of African film and developing new audiences for African cinema. African content is curated among international content, and with these types of platforms often creating a taste profile of users, viewers who highly rate specific types of genres, styles, themes and so on might now also start to watch similar types of African film suggested to them through the platforms' algorithms. This could counter the marginalization of African cinema by integrating it into mainstream film viewing.

Given the limitations of traditional distribution and exhibition of film (theatrical, DVD, festivals, television broadcast), especially in the case of the African continent and African cinema, it is important to note that these types of traditional distribution could be undermined by new digital technologies. The process whereby direct access to content makes the intermediary in a supply chain (e.g. distribution company, sales agent, cinema and festival programmer, commissioning editor) obsolete has been called disintermediation (Iordanova 2012: 17). Of course, disintermediation has been practised since the early days of Nollywood, not least through the 'subcinema' practices of piracy.[1] In addition to this, the traditional film distribution chain has never had much relevance to African cinema – very few African films follow and complete their journey along the traditional supply chain. Digital developments now make it quite easy for a filmmaker to handle both production and dissemination of their audiovisual work, thus eliminating the middleman, another example of disintermediation (Iordanova 2012: 12). As in most of the world, this is practised with various degrees of success and sophistication by African filmmakers, from short, amateur content uploaded to sites such as YouTube, to professional self-distribution strategies with considerable reach. However, although this pertains to certain instances it cannot be indiscriminately applied to the dissemination of African cinema on VOD platforms. Many of the larger platforms such as

---

[1] Piracy is continuously discussed as one of the biggest obstacles in the development of financially healthy film industries such as Africa, and piracy has now moved online as well, through what Ramon Lobato describes as the informal distribution methods of secondary markets, household-level P2P exchange as well as black markets (cited in Cunningham and Silver 2012: 33).

Netflix, Amazon Prime and MUBI that are starting to increasingly monopolize the African VOD market will still work through these intermediaries. Thus, the increased access to African cinema is only partially democratized through the process of disintermediation.

The role of film festivals in the dissemination of African film should not be underestimated, as the limited distribution opportunities for African cinema means that a festival is not only a place to get distribution but is often the distribution itself (Iordanova 2012: 20). With film festivals playing such an important role in the dissemination of African cinema, it is useful to also consider the impact of digital technologies on festivals. Digital distribution presents opportunities for festivals but cannot replace a format of film viewing that is so bound to spatio-temporality and communality. As we have seen, in the case of African cinema, it is mostly popular African cinema such as Nollywood that is being distributed digitally, while film festivals still seem to hold the niche for promoting 'art house' African cinema that would get very limited theatrical releases, and remains difficult to access otherwise (DVD, online, broadcast, etc.). It seems that online distribution will not replace film festivals anytime soon, although there has been crossover between the two distribution channels, for example, the extensive South African online film festival that was launched by AfricaFilms.tv – one of the earliest pioneering online African platforms – in 2014 in conjunction with the country's twenty-year celebrations since the end of apartheid. Often film festivals make some of their content available online, with physical screenings complemented by online availability.

Before we move on to discuss online technology in Africa and examples of African cinema online, it is important to stress that 'African cinema' is by no means a homogenous concept and should be regarded as hugely diverse and even disparate. While there are similarities, regional links and transnational connections between different film industries on the continent, there are also very specific histories of how the film industries developed in different places, and very particular cultural influences on what kinds of films are being made in particular territories. Styles, genres, themes, audiences, approaches and influences are as diverse and multiple as one could imagine from a continent with over a billion people, fifty-four countries and up to three thousand languages. This diversity also has a bearing on how and what kind of films are distributed online. The popular African cinema of Nollywood and its neighbours seems to be the most widely available online, providing access to this type of African cinema particularly for African viewers on the continent as well as in the diaspora. African documentaries are mostly distributed online by platforms that specialize in this kind of content, often categorized thematically and available as part of the menu of content available on sites that do not focus on African cinema alone. Short films, widely regarded as a stepping stone to feature filmmaking, and a format for which distribution is notoriously difficult to monetize, are often available for free online, and uploaded to YouTube by filmmakers themselves. Classic and 'art house' African cinema can mostly be found online on specially curated websites, with a focus on archiving and a cultural or artistic rather than commercial motivation.

Technology in Africa: A digital democracy or digital divide?

As we are particularly interested in how digital technology could widen access to local content on the continent itself, it is important to consider aspects of accessibility. The key to the success of African cinema being made available online clearly lies in the accessibility to and efficiency of technology on the continent, in particular the internet. The democratizing potential of digital technology should not be overestimated on a continent that still is on the wrong side of the digital divide. Nonetheless, Africa-specific digital technologies, such as mobile phone banking and utilizing mobile phones in agriculture, are more and more commonplace, with smartphones becoming affordable and ubiquitous all over the continent. Kenya has been at the forefront of the development of many of these technologies, with the conglomeration of tech entrepreneurs in the country leading to the epithet 'Silicon Savannah'. Africa is on the cusp of new ways of understanding user experience and user interface technology and design because Africa's exposure to technology is unique to the West. The continent has had an accelerated access to technology – the majority of Africans are introduced to the internet through mobile/smartphones, while they might never own a desktop computer; in the West this exposure has worked in the opposite direction.

For online access to audiovisual content this has significant implications: While it is estimated that there is approximately one cinema screen for every six million people across the continent, in 2018 a survey carried out by Mobile Africa in fifteen Africa countries (which generate more than 80 per cent of Africa's GDP) showed 'that there are precisely 216 million Internet users (18%

Internet penetration) across Africa from 960 million mobile subscriptions' (Ndiomewese 2018). In 2019, 35.9 per cent of people across the African continent had access to the internet, in comparison to 90 per cent in Europe (Internet World Stats 2019). Though this remains low, shifts are in progress and access to the internet is rapidly expanding. Research from TeleGeography – an international telecommunications research firm – shows that while internet in many parts of Africa is still slower than in the West, and limited by a lower penetration rate when compared to the rest of the world, bandwidth capacity is growing faster than anywhere else in the world (Tshabalala 2015). Undersea broadband cables, like the Sea Cable System (Seacom), the Eastern Africa Submarine Cable System (EASSy) and the West Africa Cable System (WACS), have helped multiply Africa's access to international bandwidth by twentyfold in just five years. Telecommunication companies in Africa have been working on broadband wireless access technologies in order to make internet available to the population at large. This fast-improving internet infrastructure is attracting investor demand, particularly in Nigeria and South Africa. Wireless speeds have improved, and their cost is becoming more affordable, at least for the 300 million Africans classified as middle class. The pace, however, remains slow, and this has led to a heavy focus on smartphone access on the continent.

As a result, access to 'small screen' digital information and communication technologies is rapidly increasing in Africa, including through mobile phones, tablets and laptops. In South Africa 34 per cent of mobile subscribers use smartphones, 27 per cent in Nigeria, 15 per cent in Senegal and Kenya, 14 per cent in Ghana and 8 per cent in Tanzania (Kazeem 2016). Treffry-Goatley (2011) has argued that such technologies facilitate a new kind of relationship between place and space: through their capacity to transgress frontiers and subvert territories, they are implicated in a complex interplay of deterritorialization and reterritorialization. For example, mobile phones can now be used to produce and consume audiovisual content ('prosumption'), with the internet making it possible for alternative media productions of all kinds to gain greater visibility. Research data showed that across 35 sub-Saharan African countries there were 1.56 million VOD subscribers at the end of 2017; this is projected to grow to 10 million by 2023 (Read 2018). This figure is dominated by South Africa and Nigeria who collectively account from 74 per cent of VOD subscribers (Read 2018).

Despite this evident growth and positive forecasts, issues of access remain: internet and broadband technology is still in a developing phase in

Africa, in many parts of the continent still being costly and slow; software and infrastructure for online distribution in Africa is still being built; although mobile phones and smartphones are widespread on the continent, the capacity to play full-length videos is still in development; and there are further limitations such as creating alternative payment methods for online content due to limited access to bank accounts and debit/credit cards. Entrants into Africa's VOD market also face competition from existing broadcast platforms such as the ubiquitous DStv (discussed below), Netflix and Showmax, and other challenges such as piracy, regulation and content rights and fees ('Video-On-Demand in Africa', www.jukwa.com).

African cinema online: Examples and case studies

Digital platforms for African content have proliferated on the continent and internationally and consist of many different types – there are VOD, internet streaming, digital television and internet television platforms on which films can be watched for free (often subsidised by advertising), or through a monthly subscription fee or a one-off fee per view; some platforms acquire their own contents, others merely embed free content available from elsewhere, for example, from YouTube; African content is curated as part of bigger international platforms such as Netflix, MUBI and Vimeo; and some platforms, including P2P downloading, carry content of dubious, and likely illegal, origin, with no evidence that rights have been cleared or paid to hold the content. The creation of these platforms is driven by both commercial strategies and grassroots tactics, and their purpose ranges from entertainment and financial gain, to artistic, cultural, archival and activist motivations. They appear and disappear with equal regularity; it should be noted that by the time this chapter appears in print, some of the platforms mentioned here will almost certainly no longer be in existence.

Balancing Act, a company that provides consultancy and conducts research on technological developments in Africa, published an updated report in July 2017 on VOD platforms in Africa. They identified more than 180 platforms related to Africa and Black culture. The report claims that the emerging distribution market for the African audiovisual industry is VOD. Their detailed list of 180 VOD platforms related to Africa includes VOD mobile apps, VOD via box and via the internet. The report points out that VOD provides a new, complex way of watching audiovisual content, tailored to the needs and desires of consumers

('VoD and Africa – A Review of Existing VoD Services, Drivers, Challenges and Opportunities' 2017). With multimedia digital convergence increasingly taking place across Africa, the multiplication of TV channels over the past decade and better access to broadband internet, consumers are asking for more than the traditional linear TV service, and also increasingly want to manage their viewing time.

In 2010, AfricaFilms.tv was most likely the first legal movies-on-demand service with an African focus to launch, carrying films from and about Africa and the diaspora (Cunningham and Silver 2012: 47). AfricaFilms provided a downloading service targeting Africans living abroad and world cinema aficionados. The platform acquired non-exclusive rights, a 50/50 revenue split and operated totally transparent, fair and cooperative, allowing producers to securely log onto the site to check sales, which they then invoice to the company for payment. Files were encrypted so as to prevent any illegal copying which would take away vital revenue streams from African creators. The site launched as a platform with its own independent URL, and included feature films, documentaries, soaps, filmed concerts and shows from all over Africa and the diaspora. Viewers were able to download content from anywhere in the world, depending on the territories authorized in the contracts with filmmakers/producers. Though it was a pioneering VOD platform for African contents it has had to shift and transform in a competitive market; rather than a stand-alone website they have migrated to YouTube where they now show a variety of Francophone TV series and shorts. With over 180k subscribers they still maintain an active niche within the VOD distribution market.

In addition to AfricaFilms.tv, Kenyan-based Buni.tv was another big player, and it is significant to note that AfricaFilms.tv and Buni.tv were both supported by European donor funds (such as the EU-supported ACP Cultures) and are thus different from other, purely commercially oriented platforms typically supported through corporate investment. Buni.tv offers a comprehensive and interesting case study of VOD in Africa, as the company has concluded what appears to be a full life cycle of a successful VOD platform: It launched in April 2012 as a platform offering free contents (a 'freemium' model) and quickly experienced huge growth; it subsequently launched a premium subscription service, Buni+, in March 2014.

Buni.tv features films, documentaries, television series, animations and music videos and, similar to AfricaFilms.tv, shares all revenue with content owners on a 50/50 basis (Okezie 2014). The platform is operational on the web, as well as on iPhones, Android and Blackberry smartphones across the world. It distinguished itself since its inception from most other African VOD platforms in that its contents are highly curated, placing a high premium on professionally produced audiovisual products, and 'content that feels modern, is exciting and reflects contemporary themes and ideas', in the words of Marie Lora-Mungai, Buni.tv's co-founder and CEO ('VOD alive and well in Africa' 2013). In line with this content criteria, Buni.tv has curated controversial content, such as Cameroonian director Jean-Pierre Bekolo's *The President* (2015), which was banned in Cameroon due to its contentious fictionalization of Cameroon's current dictator. The Kenyan political satire puppet show *The XYZ Show*, which regularly satirizes African politicians and comments on political happenings on the continent, is produced by Buni Media, the production arm of the company, and has an audience of 10 million on television and radio in Kenya. Buni.tv carries all the episodes of the show minutes after they have aired on television. When it launched its premium subscription service, Buni+, in 2014, subscribers could gain access to a range of high-profile African films, such as the Kenyan blockbuster *Nairobi Half Life*, and the 2008 South African crime film *Jerusalema*, for around $5 per month (Greeves 2014). In June 2016 the French network TRACE TV took over Buni.tv and has now incorporated its assets and catalogue into its own VOD offering, TRACE Play, which launched in September 2016 (Nevill 2016). In addition to the African continent, TRACE Play will be available in countries with a strong African diaspora and active Black culture, such as France, the UK, the United States and the Caribbean. Marie Lora-Mungai, the founder of Buni.tv, has stated that consolidation is needed because of the capital-intensive nature of VOD. She believes that 'high quality original scripted content (TV series and films) is the key to success for any VOD service' (Nevill 2016).

Other VOD platforms have been initiated from East Africa, including Tanzania's Tango TV (tangotv.co.tz). Tango TV is a technology company focused on integrated media streaming services. It streams African films, music videos and television shows, focusing on local content for local audiences, in this case Tanzanian films in particular. This kind of local VOD start-up has a short window in which they can establish themselves while the international companies are more focused on getting sales for their international catalogue across multiple markets (Southwood 2016).

South Africa and Nigeria are the locations where most of the digital developments for online consumption of audiovisual contents are taking place, where the strongest platforms are and also from where most data is available (Vourlias 2015). Several new VOD players entered the South African market over the last couple of years, some from partnerships with mobile telecommunication companies and others through pay TV offerings (Theron 2015). A video-on-demand survey that polled 30,000 online respondents in 61 countries in 2016 found that 63 per cent of South Africans watch some kind of VOD programming on an online device and that 79 per cent do so at least once a week. Rather than replacing traditional TV services, VOD subscriptions are supplementing established viewing habits, thus online and traditional services work in a complementary rather than mutually exclusive way. An advantage for traditional network providers is that there is no simple replacement for live news and sports programming, but where VOD prevails is in convenience (Phakathi 2016).

M-Net (originally an abbreviation of Electronic Media Network) is certainly the biggest audiovisual communications player in Africa, and was established in 1986 by Naspers, a multinational internet and media group and the largest corporate company in Africa. The service broadcasts both local and international programming, including general entertainment, children's series, sport and films. M-Net has been at the forefront of embracing new technologies in content development for new platforms. In 2006 it launched DStv mobile – a digital video broadcast of live TV channels to enabled mobile phones – and M-Mobile, which provides 3G content on-demand to mobile phones. In December 2007, M-Net launched Catch-up TV through DStv on Demand, a free video-on-demand service to PVR (personal video recorder) and PC.

DStv is MultiChoice's (a leading video entertainment company with a strong presence in South Africa and across the African continent, and a sister company of M-Net) digital satellite TV service in Africa, launched in 1995, and provides various bouquets of general entertainment, movies, lifestyle and culture, sport, documentaries, news and commerce, music and religious audiovisual content to MultiChoice subscribers. It currently has around 8 million subscribers, with the majority being based in South Africa and Nigeria. While these two countries are considered to be the most important markets for DStv, markets in countries such as Kenya, Angola, Zimbabwe, Uganda, Mauritius and Tanzania are also a focus point for DStv. The platform has various channels dedicated to African content, such as Africa Magic Showcase, Africa Magic Family and Africa Magic World. Through its VOD service called DStv Catch-Up (renamed DStv Now) customers of DStv can stream or download over 350 titles of series and films on their iPhones and iPads via its iOS app available on the Apple App Store (Okezie 2014).

In 2009 M-Net launched the African Film Library, a VOD platform featuring the world's largest collection of award-winning African film content (Graziadio 2012). Managed by DStv Online, the African Film Library constituted a treasure trove of classic and contemporary films and documentaries from across the continent, accessible to viewers worldwide through pay-per-view. The library purchased the rights to over four hundred African and South African films and included selections from influential and pioneering African directors, including the entire oeuvre of Senegalese director Ousmane Sembene. At the time of the library's launch, its founder, Mike Dearham, stated,

> The African Film Library is a testament to the work M-Net has put into making these films available and also to the strength of the African production industry. Without a doubt, the advent of digitization has catalyzed the pace and quality of our documentary production and the AFL is an important step in supporting our industry's continued growth on the world stage. In making this content digitally accessible we are able to reach audiences right across the African Diaspora as well as to individuals with an interest in the continent's wealth of culture, history and film—showcasing the quality of African film to the global audience and challenging preconceptions. (quoted in Graziadio 2012)

Sadly, the African Film Library went offline around 2013 and now only exists as a YouTube channel carrying clips and trailers with no full-length films. It is not known why the library was discontinued, with no press release issued at the time to explain its demise. One could speculate that the reason might have been financial, as M-Net on the whole is certainly focused more on commercial African content such as showcased on its Africa Magic channels. It was a worthy project with lofty ambitions, and the most extensive archive of African film to date – an invaluable resource for students, researchers and general world cinema aficionados. The burning question for African film scholars is what would happen with all the films that the rights were acquired to, and whether M-Net will make them available in another way. A VOD platform serving as an archive of African film is certainly much needed and essential to preserving the continent's rich film history for future generations.

Showmax, launched in August 2015 as a subsidiary of Naspers, is one of the fastest-growing internet-based subscription VOD platforms in South Africa. It currently has the largest subscription VOD catalogue on the continent, and is available in sixty-five countries, including a large number of African and European countries as well as in Australia, Canada and the United States. In

Africa the Showmax catalogue consists of Hollywood, British and South African content and outside of Africa it consists primarily of kykNet (an M-Net-owned Afrikaans television channel) content, targeted primarily at the Afrikaans diaspora audience. The catalogue includes approximately 15,000 TV show episodes and films, totalling almost 10,000 hours of viewing, and its sub-Saharan platform includes a Kiswahili language section and a Nollywood section, as well as an African film section that collates classic films from across the continent ('Video-On-Demand Provider ShowMax Expands to 36 Sub-Saharan Africa Countries' 2016, http://aptantech.com). It has an interface with a look and feel very similar to Netflix and has likewise started producing its own high-quality Afrikaans content for diaspora audiences. The platform is accessible across a wide range of devices, including smart TVs, PCs, smartphones and tablets, and has specifically adapted its apps to address the needs of consumers in Africa, introducing features such as downloads for viewing TV shows and films when not connected.

By far most of the online content from sub-Saharan Africa originates from Nigeria's Nollywood.[2] The biggest and most successful of these is iROKOtv, which launched in 2011, and with a library of over 5,000 Nollywood films is the world's largest legal digital distributor of African film. Unsurprisingly, it is often dubbed 'Africa's Netflix', iROKOtv is part of iROKO Partners, one of Africa's leading entertainment companies. It operates as a subscription business model where users can access Nollywood movies via an Android app in Africa, and via an app or online in the rest of the world. Starting as a freemium service, it also launched a subscription service, iROKOtv PLUS, which now generates more revenue than the advertisements on its basic service ('Video-On-Demand in Africa', www.jukwa.com). iROKOtv has, similarly to other big players in the VOD field, worked to adapt their platform to the specificities of digital technology on the African continent, specifically targeting smartphone users through a mobile site (Robson 2013). With over 50 per cent of its consumers coming from the African diaspora, this audience forms a core part of the platform's success.

Afrinolly is a Nigerian-based mobile app launched in 2011, enabling viewers to watch trailers, short films, feature films and music videos that have been

---

[2] At the time of researching this chapter, a non-exhaustive search for Nollywood content online yielded dozens of websites, including: www.africanmoviesclips.com; www.nigeriamovienetwork.com; tvnolly.com; zeratv.com; www.snagfilms.com; www.nollyland.com; www.nollywoodmovies.com; www.realnollytv.com; reelafrican.com; and http://www.un1ty.tv/.

made public by content owners. The app is available for Android, iPhone, iPad, Blackberry, Windows and Java devices. As with many of the VOD platforms discussed here, Afrinolly was launched to take advantage of the pervasiveness of the smartphone in Africa and operates exclusively in the mobile space. The platform had over 3 million downloads in 2014, with most of its contents being Nigerian.

The Netflix effect

The global phenomenon of Netflix has revolutionized audiovisual content consumption, so that viewers can now curate what they watch and when they watch it, through their extensive online film catalogue. African films are still few and far between on the platform, and Netflix's first move to include African content was through the acquisition of Nollywood films *October 1* (Kunle Afolayan, Nigeria, 2014) and *Fifty* (Biyi Bandele, Nigeria, 2014), along with a few other high-profile titles. This was mainly an attempt to cater for African diaspora audiences.

The platform only arrived in all fifty-four African countries in 2016 (Bacon 2019). This was part of a global strategy for rolling out Netflix beyond the United States and Europe. However, it was met with mixed responses from other big players on the continent mentioned above, such as Multichoice and iROKO.tv. They responded by strengthening their own market position. Naspers, South Africa's largest internet company, worked with Multichoice to roll out the Showmax platform. They recognized the threat Netflix posed to their stronghold across the continent 'as the largest pay TV operator across 15 countries in Africa', generating around $3 billion annually (Kazeem 2018). Despite this high turnover in 2018, Netflix's arrival and expansion cost them more than 100,000 premium subscribers in the same year. Multichoice CEO Calvo Mawela ascribed this to the 'unregulated competition from Netflix' and called for the platform to be regulated (Phakathi 2018). This loss of viewers took place especially among the younger generations in South Africa, who consume content on their mobile phones and are increasingly turning to international platforms such as Netflix, which are cheaper and have faster download services (Kazeem 2018).

iROKO.tv began to partner with Netflix in 2015, selling content to the platform for viewing in the diaspora. However, this shifted as Netflix began to roll out across the continent. iROKO.tv received $19 million from investors such as Canal+ and others in 2016 to begin creating original content (Chutel 2018). According to iROKO.tv founder Jason Njoku, Netflix in Nigeria and Africa does not pose a threat to his company, stating in an interview that iROKO.tv will continue to be the 'home of Nollywood' for many. In addition to this, iROKO's subscribers are predominantly based in the UK and United States with the diaspora making up over half (55 per cent) of the subscription base (Adeleke 2016). iROKO.tv provides a particular service to those interested in consuming Nollywood films, and although Netflix is increasingly acquiring a select number of Nollywood films and has produced its first Nollywood Netflix Original *Lionheart* in 2018 (directed by hugely popular Nollywood actor Genevieve Nnaji), it still does not pose a direct threat to the Nigerian market, as iROKO.tv maintains its niche. According to Alessandro Jedlowski (2019) much larger investments are needed if Netflix is going to compete with other players in Nollywood, as the dissemination of 'Nollywood films via piracy or local screening venues will continue to be the key strategy [for viewing] adopted by the largest percentage of Nigerian viewers' (Jedlowski 2019).

Subscription costs will also influence the impact Netflix has on the continent. In South Africa and Nigeria Netflix costs around $7 per month, although this is the minimum subscription and would only allow you to watch content on one device. Showmax is the same price and can be viewed in up to five devices. However, the offer of content on Netflix far outweighs Showmax with over '4,291 different shows, equating to around R0.02 per title' (Edwards 2019), so it is better value. iROKO.tv has a more flexible pricing structure that is not set to a global standard, while in the more affluent countries including the United States and UK pricing is set at $15/3 months in comparison to $5.50/year in Lagos and over $10/year in Johannesburg. This price flexibility is unique and caters geographically so that they 'reflect the purchasing power in the respective regions' (Adeyinka 2019). This customer-centred focus allows iROKO.tv to provide a more accessible model of access to VOD content, responding to the consumer needs in each geographical location.

Could content creation give Netflix its edge across the continent? Netflix has expanded and strengthened its foothold in Africa through investing in the development of original shows. As previously mentioned, *Lionheart* became the first Nollywood original production, released in 2018. In 2019, *The Boy Who Harnessed the Wind* (Chiwetel Ejiofor Malawi, 2019) was launched on the platform as the first Malawian production, along with the South Africa thriller series *Shadow*. They are also in the process of producing an animated musical from Zimbabwe entitled *Tunga*, from director Godwin Jabangwe (Fleming 2019). These films and TV series showcase local talent, bringing it to both a local and international audience. Whether this is going to interfere or boost local production remains to be seen. However, the international availability of these provides great international exposure for African cinema, taking this content to audiences who would not typically encounter films from the continent. This could have an impact on shifting tastes and viewing habits from a Western-centric appetite and help to counter the marginalization of African cinema globally.

Conclusion: The future of online distribution of African cinema

This chapter demonstrated that online VOD platforms with African content have proliferated on the continent over the past few years, for both continental and international audiences. As a result, there is now unprecedented access to all kinds of African audiovisual media, unthinkable even a mere five or six years ago. The advantages of increased accessibility to African audiovisual content are legion and include economic and cultural benefits: more content will develop and build existing and new audiences, which will in turn stimulate growth of the audiovisual industries on the continent; and an increased variety of African-produced content on platforms such as Netflix will enhance our understanding and knowledge of the continent and broaden our awareness of and taste for different types of world cinema.

Technological challenges and barriers should, however, not be underestimated, in particular in terms of online access on the continent itself, and VOD companies would have to continue creating and devising Africa-specific technologies and strategies to overcome these challenges. Africa's position within the digital divide means that the potential of online distribution is not as strong as in other parts of the world, even though digital technologies and internet access on the continent continue to develop at a fast pace. When we recently posed the question to African filmmakers' part of an online social media group, the African Film Consortium, it became clear that at the time of writing, online distribution is seen as complementary and supplementary to traditional distribution channels such as DVD, television and cinema.

There also seems to be a need to diversify online African content. While iROKOtv is the most successful platform to capitalize on the popularity of

Nollywood in Africa and among its diaspora, the audiovisual offer would have to diversify in order to cater to the tastes of audiences in all of Africa's fifty-four countries, among African diaspora communities and general viewers of world cinema. The Netflix effect still remains to be seen, but it is creating competition, particularly in South Africa and Nigeria where local market leaders are having to up their game. Much of this depends on price, data provision and accessibility. Despite the challenges, however, from the current rich and varied landscape of VOD developments on the continent, it would appear that online access to African audiovisual content could potentially finally break the gridlock that African film distribution has faced since its inception.

References

Adeleke, D. (2016), 'What Impact Does Netflix in Africa Have on iROKO?', *Techcabal*, 7 January. Available online: https://techcabal.com/2016/01/07/what-impact-does-netflix-in-africa-have-on-iroko/ (accessed 2 May 2019).

Adeyinka, F. (2019), 'Is Iroko TV Pricing Strategy Sustainable?', *36 States*, undated. Available online: https://www.36-states.com/businessculturetechnology/irokotv (accessed 2 May 2019).

Bacon, M. (2019), 'Netflix's Involvement in Africa', *Medium*, 4 January. Available online: https://medium.com/datadriveninvestor/netflixs-involvement-in-africa-cdc1234c2d9b (accessed 2 May 2019).

Chutel, L. (2018), 'Netflix Is Making Dozens of New Shows around the World, but Africa Is Getting Left Behind', *Quartz Africa*, 17 May. Available online: https://qz.com/africa/1279754/netflix-africa-dstv-multichoice-irokotv-and-nollywood-could-win-over-netflix/ (accessed 2 May 2019).

Cunningham, S., and J. Silver (2012), 'On-line Film Distribution: Its History and Global Complexion', in D. Iordonava and S. Cunningham (eds), *Digital Disruption: Cinema Moves On-line*, St Andrews: St Andrews Film Studies, 33–66.

Edwards, C. (2019), 'Netflix South Africa versus the World: What You Get for Your Money', *South African*, 27 February. Available online: https://www.thesouthafrican.com/netflix-south-africa-versus-the-world-what-you-get-for-your-money/ (accessed 2 May 2019).

Fleming, M. (2019), 'Netflix Wins "Tunga", Animated Musical from Zimbabwe – Born Newcomer Godwin Jabangwe; First Deal Out of Talent Hatchery Imagine Impact 1', *Deadline*, 14 February. Available online: https://deadline.com/2019/02/tunga-netflix-animated-musical-zimbabwe-newcomer-godwin-jabangwe-imagine-impact-1-1202557570/ (accessed 2 May 2019).

Graziadio, M. (2012), 'MNet Offers African Film Library on Demand', *Film Contact*, undated. Available online: https://www.filmcontact.com/news/south-africa/mnet-offers-african-film-library-demand (accessed 25 July 2016).

Greeves, N. (2014), 'Leading African VOD Platform, Buni TV, Launches Premium Subscription Service Buni+ Today', *Shadow and Act*, undated. Available online: https://shadowandact.com/leading-african-vod-platform-buni-tv-launches-premium-subscription-service-buni-today (accessed 20 June 2016).

Internet World Stats (2019), 'Internet Penetration in Africa March 31, 2019', *Internet World Stats*, undated. Available online: https://www.internetworldstats.com/stats1.htm (accessed 2 May 2019).

Iordanova, D. (2012), 'Digital Disruption: Technological Innovation and Global Film Circulation', in D. Iordanava and S. Cunningham (eds), *Digital Disruption: Cinema Moves On-line*, St Andrews: St Andrews Film Studies, 1–31.

Jedlowski, A. (2019), 'Netflix Is Romancing Nollywood. Will It Last?', *Bright*, 24 January. Available online: https://brightthemag.com/what-netflix-involvement-in-nigeria-film-industry-means-nollywood-africa-88a3b449b9e0 (accessed 2 May 2019).

Kazeem, Y. (2016), 'No Matter Where Netflix Goes in Africa It Will Run into These Two Problems', *Quartz Africa*, 14 January. Available online: https://qz.com/africa/589907/no-matter-where-netflix-goes-in-africa-it-will-run-into-these-two-problems/ (accessed 2 May 2019).

Kazeem, Y. (2018), 'Naspers Is Spinning Off Its Multichoice Video Business to Focus on the Internet', *Quartz Africa*, 19 September. Available online: https://qz.com/africa/1393984/naspers-spins-out-multichoice-showmax-as-netflix-bears-down/ (accessed 2 May 2019).

Mwansa, K. (2016), 'Netflix in Africa: Why Video-On-Demand Startups Will Still Flourish', *AFK Insider*, 8 January. Available online: http://afkinsider.com/109585/netflix-in-africa-why-video-on-demand-startups-will-still-flourish/ (accessed 20 June 2016).

Ndiomewese, I. (2018). 'How Do You Capture a Market Like the African VoD market?', *Techpoint Africa*, 1 March 2018. Available at: https://techpoint.africa/2018/03/01/of-the-african-vod-market-and-what-operators-need-to-know-in-order-to-win-big/ (accessed 2 May 2019).

Nevill, G. (2016), 'TRACE TV's Buyout of Buni.tv Powers Up Africa's VOD Market', *Media Online*, 22 June. Available online: http://themediaonline.co.za/2016/06/trace-tvs-buyout-of-buni-tv-powers-up-africas-vod-market/ (accessed 22 June 2016).

Okezie, L. (2014), '15+ Online Video-On-Demand Platforms for Africa Worth Watching in 2014', *Telecomist*, 15 January. Available online: http://techloy.com/2014/02/01/15-online-video-on-demand-platforms-africa-worth-watching-2014/ (accessed 20 June 2016).

Phakathi, B. (2016), 'Almost Two-Thirds of South Africans Use Video-On-Demand', *Business Day Live*, 25 April. Available online: http://www.bdlive.co.za/business/media/2016/04/25/almost-two-thirds-of-south-africans-use-video-on-demand (accessed 22 June 2016).

Phakathi, B. (2018), 'MultiChoice Calls for Netflix to Be Regulated', *Business Live*, 12 July. Available online: https://www.businesslive.co.za/bd/companies/2018-07-12-multichoice-calls-for-netflix-to-be-regulated/ (accessed 2 May 2019).

Read, C. (2018), 'Streaming Video-On-Demand to Boom in Africa: Report', *Connecting Africa*, 25 June. Available online: http://www.connectingafrica.com/document.asp?doc_id=744301 (accessed 2 May 2019).

Robson, S. (2013), 'Video on Demand Poised to Change How Africa Watches', *BBC News*, 29 October. Available online: http://www.bbc.co.uk/news/business-24706209 (accessed 20 June 2016).

Southwood, R. (2016), 'Tanzania's Tango TV, One of Africa's New Breed of VoD Start-Ups Looks to Establish Itself with Local Content Up against International Offerings', AllAfrica, 14 January. Available online: http://allafrica.com/stories/201601141553.html (accessed 22 June 2016).

Theron, H. (2015), 'Video-On-Demand in Africa', *Red Touch Media*, 14 June. Available online: http://www.redtouchmedia.com/video-on-demand-in-africa/#.V0ynQWgrK00 (accessed 25 July 2016).

Treffry-Goatley, A. (2011), 'Digital Cinema: An Alternative Model for Post-Apartheid Cinematic Production and Consumption?' *Ilha do Desterro*, Florianópolis, 61: 315–53.

Tshabalala, S. (2015), 'Africa's Internet May Be Slow, but Bandwidth Capacity Is Growing Faster Than Anywhere Else', *Quartz Africa*, 28 August. Available online: http://qz.com/490212/africas-internet-may-be-slow-but-bandwidth- capacity-is-growing-faster-than-anywhere-else/ (accessed 20 June 2016).

'Video-On-Demand in Africa' (publication date unknown). Available online: http://www.jukwa.com/video-on-demand-in-sub-saharan-africa/ (accessed 20 June 2016).

'Video-On-Demand Provider ShowMax Expands to 36 Sub-Saharan Africa Countries' (2016), *Aptantech*, 16 May. Available online: http://aptantech.com/2016/05/video-on-demand-provider-showmax-expands-to-36-sub-saharan-africa-countries/#.V0ynRGgrK00 (accessed 25 July 2016).

'VOD alive and well in Africa' (2013), *Screen Africa* 3 May. Available online: https://www.balancingact-africa.com/reports/broadcast/vod-and-africa---a-review-of-existing-vod-services-drivers-challenges-and-opportunities-update (accessed 20 June 2016).

'VoD and Africa – A Review of Existing VoD Services, Drivers, Challenges and Opportunities' (2017), *Balancing Act*, 4 July. Available online: https://www.balancingact-africa.com/reports/broadcast/vod-and-africa---a-review-of-existing-vod-services-drivers-challenges-and-opportunities-update (accessed 2 May 2019).

Vourlias, C. (2015), 'Video-on-Demand Race Heats Up in Africa', *Variety*, 29 October. Available online: http://variety.com/2015/tv/markets-festivals/video-on-demand-race-heats-up-in-africa-1201629230/ (accessed 22 June 2016).

9

Reset mode: African digital video films as expanded cinema

Sheila Petty

Africa has always been a continent of storytellers, and for many generations and throughout history, African societies relied on oral methods of transmission of knowledge and stories to preserve historical records of cultures.[1] Ownership of a narrative is generally unheard of because oral tradition is considered a collective project that connects speakers and listeners in a 'communal experience' (Hanson 2009). Once a story has been told, it is impossible to take it back, because it is already circulating in a variety of ways among communities. These principles of oral tradition 'form the foundation' of many African societies and have filtered, in various ways through the years, into audiovisual production on the continent (2009).

Cinema in most areas of the African continent was born alongside nations' independence. In British-colonized areas, the film units were not maintained due to other pressing needs and in French-colonized areas, a form of dependency was maintained through the French Ministry of Cooperation especially during the 1960s and 1970s which stipulated how Africans would create their cinema projects. The major production imperative during the 1960s and 1970s was the decolonization and reappropriation of African cultural space, ideology and images. By the 1980s and 1990s, nations' IMF debt load and devaluation of African currencies made it increasingly difficult for Africans to shoot films in Africa and many filmmakers began to pursue north–south co-production partnerships with European nations (NeuCollins 2007). Furthermore, as the celluloid-based (and often state-controlled) infrastructure of many African nations has

---

[1] This chapter is a significantly revised version of the previously published work entitled 'Digital Video Films as "Independent" African Cinema, in Independent Filmmaking around the Globe. Eds. Doris Baltruschat and Mary P. Erickson, University of Toronto Press, 2015: 255–69.

eroded, many, including Nigerian filmmaker Tunde Kelani, believe that Africa's audiovisual sectors can thrive by embracing the digital video revolution. Kelani maintains that high-quality production does not necessarily require shooting on celluloid (which relies mainly on foreign post-production facilities and is payable in non-African currencies) and that low-cost digital technologies can provide a suitable alternative (Kelani 2008: 90–1). Indeed, independent digital video filmmaking has afforded directors a great deal of freedom to challenge and reconfigure established modes of production, platforms, distribution and exhibition in a globalizing Africa, allowing artists to tell their stories in their own culturally appropriate ways so that art and life are interconnected just as they are in African systems of thought.

In a recent publication on African filmmaking, scholar Jonathan Haynes describes how Nollywood, as a commercial video industry in Africa, 'saturate(s) Nigerian social space' and is an example of 'globalization from below' (2017: 82, 83). Haynes's statement is intriguing in the sense that it implies an expansion beyond the medium of film/video itself to a fusion of art, entertainment and life with a society's whole cultural fabric. This observable fact is actually expanded cinema, described by some as the explosion of the screen outward, 'toward immersive, interactive, and interconnected forms of culture' (Marchessault and Lord 2007: 7). Jackie Hatfield has also been important in defining 'cinema' in the digital era to signify a 'wide-ranging historical and philosophical discourse', rather than 'film' per se: 'Importantly', she writes, the term 'cinema' is no longer 'yoked to the material conditions of a medium, and the cinematic experience can cross media boundaries and be achieved through a range of media combinations. A cinematic configuration could involve intermedia, performance, spectacle, video, art and technology in addition to film, and could be located within the "black box" of the theatre or the "white cube" of the gallery' (2011: 262). It can be located in particular sites, or constructed translocally and even transnationally.

This, in many ways, describes the Nollywood video phenomenon, its expansion and evolution and its many offshoots such as Ghana (Ghallywood), Cameroon (Collywood), Kenya (Riverwood), Tanzania (Bongowood) and Uganda (Ugawood). These have all been studied extensively through analyses of industry production; historical, global and transnational factors leading to production, audience reception, distribution and exhibition patterns.[2] In what

---

[2] See, for example, the extensive scholarship of Moradewun Adejunmobi, Jonathan Haynes and Onookome Okome.

follows, I want to take a different approach and consider several expanded cinema initiatives on the continent that 'explode screens' and saturate social space, beginning with Nollywood and then probing some examples from Ghana and Burkina Faso.

The Nollywood phenomenon

Nigerian-based video film, often referred to by the sobriquet 'Nollywood' film, denoted, in its infancy, a strand of low-budget film within African cinema that is based on popular culture and promotes a production model involving market-driven entrepreneurial financing, independent of state funding, and product placement as a means of financing. Nollywood has long been controversial among African cinema film scholars, who seem divided on the authenticity and cultural worth of an industry noted for its ability to churn out low-budget, straight to video or DVD film product at what seems to be an astounding rate. Ikechukwu Obiaya, for example, lauds Nollywood for its populist approach, describing it as 'created by the people for the people' (2010: 321). Others, such as Olivier Barlet, have lamented that the popularity of such works might spell 'the end of African auteur cinema' (2010: 81). Regardless of the boom and gloom surrounding Nollywood cinema, it has nevertheless demonstrated a profound resilience grounded in an extraordinary relationship with technological advancement and has made significant inroads across the African continent as a production and distribution model.

It is widely acknowledged that Nollywood has its roots in the traditions of Yoruba Travelling Theatre, which in turn derives from church year end and harvest performances as well as 'Yoruba *alarainjo* (or *apidan*) masquerade performance practices that predate colonialism by centuries' (Ogundele 2000: 92). At its height in the early 1980s, at least a hundred theatre companies travelled Nigeria, bringing to audiences a mixture of Christianity and folk-based productions (Ogundele 2000: 91).[3] The first link to Nigerian video film is found in the 1970s, when leading Nigerian dramatist Hubert Ogunde pioneered the use of film inserts during the plays. These were intended to connote 'fantasy actions or elements (transformation

---

[3] It is interesting to make the comparison with Amazigh video films, which came to prominence in southern Morocco during the 1990s. Many theatre actors from travelling troupes were solicited to act in the videos, with some going on eventually to direct video productions.

of human being into animals, for instance), that were meant to convey the supernatural dimensions of Yoruba cosmology' which could not realistically be portrayed during live performances (Ogundele 2000: 95). Later, recognizing the potential of television for spectacle and sensationalism, Ogunde began producing full-length, low-budget feature films on video, taking the first tentative steps in the development of Nollywood (Ogundele 2000: 96).

The second influence on the development of the Nigerian video film industry comes from Ghana, which pioneered the development of a market-driven, low-budget video film industry based on popular local cultural interests. Often created by 'private producers' without formal film training, these films are distributed through a network of 'small video theatres' and home sales, making them very popular and potentially lucrative (Meyer 1999: 93). Olivier Barlet credits producer Holy Rock as the first to see the potential of adopting the Ghanaian production model when he received a large shipment of blank video tapes and commissioned a Yoruba language film on VHS (2008: 121). The Igbo language video film, *Living in Bondage* (directed by Chris Obi Rapu), followed in 1992, and focused on a man who makes a deal with the devil to advance his social and economic position. This is arguably Nollywood's first financial and popular success (Barlet 2008: 121–2). This film and the others that followed are supported by '15,000 video clubs' and 'individual cassette sales, which can reach up to 200,000 copies of the same film' (Barlet 2008: 122). In addition to private financing, additional production financing comes from product placement, including virtually any marketable item that can be placed in front of the spectator (Barlet 2010: 87–8).

The third element delineating the rise of Nollywood includes a series of cultural factors. As Olivier Barlet explains, the collapse of Nigerian currency made celluloid film production prohibitively expensive versus the much less expensive alternative offered by video production. In addition to the collapse of the currency, social conditions deteriorated, resulting in many Nigerians choosing to stay in at night, no doubt contributing to 'the sharp rise in the number of VCRs and V-CD players in homes' (Barlet 2008: 125–6).

Finally, the presence of multiple ethnic groups and languages, including Hausa, Yoruba and Igbo, provided ready-made audiences predisposed to video films focusing on local folklore and imperatives (Barlet 2008: 125). Manthia Diawara cautions that 'even in Nigeria, Nollywood videos are not to be confused with the Yoruba videos', which are mostly historical and which employ acting and narrative techniques firmly ensconced in Yoruba theatre traditions (2010: 169). The Nollywood product, according to Diawara, represents 'stories of mobility' and 'is full of the elements that facilitate the projection of the spectator's fantasies or fears onto the screen, and thus constitute narrative desire and identification'. These films are star-driven, rely heavily on spectacle and melodrama, and use Nigerian English (Diawara 2010: 170, 179).

It is not only the Nollywood-style storytelling which has contributed to the industry's boom, but technological, distribution, marketing and cultural factors have also helped fuel Nollywood's rise. Technological elements include affordable production and home equipment, now including DVD and VCD players and recorders. Perhaps more to the point, Nollywood became an aggressive marketing machine that saw the potential of making its product available to more than a Nigerian-based audience. Innovative marketing and distribution methods include selling DVDs in hair salons and street stalls, by hawkers, through video-clubs or by promotional events and posters, press coverage including magazines, sponsorships by automobile and beverage companies, and in hotels. With 'a declared production of nearly 700 films' in approximately ten years, Nollywood has been promoted along cultural lines, with Hausa films finding an audience in Niger, and Yoruba films finding secondary markets in Benin and Togo (Barlet 2008: 125). Dubbing in French has opened up opportunities in sub-Saharan Francophone countries and dubbing in English has opened the market up to the Nigerian diaspora who access films via distribution websites (Barlet 2008: 125). On this topic, Allessandro Jedlowski has produced an enthralling account of the rise in circulation of Nigerian video films in Ivory Coast. His extensive field research uncovered how Ivorian 'marketers' such as Ibrahim Sangaré established themselves in the early 2000s on the outskirts of Lagos, purchased VCD copies of Nigerian video films and distributed them in Abidjan, first in English and various Nigerian dialects, and then with French subtitles when the product became popular. By the late 2000s, Sangaré no longer had to travel to Nigeria for product because he could buy Nigerian video films already dubbed into French via an intermediary in Lomé, Togo. Jedlowski maintains that this practice continued until 2010 when Ivory Coast's political and economic structures began to crumble and the cost of VCDs became too onerous for local populations (2017: 266–7).

Onookome Okome has argued that the Nigerian video film is instrumental in forging the local–global connection between transnational communities and home (Okome 2004: 5). Finally, the low production budgets (especially as the industry took hold in the 1990s and 2000s), typically US$ 8,000 to produce a ninety-minute video film, necessitate volume sales and, as a result, Nollywood films are among the most competitively priced, certainly undercutting the rental/purchase cost of African auteur, American, Asian and Indian films (Oladunjoye 2008: 64). Increasingly, Nollywood is successfully exploiting streaming as a means to reach an African and Nigerian diasporic audience. A recent study of Nollywood's presence online conducted by Ikechukwu Obiaya finds that Nollywood 'commands a fairly high online presence', including 'twelve websites, fifteen blogs and 107 Facebook groups all fully dedicated to' topics centring on all aspects of Nollywood film including reviews, performers, and 'industry news' (2010: 325). What this indicates is a computer-literate international audience prepared to consume Nollywood films through an internet medium. Interestingly, this wide audience base includes Nigeria-based members who, statistically, have a higher percentage of internet users than the African average. For example, Africans constitute only 3.4 per cent of worldwide users (Obiaya 2010: 325). With 10 million potential users, Nigeria's national average includes 6.8 per cent internet coverage in its own population and represents 18.5 per cent of all African internet users (Obiaya 2010: 325). This suggests that, as a nation-building infrastructure, Nigeria remains committed to the development of technological advancement.

A quick search of YouTube for 'African films' retrieves a vast number of items bearing the Nollywood brand. For example, out of twenty-five possibilities drawn up by one search, at least two-thirds either promoted Nollywood films or offered sites that allowed the streaming of select films. Ironically, a search for 'African cinema' unearthed more traditional offerings pertaining to African auteur cinema. The contrast between these two phrases bears out the struggle perceived by Olivier Barlet and other African Film Studies scholars that Nollywood has become a sort of low-budget predatory colonizer that has 'invaded markets in neighboring countries (Ghana, Cameroon, Niger, Benin, and the African market in general) thanks to dumping and aggressive sales practices' (Barlet 2008: 126). Certainly, some of these complaints are accurate, and a look at Nollywood's presence on YouTube demonstrates why this is so.

Streamed Nollywood product on YouTube includes clips, trailers and full-length feature films. Some of the trailers are clearly professionally produced, including slick production values and centring on highlights from the films they promote. Others take the form of simple clips, often promoting the film they've been taken from by simply presenting a dramatic or climactic scene without further context. Full-length feature films are presented in a series of clips as per the limitations of YouTube's technology. Streaming quality can be quite uneven and, given the weaker production values of some films, quite problematic. However, as a marketing and fan resource, the streaming of Nollywood film on YouTube offers an effective way of building an international audience.

Another way for Nollywood producers and distributors to access African diaspora and international audiences is through so-called fan sites, forums and e-zines. Often promoting free access to streamed Nollywood films, such fan sites and forums are geographically mobile, allowing fans and other interested parties to connect worldwide (Obiaya 2010: 326). Another function of such sites is the ability to provide audience feedback and, as Obiaya notes, 'the technology has permitted a shift in the balance of power between media producers and consumers, in that the audience can now compete online with the producers' (2010: 327). Thus, the forum format coupled with the streaming of Nollywood film provides both a local and transnational hub around which audiences can coalesce.

An example of such a community may be found on Naijapals.com and Naijarules.com. The term 'Naija' is a colloquial term for Nigeria, and signals the site's interest in Nigerian culture (Obiaya 2010: 326). As is the case with many of these sites, Naijapals.com offers a wide range of foci, including Nigerian entertainment, politics, celebrity gossip, music and Nigerian and African films. Under the category of videos, Naijarules.com provides a free video streaming and/or download service for members of the site. A quick perusal of films such as *Freefall* and *Freefall 2* demonstrates the tendency of Nigerian video filmmakers to make sequels of successful films, following the US system and thus capitalizing on ready-made audiences. Other notable examples include *Living in Bondage 1, 2 and 3*; *Glamour Girls 1 and 2*; and *Issakaba 1, 2, 3 and 4*.

Sites like Naijapals and Naijarules, while clearly assisting Nollywood film with promoting their products, raise some concerns about one of the most debilitating activities in the film industry, namely pirating. On free streaming sites like Naijapals, Naijarules and YouTube, it is often difficult to find attribution for the films housed on-site. As Barlet notes, 'Video pirating is rampant' in Africa and relates the allegation that 'Nigerians even go as far as changing the credits and adding scenes with their own actors in order to give the films greater commercial appeal when they pirate Ghanaian films' (Barlet 2008: 129). Streaming pirated films purportedly adds to the loss of revenues in Nollywood film, and seems virtually unstoppable although Nollywood producers have had occasion to require their films be removed from such sites. Opinion is mixed on the issue of piracy. As an industry until itself, it keeps many people (upwards of 20,000 in Kano alone) employed. Some producers, however, such as the Ghanaian director/producer Socrate Safo, believe that although it is impossible to fight pirates, it is possible to undermine them by flooding the markets with CDs or DVDs when a film is first released (Oladunjoye 2008: 66–7).

Another venue for African film is the AfricanMovieChannel.com (AMC), which came into existence in the UK in 2006 as a pioneering effort to provide the first television channel 'dedicated to African movies from Nollywood (the very popular Nigerian film industry)' outside Africa (http://www.africanmoviechannel.tv/). Although other African films may be represented here, the focus of the channel remains primarily on Nollywood film. The fact that the UK was the site for such an endeavour is not surprising, given that it possesses one of the largest Nigerian diasporic communities in the world, estimated in 2009 at 154,000 (http://www.africanmoviechannel.tv/). The obvious attraction here is an international market with a ready-built audience and expansion. As well, unlike Naijapals, Naijarules and YouTube, AMC is a fee-for-service site which sells its offerings via online downloads, worldwide streaming and television syndication (http://www.africanmoviechannel.tv/). Films are purchased in 'credit packages', the least expensive of which is fifty credits for £5. Given that an individual streaming of a film costs approximately ten credits, the cost of procuring a film is relatively inexpensive. In addition to films, AMC also offers streaming and download services for other types of programming, including television series, documentaries and talk shows originating in Africa.

Nollywood scholar Moradewun Adejunmobi has recently argued that by 2016 some of the more popular streaming platforms for African films include iROKOtv and ibakatv, the latter focusing exclusively on Nollywood product (2019: 223). She considers iROKOtv as 'the most important streaming platform dedicated to Nigerian content', boasting the world's most extensive listings of Nollywood films since its debut in 2011 (Adejunmobi 2019: 223–4). The site has constantly transformed over the past eight years, beginning with a heavy focus on streaming straight to video product and gradually obtaining 'locally produced cinema features from Ghana and Nigeria' as well as 'licensing its own television series for circulation on Pay TV' (Adejunmobi 2019: 226). Adejunmobi explains how, following its establishment, iROKOtv offered two types of streaming services: one free to the public but paid through advertising and an ad-free 'premium subscription service' (Adejunmobi 2019: 224). The free service eventually proved unsustainable and was dropped in favour of a 'paid subscription' only where subscribers can request specific 'quality' content (Adejunmobi 2019: 229–31). The founding and rise of iROKOtv coincided with New Nollywood's rise around 2009/10 when some Nigerian directors turned their attention to larger-budget productions featuring 'higher production values for theatrical exhibition' (Adejunmobi 2019: 224). Adejunmobi further argues that 'curiously' none of the seminal films such as Kunle Afolayan's 2009 *The Figurine* or those 'of Tunde Kelani had ever been on iROKOtv' as of late 2016 (2019: 232).

Given the strong presence of Nollywood films on the internet and the variety of streaming options available, it seems there is a possibility that Nollywood and its transformation into New Nollywood have emerged as the 'first' face of African cinema. Regardless of detractors who question whether such manifestly commercial and popular cinema could ever authentically represent African needs and imperatives on the world's screens, Nollywood cinema has clearly exploited technology in a calculated way in order to bring its products to a local and international audience. Although somewhat grudgingly, Barlet admits that Nollywood video film's 'democratization of image production' signals that digital film has given 'Africa the potential to produce its own images without foreign backing' (2008: 127–8). Indeed, what began as a popular art has transformed into a formidable industry within the field of African screen media, commanding considerable academic attention on par with the celluloid art films produced in other areas of the continent.

Ghallywood video scene

In her comprehensive study of Ghana's commercial video industry, Carmela Garritano laments how the global emphasis on Nollywood has obfuscated the 'transnational interaction' between the Ghanaian and Nigerian media industries (2013: 3). Garritano makes the point that many of the video and media industries on the continent share 'points of intersection with and divergence from Nollywood' (2013: 3). Each 'wood' might possess its own distinct stylistic signature, but they all share the common goal of storytelling and entertainment (Garritano 2013: 3, 9). Garritano describes this as 'minor transnationalism' whereby national borders are increasingly porous as video films or home movies saturate multiple sites of social space (2013: 156).

Ghana provides one of the most striking examples of the development of a video film industry in the late 1980s with the creation of low-budget video films (Meyer 1999: 93). Spurred on by the inexpensiveness, accessibility, portability and ease of post-production made possible by video technology, the Ghanaian film industry was revitalized and a new set of narrative and aesthetic imperatives, albeit controversial ones, entered the lexicon of African cinema (Meyer 1999: 94–5). Manthia Diawara describes Ghanaian videos as 'remakes of [Kwah] Ansah's films, but without the same dramatic tension, with less characterization, fewer special effects, more slowly paced narratives, and predictable, didactic endings' (2010: 169). What Diawara is inferring here, via a reference to one of Ghana's most well-known cinema (celluloid) directors, is that Ghanaian video films tend to take up Ansah's project in his two groundbreaking films, *Love Brewed in the African Pot* (1980) and *Heritage Africa* (1988), of rehabilitating African history and identity via the African male protagonist's 'correct' choices vis-à-vis tradition and heritage (2010: 169). Birgit Meyer has argued that the comparison of 'tradition' and 'heritage' in *Heritage Africa* with the plots in video films merits a much more complex analysis than simple rehabilitation or retrieval from 'colonial brainwashing'. She demonstrates how, in video films, 'tradition' and 'heritage' were 'framed differently' and were a 'major source of trouble and anxiety – indeed, a burdensome "legacy" more than simply "heritage" – that had to be gotten rid of' (Meyer 2010b: 13). Ultimately, Meyer advocates for more flexible understandings and applications of these notions so they are not fixed definitively to the colonial past, as demonstrated in Ansah's work (2010b: 19).

Interestingly, Ansah's films are the prototypes of 'appropriate representations' sanctioned by the 'once state-owned Ghana Film Industry Corporation (GFIC)' (Meyer 2010b: 8). However, from its inception in 1957 to its closure in 1996, the Ghana Film Industry Corporation only produced thirteen feature films on celluloid (among the numerous documentaries and newsreels produced). With the introduction of television and subsequently video technology, local entrepreneurs considered video as a way to revitalize the local cinema industry. Kwah Ansah himself declared in 2002, 'Film or celluloid is expensive, and ideally that's the format by which I would prefer telling my story, but realistically no African filmmaker on his own can afford celluloid as things stand now. And neither can we wait for our mismanaged economies to be revamped before telling our stories' (Ukadike 2002: 17).

Although the Ghanaian video industry began well before Nollywood, it was slow to develop compared to the Nigerian industry, which finally overtook that of Ghana by the late 1990s. This was mainly due to the fact that, in the beginning, many viewers preferred Nigerian videos. Meyer argues, for example, that style, fashion and the latest fads are highly prized values in Ghana and that, for a long period, Ghanaian video films appeared modest and 'old-fashioned' compared to the flashy Nigerian product. But even more importantly, Ghanaian viewers tended to prefer the stories and content of Nigerian movies because the 'films resonated more than Ghanaian ones with the concerns of people in the street' (Meyer 2010a: 54). The depiction of melodramatic excess, opulent displays of wealth, stories centred around issues of witchcraft and juju (sorcery) versus Christianity were especially attractive to viewers who considered juju a part of everyday life. And thus, Nigerian product continued to be dumped on the Ghanaian market (to a large extent by Ghanaian business people because it was more profitable than Ghanaian movies) (Meyer 2010a: 53–4). Pierre Barrot cites the Ghanaian director/producer Socrate Safo who claims that, at the end of the 1990s, there were forty-seven registered Ghanaian producers, and by 2004 there were only seven. As well, by the same year, eighteen out of twenty-six officially registered active distributors were Nigerian (Barrot 2008: 44). In another context, Safo has described how Nigerian directors pirate Ghanaian videos, change the credits and embellish the stories with scenes using Nigerian actors in an attempt to heighten commercial and audience appeal (Barlet 2008: 129). Garritano explains that by 2008, Ghanaian and Nigerian media industries were working hand in hand to discourage piracy in local markets. She describes how delegations from the two nations encouraged regional co-productions and developed 'strategies for legitimizing and regulating the marketing and distributing of movies in both countries' (Garritano 2013: 165). With no real follow-through, however, or support from business or government in either country, to resolve copyright and piracy issues, 'transnational collaboration' had to find its way through another venue (Garritano 2013: 165). Garritano discloses that by the early 2000s, some Ghanaian video directors were keen to work with Nigerian producers believing this would bring larger production values and Hollywood glitz to their films, which Garritano describes as 'Ghanaian films with "Nollywood" style' (2013: 169).

A similar situation was developing in Anglophone Cameroon around the same time period when Nollywood stars were being deployed to act in Collywood productions in order to boost marketing and sales. Stéphanie

Dongmo argues that in 2003, the newly formed production company 'Splash' invited Nigerian film stars to act in the film *Peace Offering*, shot in Bafut, Cameroon (2010). Dongmo further asserts that it's easy to see the enormous influence of Nollywood on Collywood because the films embrace the same genres (supernatural, drama, romantic-comedy, thriller, epic, historical), similar aesthetics and special effects, and similar turns of phrases. According to Dongmo, in 2005, Collywood co-founder and producer Agbor Gilbert Ebot, having worked in Nigeria, recruited well-known Nollywood actors such as Olu Jacobs, Emma Ayagolu and Zack Orji, to film *Before the Sunrise* with Cameroonian actors. Its lavish decor and production values could lead a viewer to believe the action is taking place in Nigeria, except for the fact that almost every sentence contained the word 'Cameroon' to drive home the difference (Dongmo 2010: n.p.).

In her study of Tanzania's Bongowood, Ann Overbergh cautions that local video industries should not simply be considered copies of the Nollywood experience, and that Nollywood should serve, at most, as a 'comparative benchmark' for critics and audiences, who should, in turn, focus their attention on 'local specificity' (2015: 138). As Overbergh explains, Nollywood is but one influence among many: local Tanzanian traditions and myths, and Western cinema models (especially Hollywood). Swahili, as a common language spoken throughout East Africa, facilitates the dominance of Bongowood as 'the biggest local video industry', saturating the sociocultural spaces (to return to Haynes's concept) of this region of the continent (2015: 138). Overbergh's work points to an important consideration in the context of expanded cinema. She intimates that Nollywood has provided the economic model, and enjoys a global audience due to a large Nigerian diaspora who consume the videos in English (Overbergh 2015: 138). What makes the Tanzanian example fascinating, however, is the fact that a product produced in an Indigenous African language (rather than a colonial language) has such enormous reach across the continent, perhaps as much or even more so than any other video film production in an Indigenous African language.

Aboubakar Sanogo writes of African cinephilic traditions and attitudes 'such as renaming oneself, adopting the demeanors of actors, knowing songs by heart, changing accents, frantically watching films over and over again, reciting lines by heart, reenacting scenes and sequences with gestures, words, and swear words' and wonders if these are possible mechanisms for forging 'a continental and global cinephilia for African-produced cinema' (2009: 228). Although these traditions were created as viewer responses to Hollywood, Bollywood and Hong Kong films, they increasingly pertain to Nollywood, according to Sanogo, and thus, I would argue, Ghanaian video films (2009: 228). Video producers now speak with pride of a 'Ghallygold' industry where Ghanaian audiences are prepared to pay more for Ghanaian video films than Nollywood films (Meyer 2010a: 55–6).

The 'New Actors' – video film auteurs

A number of filmmakers across the continent have turned to independent digital video production in an effort to reach audiences through popular genres, experimental or alternative production models. Burkinabé scholar Justin Ouoro terms these directors, 'nouveaux acteurs/new actors' because their productions assist in breathing new life into almost defunct cinemas and they coexist with other directors who are only visible during the biannual Festival Panafricain du Cinéma de Ouagadougou (2017: 211). He writes that despite the 'années de gloire/glory years' of the 1990s in Burkina Faso when award-winning directors such as the late Idrissa Ouédraogo, Gaston Kaboré and the second generation, including Dani Kouyaté, Fanta Régina Nacro, Abdoulaye Dao and Issa Traoré, led the charge on the African continent with innovative celluloid productions that garnered international recognition, a number of factors including economic structural adjustment programmes, distribution difficulties and the increasing popularity of small screens led to the eventual demise of a once-burgeoning cinema industry – the pride of Africa (Ouoro 2017: 210–11). According to Ouoro, by 2016, there were only eighteen cinemas in Burkina Faso, as opposed to the fifty-three it counted in 1990 (Ouoro 2017: 211).

Technological advancements, coupled with the economic factors cited above, led to some innovative creation by a small group of media producers. Key among these is Boubakar Diallo, who began his career as a journalist, creating the weekly satire newspaper, *Le Journal du Jeudi*. After publishing two detective novels and numerous screenplays, he turned to filmmaking in 2004 with the thriller, *Traque à Ouaga?/Pursuit in Ouaga*, and the romantic comedy, *Sofia*. These were immediate hits with huge audiences and Diallo has claimed that genre movies are the way to attract audiences: 'If people aren't going to see movies, it's because we're not showing what they want to see' (Diallo quoted in Barlet 2010: 88). He has attempted almost all cinematic genres from the political thriller, *Code Phoenix*

(Phoenix Code) (2005), to the western, *L'Or des Youngas* (The Youngas Gold) (2006), to the fantasy film *Julie et Roméo* (Julie and Romeo) (2011), a 'remake' of the Shakespearean production. Produced quickly and on very low budgets of €40,000–50,000 per feature, the video films are financed through promotion of bottled water, cellular telephones, mopeds and so on (Barlet 2010: 87).

Interestingly, other independent filmmakers such as Franco-Tunisian Nadia El Fani have tested alternative funding models that involve multiple co-production via the internet in order to cover post-production costs. She sent a mass email to all her friends and acquaintances inviting them to become co-producers for €35 each. All who donated were listed in the credits of her 2012 documentary, *Même pas mal/No Harm Done* (Martin 2013). The Burkinabé filmmaker and television director/producer Apolline Traoré was able to complete her digital feature film *Moi, Zaphira/I, Zaphira* in 2012 by using all the money she made through directing/producing television serials for the state-run television station.

Diallo has been described as an 'auteur' video filmmaker who speaks and thinks like an entrepreneur. He has been heard to say, 'All activity should possess an economic logic. The day the subsidy tap runs dry, African cinema will no longer exist. However, as far as I'm concerned, from Dakar to Libreville, there is only one audience. It's a shame to not capitalize on that. (*Toute activité doit avoir une logique économique. Le jour où le robinet des subventions est coupé, il n'y a plus de cinéma africain. Or, pour moi, de Dakar à Libreville, il y a un seul et même public. C'est dommage de ne pas s'appuyer dessus.*)' (Lequeret 2005). Elisabeth Lequeret goes on to claim that for Diallo, video is much more than just an aesthetic choice. It allows him artistic licence and independence while being able to produce films quickly and regularly, often completing two features per year (2005). This is in stark contrast to filmmakers working in 35mm, many of whom would struggle to complete one feature every ten years![4]

I would argue that Diallo is at the forefront of an expanded cinema movement in Burkina Faso because he works to saturate social and cultural space of his community with stories about his community and for his community in forms and genres they can relate to. In this way, his work reaches local audiences first, and all year-round, rather just during the Fespaco festival every second year, when film aficionados from around the globe converge on Ouagadougou to

---

[4] According to Tunde Oladunjoye no feature-length 35mm films were released in Nigeria between 1994 and 2006 (2008: 68).

screen African films that the general population will never have the means to access. Diallo claims that the neologism 'Ouagawood' aptly reflects the notion of building on the Nollywood experience to expand Burkinabé cinematic space beyond Fespaco (Ouoro 2017: 213). He is joined in this quest by compatriot filmmaker Boubacar Sidnaba Zida, who, like Diallo, draws on themes of the Burkinabé collective imagination, releasing his wildly popular video *Un fantôme dans la ville* (Phantom in the City) in 2009 (Ouoro 2017: 213).

Conclusion

Although initially forged in the spirit of entrepreneurship, African digital video films demonstrate that art, culture and life are as interconnected in the entertainment industries as they are in African systems of thought. Their very localization of cultural forms demands active interaction, and in this way is a much more immersive (saturated space) experience as people share an interest in the genres, archetypes and themes explored in the films. It remains to be seen how artistic creativity and entrepreneurship will merge in future productions. Will video film directors manage to further eschew colonial imposed forms of space–time continuums and explode the temporal in order to foreground social and spatial experiences, thus resetting and redirecting global media flows?

Acknowledgements

Special thanks to the late Donna-Lynne McGregor for her assistance with this chapter. Thanks also go to the Social Sciences and Humanities Research Council of Canada for sponsoring this research.

References

Adejunmobi, M. (2019), 'Streaming Quality, Streaming Cinema', in K. Harrow and C. Garritano (eds), *A Companion to African Cinema*, Hoboken, NJ: Wiley-Blackwell, 219–43.

Barlet, O. (2008), 'Is the Nigerian Model Fit for Export?' in P. Barrot (ed.), *Nollywood, the Video Phenomenon in Nigeria*, Bloomington: Indiana University Press, 121–9.

Barlet, O. (2010), 'Africultures Dossier', *Black Camera, an International Film Journal*, 1 (3): 63–102.

Barrot, P. (2008), 'Audacity, Scandal & Censorship', in P. Barrot (ed.), *Nollywood, the Video Phenomenon in Nigeria*, Bloomington: Indiana University Press, 43–50.

Diawara, M. (2010), *African Film: New Forms of Aesthetics and Politics*, Munich: Haus der Kulturen der Welt; Berlin: Prestel Verlag.

Dongmo, S. (2010), 'Collywood, le Hollywood du Cameroun', *Africine.org*, 15 July. Available online: http://www.africine.org/?menu=art&no=9594 (accessed 26 June 2019).

Garritano, C. (2013), *African Video Movies and Global Desires: A Ghanaian History*, Athens, OH: Center for International Studies, Ohio University.

Hanson, E. (2009), 'Oral Traditions', *Indigenousfoundations.arts.ubc.ca*. Available online: https://indigenousfoundations.arts.ubc.ca/oral_traditions/ (accessed 21 May 2019).

Hatfield, J. (2011), 'Expanded Cinema: Proto-, Photo and Post-Photo Cinema', in A. L. Rees, David Curtis, Duncan White and Steven Ball (eds), *Expanded Cinema: Art, Performance, Film*, London: Tate Gallery, 262–6.

Haynes, J. (2017), 'Anglophone West Africa: Commercial Cinema', in K. W. Harrow (ed.), *African Filmmaking: Five Formations*, East Lansing: Michigan State University Press, 81–115.

Jedlowski, A. (2017), 'Les transformations de la circulation de films vidéos nigérians en Côte d'Ivoire', in P. Caillé and C. Forest (eds), *Regarder des films en Afriques*, Villeneuve d'Ascq: Presses Universitaires du Septentrion, 259–73.

Kelani, T. (2008), 'Spielberg and I: The Digital Revolution', in P. Barrot (ed.), *Nollywood, the Video Phenomenon in Nigeria*, Bloomington: Indiana University Press, 90–2.

Lequeret, E. (2005), 'Fespaco 2005: Boubacar Diallo, portrait d'un pionnier', *RFI.fr*. 23, February. Available online: http://www.rfi.fr/actufr/articles/062/article_34306.asp (accessed 13 February 2013).

Marchessault, J., and S. Lord, eds (2007), *Fluid Screens, Expanded Cinema*, Toronto: University of Toronto Press.

Martin, F. (2013), Email communication with the author. 17 March 2013.

Meyer, B. (1999), 'Popular Ghanaian Cinema and "African Heritage"', *Africa Today*, 46 (2): 93–114.

Meyer, B. (2010a), 'Ghanaian Popular Video Movies between State Film Policies and Nollywood: Discourses and Tensions', in M. Saul and R. Austen (eds), *Viewing African Cinema in the Twenty-first Century: Art Films and the Nollywood Video Revolution*, Athens: Ohio University Press, 42–62.

Meyer, B. (2010b), '"Tradition and Colour at Its Best"'; "Tradition" and "Heritage" in Ghanaian Video-Movies', *Journal of African Cultural Studies*, 22 (1): 7–23.

NeuCollins, M. (2007), 'Contemporary African Cinema: The Emergence of an Independent Cinema in Nigeria', Speaking of Art blog. 20 April. Available online: http://speakingofart.wordpress.com/2007/04/20/contemporary-african-cinema-the-emergence-of-an-independent-cinema-in-nigeria/#more-8 (accessed 3 March 2013).

Obiaya, I. (2010), 'Nollywood on the Internet: A Preliminary Analysis of an Online Nigerian Video-film Audience', *Journal of African Media Studies*, 2 (3): 321–38.

Ogundele, W. (2000), 'From Folk Opera to Soap Opera: Improvisations and Transformations in Yoruba Popular Theater', in J. Haynes (ed.), *Nigerian Video Films*, Athens: Ohio University Center for International Studies, 89–129.

Okome, O. (2004), 'Women, Religion and the Video Film in Nigeria', *Film International*, 2 (1): 4–13.

Oladunjoye, T. (2008), 'Jumping on the Bandwagon', in P. Barrot (ed.), *Nollywood, the Video Phenomenon in Nigeria*, Bloomington: Indiana University Press, 62–9.

Ouoro, J. (2017), 'Acteurs et public du cinéma au Burkina Faso: une nouvelle dynamique de la pratique cinématographique', in P. Caillé and C. Forest (eds), *Regarder des films en Afriques*, Villeneuve d'Ascq: Presses Universitaires du Septentrion, 209–21.

Overbergh, A. (2015), 'Innovation and Its Obstacles in Tanzania's Bongowood', *Journal of African Cinemas*, 7 (2): 137–51.

Sanogo, A. (2009), 'Regarding Cinephilia and Africa', *Framework*, 50 (1/2): 226–8.

Ukadike, N. F. (2002), *Questioning African Cinema: Conversations with Filmmakers*, Minneapolis: University of Minnesota Press.

10

Netflix and Africa: Streaming, branding and tastemaking in non-domestic African film markets

Alexander Fisher

In February 2018, Netflix launched its 'Strong Black Lead' initiative, formed of a collection of film and television titles that operate within 'a sub-brand of Netflix that amplifies content specifically targeted to various slices of the Black experience' (Ibrahim 2020). Just over two years later, the same company also launched its 'Made in Africa' collection, a curated inventory of African films drawing from both recent and older, more well-known material, whose inventory was made globally available. Timed to coincide with Africa month in May 2020, the collection's release included a number of 'Netflix Originals', including the television series *Queen Sono* (Kagiso Lediga, South Africa, 2020–present) and *Blood & Water* (Nosipho Dumisa et al., South Africa, 2020–present), alongside now-canonical feature film titles such as *Tsotsi* (Gavin Hood, South Africa, 2005) and *Jerusalema* (Ralph Ziman, South Africa, 2008). Additionally, several non-domestic features and documentaries – either largely or completely filmed in Africa – were included alongside the domestically produced content, including the Leonardo DiCaprio-backed *The Ivory Game* (Kief Davidson and Richard Ladkani, 2016) (Seabi 2020). Around a month later in June 2020, in the midst of global protests surrounding racial disparity, Netflix launched a further globally available[1] initiative known as 'Made by Africans, Watched by the World' which, as Kenya-based filmmaker Fred Onyango puts it, aims 'to showcase content that centres black stories but ... it will be by and about Africans' ('Made

---

[1] The research presented in this chapter was carried out using Netflix's UK site during the period of August 2020–August 2021. Since Netflix has made its African inventory globally available, it is assumed that the content accessed via the UK site is available in all other regions. For a detailed discussion regarding the problems of regional inventory differences when researching Netflix, see Lotz (2021: 195–215).

by Africans, Watched by the World' 2020). As a result, domestic African titles – that is, those made domestically, for domestic markets – have now been given an unprecedented level of global discoverability and accessibility, rubbing shoulders with internationally targeted productions, produced both within the continent and beyond.

While African film has been proliferating online for well over a decade now, its steady transferral from informal to formal distribution modes, and eventually into the hands of the global players, has transformed it from being a cinema that one must 'find' to a cinema that one 'receives'. This is evident in the marketing and PR surrounding Netflix's African initiatives, and the ways in which the site's algorithms can steer users to African material. It has also thrust the products of domestic African film industries into the cultural imaginary at a global level, extending the notion of 'African cinema' well beyond the internationally oriented material that traditionally reached foreign shores via the art house circuit.

Yet, beyond this 'cybertopian' perspective, Netflix's distribution of African content also raises critical questions regarding the gatekeeping role of global tech firms, who now determine the kinds of material that represent the international 'front' of African film, and in turn how they shape ideas about what African cinema 'is', in turn functioning as tastemakers. In this regard, the following analysis is shaped by Ramon Lobato's argument that 'Distribution lends itself to critical/cultural critique as well as industrial analysis because it ultimately functions to regulate access to texts, the conditions under which they are accessed and the range of texts available', and as a result 'distribution works to shape film culture in its own image' (2009: 169). Moreover, for many years now, Netflix's activities have extended well beyond the role of intermediary to become those of producer. This holds true in the African context where, as well as purchasing global distribution rights for content, the company is also backing production in the form of its original productions such as the aforementioned *Queen Sono* (Ritman 2020). Thus, the example of Netflix is particularly apt at a time when the once-democratizing 'disintermediation' promised by online film distribution becomes a reintermediation in which films and filmmaking fall into the hands of ever-larger and more powerful intermediaries. Yet, these global players are – almost by definition – in a position to influence at a global level, now more than ever possessing the ability to make or break the international fortunes of a given film culture. This has resulted in a paradoxical situation in which marginal cinemas are offered a wider platform than ever before, at the same time as their long-term sustainability and preservation is increasingly tied to the demands of the market.

Indeed, Netflix's recent African initiatives clearly correspond to the company's business strategies, which were firmly established within the company long before it distributed its first African films. In particular, the company has consistently established a brand that positions it as a disrupter in the arena of film distribution, pursuing ventures that are perceived as 'edgy' or 'risky', giving the impression that it works against the grain of mainstream corporate culture. As Kevin McDonald and Daniel Smith-Rowsey suggest in the introduction to their edited volume *The Netflix Effect* (2016), 'Perhaps owing to its historically antagonistic relationships with Blockbuster and the Big Six media companies, Netflix often accentuates its status as an outsider, upstart, disruptor, underdog, and even as a direct threat or "game changer" to the entire status quo' (2016: 4). However, this strategy is clearly at odds with Netflix's position as a multinational tech giant, in which it is precisely the opposite of an 'upstart', 'outsider' or 'underdog'. As McDonald and Smith-Rowsey go on to assert, 'on the one hand, Netflix suggests a kind of corporate outlier, one that – by many counts, most especially its own – aims to buck the status quo. On the other hand, Netflix is in many ways a paragon of global capitalism in the twenty-first century' (2016: 10). It is this paradoxical relationship, between the image of disruptor and the capitalist reality, that both generates and undermines the cybertopian perspective with which one might be tempted to approach Netflix's intervention into African screen production and distribution. While an abundance of diverse material is now reaching international audiences, there is a clear correlation between the ideological character and timing of Netflix's initiatives, and the business practices it has openly established over the course of many years.

From this perspective, 'Strong Black Lead', 'Made in Africa' and 'Made by Africans, Watched by the World' may all be traced to Netflix's alignment of its business strategy to two major economic and social shifts, allowing the company to both generate and meet new forms of market demand. Firstly, the company has built much of its business on utilizing the economics of 'long tail' markets via its SVOD (subscription video on demand) model, as facilitated by the technologies of streaming video, in which the long-term consumption of film material may afford its profitability (see Anderson 2006). This is particularly relevant to marginal and niche content, that would typically fail financially within orthodox distribution structures. Secondly, the company has responded to shifting attitudes towards the representation of race in the light of the growing global consciousness surrounding racial equality, offering representations of difference and diversity beyond the stereotypes and exclusions sustained by the 'western frame'. It is against these two interlinking shifts that Netflix has been able to capitalize on, and extend, its established foothold in African film production, further monetizing the material at the same time as the company 'brand' benefits from the cultural kudos of reaching new, international audiences, hungry for alternative representations.

Thus, by 2020, Netflix was well placed to respond to the new market demand for diversity. Despite disparities in communication infrastructure across the continent, the company is clearly positioning itself as the key global player in the continent's contemporary screen industries (see Kazeem 2016), having established an intracontinental dialogue between African screen cultures well before it began to market them at a global level. As 'Made in Africa' launched, the company was already commissioning a second season of *Queen Sono*, was ready to premier *Blood & Water* and had finalized a deal with Mo Abudu's EbonyLife in Nigeria for the production of a range of locally produced projects, including two series ('Made by Africans, Watched by the World' 2020; Bacon 2019). By March 2020, Netflix had also signed a deal with John Boyega's UpperRoom Productions for the development of several non-English-language projects in East and West Africa (Ritman 2020). Additionally, it had previously secured distribution rights for the forthcoming Zimbabwean musical animation *Tunga* (Fleming 2019). However, the company had also been rapidly extending its interests in independent material, licensing titles such as *Kalushi* (Mandla Dube, 2016, South Africa), *King of Boys* (Kemi Adetiba, 2018, Nigeria), and *Potato Potahto* (Shirley Frimpong-Manso, 2017, Ghana), and had ventured into territories where feature filmmaking was scarce, for example, in its acquisition of distribution rights for *Resgate* (Mickey Fonseca, Mozambique, 2019) ('Made by Africans, Watched by the World' 2020). Moreover, Netflix had acquired distribution rights to a number of titles aimed at the international art house circuit; these included the Palme d'Or–nominated *Atlantics* (France/Senegal/Belgium, 2019), directed by Mati Diop (the niece of celebrated Senegalese film pioneer Djibril Diop Mambéty), and the Ghanaian production *The Burial of Kojo* (Blitz Bazawule, 2018), which received the award for 'Best Narrative Feature (World Cinema)' following its premier at the New York's Urban World Film Festival.

The effect of Netflix's distribution of African domestic production is perhaps most readily demonstrated by the success of *Cook Off* (Tomas Brickhill, Zimbabwe, 2017), which has almost come to promise a renaissance of filmmaking in its country of origin, Zimbabwe. Dominated by Hollywood activity in the 1980s, and subsequently donor-funded filmmaking in the 1990s, Zimbabwe has struggled to establish a commercially viable domestic cinema, a situation exacerbated by economic decline from the turn of the millennium onwards. Thus, unsurprisingly, *Cook Off* was made on a shoestring budget of just US$ 8,000; yet it has received global attention through a distribution deal with Netflix, whose interest may well have been perked by the film's overtly Zimbabwean flair. Featuring 'an all-Zimbabwean cast of young actors, veterans of the industry, and distinguished figures in music, comedy and poetry' (Vickers 2020), *Cook Off* establishes distinct local credentials, while simultaneously eschewing the didacticism that preoccupied donor-funded productions. This is notable in the casting of Jesesi Mungoshi in a supporting role, an actor already associated with Zimbabwean screen production through her role as the eponymous lead in *Neria* (Godwin Mawuru, Zimbabwe, 1992), the most well-known of the donor-funded films to come out of the country. Often referred to 'development films', these films were typically funded by NGOs involved in public health and social matters, and were widely criticized for their clear lineage to the colonial era 'development ideology', particularly as found in the output of the British Colonial Film Unit (Fisher 2010). As a result, their local specificity was overshadowed by the spectre of neocolonialism, and it remains difficult to justify a reading of such films within the generally accepted terms of 'national cinema'. In contrast, *Cook Off* is unburdened by social concerns, structured as a light-hearted romcom that potentially signals a commercial cinema produced for domestic market demand, rather than for social purposes or the international art house circuit. It is this nationally specific flavour that makes *Cook Off* a case in point for this discussion, becoming emblematic of an era of African screen production in which the rise of commercial cinema appears to be generating room for 'the national' in the continent's output and, perhaps even more importantly, room for a notion of the national that is able to circulate intra-continentally and internationally, as well as domestically.

The precarity of African films online

The arrival of Netflix on the African film scene follows a chain of events that have seen the sustained intermediation of the domestic African screen industries, many of which initially followed the model of Nollywood inasmuch as they were founded upon informal distribution structures (with material disseminated by filmmakers themselves via VHS, DVD and VCD) (Bisschoff 2017: 262; Lobato 2010: 337–54). Since then, numerous formal and informal video on demand services have emerged, coalesced and faded, with distribution increasingly falling into the hands of the multinationals (see Adeleke 2016; Ebelebe 2019; Mwansa 2016; Sawadogo 2017). As the continent's film cultures come under the aegis of increasingly fewer big players, the security of their long-term preservation and accessibility does too, a problem summarized in Wheeler Winston Dixon's observation that 'as events have proved, with streaming technology, even when you buy something, you don't really own it' (2014: 8). Indeed, one of recent history's most significant threats to African film's long-term preservation occurred with the failure of the African Film Library, an initiative of the South African pay-to-view TV channel M-Net. Promising to offer over six hundred African films for streaming on demand, AFL's inventory was drawn predominantly from the canon of African auteur-based films, represented by the likes of Ousmane Sembene, Idrissa Oudraogo and Djibril Diop Mambéty (Cooper 2012). Had it been successful, the website would have offered a comprehensive cross-section of African film history, but unfortunately the project was abandoned before the site was even functional. As I have discussed elsewhere (Fisher 2018), M-Net's disbandment of this project represented a major blow to the accessibility and discoverability of the content, but perhaps more importantly it raised critical questions regarding the future preservation of the material; M-Net had presumably secured the films' rights in perpetuity, a monopoly which restricts the 'safety net' of ongoing reproduction and dissemination of the works through DVD and other physical media.

Thus, the case of the African Film Library was an early challenge to the cybertopian narrative in which the availability of niche and marginal material would vastly improve, demonstrating how easily this could result in a threat to their long-term preservation, with the ever-increasing dependency on online retrieval of material giving unprecedented control of access to its new, more powerful gatekeepers, in turn placing its preservation at the beck and call of commercial demands (Fisher 2018). These problems hold true for Netflix's inventory, which will be secure provided the company continues to benefit financially, but whose preservation could be under threat if it does not. At this point, the availability of the material is propelled by a combination of its domestic and/or global profitability within the paradigm of long tail markets, alongside demand and marketing niches created by current attitudes surrounding race and representation in film. The prevalence of either of these things cannot be guaranteed, and the precariousness of an archiving model based on financial return always creates concerns for the future preservation of material.

African film and Netflix's business model

Netflix's strategy regarding its African output aligns with the company's approach to several other forms of 'cheaper' content, in particular older material with niche appeal. A comparable case is the company's noir inventory, which 'is more commonly associated with Netflix's Long Tail business model, with its ability to drive viewers to older, more specialized types of content that is cheaper to license and therefore a more cost-effective business strategy' (McDonald and Smith-Rowsey 2016: 9). The company's incursion into African content continues this existing business strategy, capitalizing on a tried and trusted distribution model that draws from a ready-made inventory of cheap-to-license material whose niche appeal will result in the accrual of profit over time.

The commercial imperative underpinning these kinds of strategies cannot be overstated, and yet, as Sudeep Sharma shows, has frequently been overlooked. Discussing Netflix's increasing involvement in the production and distribution of documentary, Sharma points out that 'As a source of streaming documentary, Netflix has been celebrated because the popularly understood model for the service has been that of the *library*' (Sharma 2016: 144). However, as Sharma goes on to argue, this comparison with traditional modes of archiving overlooks the fact that Netflix's inventory is fundamentally shaped by its business strategy, in contrast to the altruistic notion of the library whose collections are held for the common good, and thus largely decoupled from commercial pressures. Whereas a not-for-profit archive will add niche material to its catalogue in order to broaden the representations within that archive, 'Netflix's choices are driven by commercial needs' (Sharma 2016: 144), in particular those that may be met by the long tail potential of its inventory.

This analysis holds true for Netflix's addition of marginal content in the form of its African ventures, with the breadth of its material accruing the company's 'brand' a level of kudos, particularly in its broadening representations of difference. This adds another dimension to its strategy, in addition to its utilization of long tail markets; when considered in relation to its brand, Netflix's extensive African titles amplify the diversity of its inventory. Thus, the value of the content lies not only in its ability to generate long tail income in its own right but also in the prestige it brings through its similarity to the socially driven projects of the library or archive. Moreover, the example of Netflix's documentary content demonstrates one of the ways in which the company positions its brand as offering quality, worthwhile content, aligning the company's inventory with ideas of public service broadcasting, in addition to notions of film archiving and preservation. As Sharma observes, this sense of quality counteracts the ideas of 'repetitive viewing' (or 'binge viewing') that are often associated with SVOD, and in turn their connotations of 'sickness' (Sharma 2016: 145).

The alignment of Netflix's African initiatives with its branding strategy comes into even sharper focus in view of the company's more recent attempts to establish a 'progressive' image, for which 'Made by Africans, Watched by the World' forms a case in point. Indeed, the promotional trailer for the venture clearly intersects with this strategy, opening with Nigerian actor and director Genevieve Nnaji addressing the camera with the words: 'Have you ever had someone tell your story, take your voice, and replace your face, until no one else can see or hear your?' Significantly, this overt affiliation with contemporary discourses surrounding representation is quite distinct from previous ventures promoting African culture, such as the BBC's 'Africa Lives' season in 2006. Whereas the BBC's initiative centred on offering positive representations of the continent (thus countering stereotypical associations with underdevelopment (see Magombe 2006)), Netflix's approach questions the act of representation itself, overtly aligning its ventures with the notions of cultural decolonization that have firmly established themselves within contemporary discourses surrounding racial equality. In turn, this approach corresponds to branding trends that have increasingly become a characteristic of corporate culture at large.

Indeed, a pre-existing example of Netflix's approach is identified by Brittany Farr in her analysis of the company's original series *Orange Is the New Black*, in which the 'show's creators were able to mitigate the risks of content creation, in part, by strategic appeals to diversity' (Farr 2016: 155). Indeed, it is paradoxical that the very 'edginess' engendered in productions such as *Orange* is in fact quite the opposite when it comes to commercial risk, representing a cautious business strategy rather than a radical one. As Farr goes on to assert, 'The success of *Orange Is the New Black* proves a point made by Herman Gray and other media scholars: the recognition of difference within contemporary media is good business practice. It is one strategy, of many, used to create marketable representations and manage the riskiness of participating in an ever-less regulated sphere of capitalism' (2016: 155–6). Thus, the emphasis on difference, social significance and aesthetic 'quality' that underpins Netflix's 'Strong Black Lead', 'Made in Africa' and 'Made by Africans, Watched by the World' initiatives represents a clear continuation of the company's branding, while also bolstering its image as an outsider and disruptor in its sector. The brand kudos garnered by these qualities simultaneously effaces the commercial imperative that underpins the choices of inventory, with the apparent range and diversity of its content – the majority of which falls outside prevailing notions of 'the commercial' – implying that its social and historical significance usurps any commercial concerns.

The impact of Netflix's brand image on global tastemaking in African films

The strategies outlined above are in evidence when browsing the company's current inventory of African titles, which clearly attempts to diversify its range, offering content produced for both domestic and international markets. Moreover, the scope of its catalogue is becoming increasingly focused on regional industries, encompassing titles produced for domestic consumption in Ghana, Kenya, Nigeria, South Africa and Zimbabwe, among others. A promising aspect of this range is its potential to promote taxonomies of African films at more culturally specific levels, avoiding the tendency to homogenize discrete film cultures under the banner of an extremely large and diverse continent. Yet, despite the increasing scope for cultural specificity in the company's ever-expanding catalogue of domestic content, the 'country of production' tags used by Netflix for categorizing African titles remain homogenized, and at the time of the writing are limited to 'African Films' and 'Nollywood', with both categories corresponding to, and producing results for, the latter. Thus, the 'African Films' tag in Netflix UK offers no way of filtering African content to a culturally more granular level, being attached to titles that range from the East African romcom of *Cook Off* through to the West African 'art film' of *Atlantics*.

Moreover, the scope of Netflix's 'African Films' category significantly stretches the definition of the term, encompassing European and North American co-productions such as *Beast of No Nation* (Cary Joji Fukunaga, United States/Ghana, 2015) and *A United Kingdom* (Amma Asante, Czech Republic/UK/France/United States, 2016), which are highly questionable as examples of the 'African frame'. Indeed, this approach runs in direct opposition to the political conception of 'African film' put forward by multiple generations of African filmmakers and critics, who have often been concerned with ideas of authenticity in African cinema, with the 'gold standard' being a cinema produced 'by Africans, for Africans', for which Ousmane Sembene is often cited as the founding father. Indeed, filmmakers such as Sembene are notably absent from Netflix's inventory which is, in the main, constituted of more recent material, principally targeted at domestic markets.[2] Likewise, Netflix's conceptualization of 'African Films' is characterized by media convergence, with produced-for-television movies, series and documentaries falling into the category. Thus, despite its emphasis on content intended for domestic markets, and the possibilities of national–cultural specificity this provides, Netflix's tagging system paradoxically positions 'African Films' as a continuous category which is established in terms of both cultural homogenization and media convergence, obscuring cultural specificity at the same time as it effaces the idea of 'film' as a medium-specific dimension of screen culture.

In broad terms, this paradoxical homogenization of an increasingly heterogeneous body of material might be understood as characteristic of modern times, emblematic of the internet's acceleration of 'glocalization'. However, Fred Onyango senses something more specific taking place here regarding the very notion of African cinema itself; whereas previously the question 'what is an African film' was largely limited to the preoccupations of African film scholars, Netflix's initiatives have the potential to reinvent these questions as the transnational exchange of cultural production is radically altered in the digital age. As Onyango asserts,

> The wider reality is that Africanness in cinema has become an identity to play with. Hollywood tends to treat Africa as a homogenous location with unspecified cultures and accents. While we Africans can admire Beyoncé Knowles-Carter's *Black Is King* or Ryan Coogler's *Black Panther*, the wall-to-wall fan adulation in the west doesn't tell the full story. African audiences know these films get accents wrong and don't accurately portray their traditions and cultures. For the most part, these stories are targeted at the black American experience, and to amplify their nuances and concerns. The black American experience may overlap with what African audiences consider relatable, but for the most part the social and especially political concerns do not entirely mesh. (2020)

---

[2] It is possible that M-Net's acquirement of the rights to the films of Sembene et al. is impacting their availability to other online distributors.

This idea of 'an identity to play with' perhaps reveals itself in the particular formations of the homogenization/heterogenization duality found in Netflix's African inventory, and its related metadata. It is also a duality that feeds into the 'paratext' of web journalism's responses to Netflix's initiatives, which are indicative of the company's role in tastemaking. Indeed, these have recently proliferated, generating numerous articles whose notion of the continent's cinema is entirely shaped by – and even invoked by – the idea of 'African films on Netflix' (any discussion of African films *not* on Netflix is ubiquitous in its absence). One example is the US website *Cinema Escapist*, which lists 'The 11 Best African Movies on Netflix'. First and second places are occupied by *The Burial of Kojo* and *Atlantics*, with *The Boy That Harnessed the Wind* (Chiwetel Ejiofor, 2018, UK/Malawi) and *Lionheart* (Genevieve Nnaji, 2018, Nigeria) occupying fourth and fifth places, respectively ('The 11 Best African Movies on Netflix' 2020). Meanwhile, writing in the *New African* in April 2021, Michael Renouf lists the '10 best African films streaming on Netflix', including Nigerian director Kemi Adetiba's hugely successful first feature *The Wedding Party* (Nigeria, 2016) and *The Boy Who Harnessed the Wind*, but extends the scope of 'African film' to Disney's *Queen of Katwe* (Mira Nair, United States, 2016) and *A United Kingdom*, alongside *Queen Sono* (actually a series rather than a feature) (Renouf 2021). Likewise, in November 2020, the website *African Vibes* offered '10 Must-Watch African Movies On Netflix', which lists the '2016 South African Movie' *Kalushi* in its top spot, '2019 Namibian Movie' *Baxu and the Giants* (Florian Schott, Namibia, 2019) in second place and '2018 Nigerian Drama Film' *Diamonds in the Sky* (Kunle Afolayan, Nigeria, 2018) in fifth position (Gitari 2020). Thus, the influence of Netflix in determining the global conceptualization of African cinema becomes abundantly clear in web journalism's responses, provoking articles that are in *themselves about* Netflix's inventory, accepting the notion of 'African Films' encompassed within the platform's branding, marketing and metadata.

Where the influence of Netflix's metadata seems less obvious is in web journalism's apparent emphasis on national production contexts. Within the production details and blurb offered in these lists, there are frequent references to countries of production. Moreover, in some cases, their national contexts are fleshed out with nods to the films' backers (such as the 'British Producers' in *Cinema Escapist*'s mention of *The Boy Who Harnessed the Wind*) or biographical details of the filmmakers (such as Mati Diop's filmmaker familial lineage in the same website's mention of *Atlantics*) ('The 11 Best African Movies on Netflix'

2020). Thus, the homogenizing effects of the 'African Films' tag are perhaps counteracted by the sheer range and diversity of its corresponding material, offering a heterogeneity of content that filters through to web journalism as an awareness of national specificity and departing – to a degree – from the predominant image of 'Africa as a homogenous location with unspecified cultures and accents' (Onyango 2020).

More obviously influenced by Netflix's metadata is net journalism's awareness of genre in African film (exemplified in the *African Vibes* list), which is clearly invoked by the company's use of genre categorizations as a central component of its tagging system. Indeed, Netflix's former involvement with Nollywood places it at the heart of the emerging genre cinemas in the continent (which are analysed in detail by Jonathan Haynes in *Nollywood: The Creation of Nigerian Film Genres* [2016]). Thus, the website *Ranker* cites fifty titles in their list of 'The Best African Films on Netflix' which, according to its author, 'run the gambit [sic] from goofy comedy to exciting thriller' (Bancroft 2021). In first place is the New Zealand/US/South Africa co-produced sci-fi movie *District 9* (Neill Blomkamp, 2009), while the Nigerian crime comedy *Sugar Rush* (Kayode Kasum, Nigeria, 2019) comes in at fifth place (Bancroft 2021). The prevalence of genre here is particularly evident in Bancroft's words on the diversity of African films, and in three of the four website lists mentioned above, the films' genres are included. Thus, just as a paradox has emerged between increasing cultural homogenization and cultural heterogeneity in Netflix's inventory and cataloguing of African titles, so a related paradox has surfaced in relation to style and form. While Netflix's tagging system has homogenized 'African Films' and 'Nollywood' as genres in themselves, there is also an emerging visibility of a more orthodox genre taxonomy, shifting the concern from questions of cultural representation to questions of storytelling, cinematic pleasure and taste.

From this perspective, the 'genre' of 'African Films' does not necessarily point to a set of movies characterized by representations outside the 'western frame' but rather functions as a marker of taste that leads to a subset of (more orthodox) genres based around scenario and story. This is perhaps most evident in the appearance of *District 9* (tagged 'African Films' in Netflix) at the head of *Ranker*'s list; while the movie could barely be described as representative of African voices in the sense proposed by Netflix's recent African ventures, its appeal to particular formations of cinematic taste embodies a trend identifiable in the continent's production at large, as its screen cultures become increasingly removed from issues of social justice and more aligned with notions of entertainment. However, a further layer of complexity is emerging in relation to ways in which nation and genre can interact in the categorization of material. For instance, both genre and national categories coalesce in the *Ranker* list (e.g. 'Nigerian drama'), offering the potential for a complex web of genre/nationality combinations, each of which connotes their own film styles and narrative characteristics.

Conclusion

There is no doubt that Netflix's initiatives have allowed African cinema – at least in the short term – to arrive at a level of non-domestic discoverability and accessibility that is transforming perceptions of the continent's cinema within the cultural imaginary. Yet it is also abundantly clear that the company's inventory is structured through underlying commercial imperatives surrounding brand image and marketing, as well as the need for metadata that fuels the company's algorithms. The significance of these issues in propelling Netflix's African ventures cannot be overstated, since they demonstrate the ongoing and ever-increasing role of the market in determining the global conceptions of regional cinemas, influencing how they are framed, categorized and organized.

In the light of this, the contradictions and paradoxes in Netflix's evolving conception of 'African Films' might be most readily explained through the tensions generated by the company's contradictory position as a capitalist, global corporation versus its brand image as outlier and upstart, all of which are in evidence at a micro level in the interrelations between the company's marketing, inventory and metadata. From this perspective, Onyago's notion that 'Africanness in cinema has become an identity to play with' is actually more a result of the way Netflix uses the 'African Films' and 'Nollywood' category tags to manage the increasing fragmentation of the African content it acquires. In turn, these categories are determined by patterns in market demand, rather than through a desire to develop conceptual understandings of the material along the lines of cultural specificity. The pressing question, then, is whether Netflix's expanding inventory, and the necessity for its organization through metadata, can leave room for more nuanced, culturally specific taxonomies of African screen production, particularly at the level of the national. As the company develops its brand identity by continually adding to its inventory, an ever-greater expanse of African material is becoming available, along with increasing complexities in organizing and indexing that content. Thus, while previously the homogenizing 'African Films' tag might have been sufficiently specific as a marker of African content, the greater fragmentation and diversity of material falling under the scope of that tag render it increasingly inadequate, as it comes to encompass material that ranges from home-grown titles produced for both domestic markets, to foreign-produced content that barely offers a domestic perspective. It remains to be seen whether this expansion will eventually generate more culturally specific taxonomies of African film cultures, but at this point it has most certainly offered a challenge to prevailing perceptions and definitions.

References

'The 11 Best African Movies on Netflix' (2020), *Cinema Escapist*, 7 August. Available online: https://www.cinemaescapist.com/2020/08/best-african-movies-netflix/ (accessed 1 February 2021).
Adeleke, D. (2016), 'What Impact Does Netflix in Africa Have on iROKO?', *Techcabal*, 7 January. Available online: https://techcabal.com/2016/01/07/what-impact-does-netflix-in-africa-have-on-iroko/ (accessed 18 July 2019).
Anderson, C. (2006), *The Long Tail: Why the Future of Business Is Selling Less of More*, New York: Hyperion.
Bacon, M. (2019), 'Netflix in Africa', *Medium*, 4 January. Available online: https://medium.com/datadriveninvestor/netflixs-involvement-in-africa-cdc1234c2d9b (accessed 19 July 2020).
Bancroft, J. (2021), 'The Best African Films on Netflix', *Ranker*, 6 May. Available online: https://www.ranker.com/list/best-african-movies-on-netflix/grayson-titan (accessed 4 June 2021).
Bisschoff, L. (2017), 'The Future Is Digital: An Introduction to African Digital Arts', *Critical African Studies*, 9 (3): 261–7.
Cooper, S. (2012), 'M-Net Launches VOD African Film Library', *Screen Daily*, 26 March. Available online: https://www.screendaily.com/m-net-launches-vod-african-film-library-/5039239.article (accessed 19 July 2019).
Dixon, W. W. (2013), *Streaming. Movies, Media and Instant Access*, Lexington: University Press of Kentucky.
Ebelebe, U. B. (2019), 'Reinventing Nollywood: The Impact of Online Funding and Distribution on Nigerian Cinema', *Convergence*, 25 (3): 466–78.
Farr, B. (2016), 'Seeing Blackness in Prison: Understanding Prison Diversity on Netflix's *Orange Is the New Black*', in K. McDonald and D. Smith-Rowsey (eds), *The Netflix*

Effect: Technology and Entertainment in the 21st Century, New York: Bloomsbury Academic, 155–70.

Fisher, A. (2010), 'Funding, Ideology, and the Aesthetics of the "Development Film" in Postcolonial Zimbabwe', *Journal of African Cinemas*, 2 (2): 111–20.

Fisher, A. (2018), 'African Cinema On Demand? The Politics of Online Distribution and the Case of the African Film Library', *Journal of African Media Studies*, 10 (3): 239–50.

Fleming, M. (2019), 'Netflix Wins *Tunga*, Animated Musical from Zimbabwe – Born Newcomer Godwin Jabangwe; First Deal Out of Talent Hatchery Imagine Impact 1', *Deadline*, 14 February. Available online: https://deadline.com/2019/02/tunga-netflix-animated-musical-zimbabwe-newcomer-godwin-jabangwe-imagine-impact-1-1202557570/ (accessed 19 July 2020).

Gitari, K. (2020), '10 Must-Watch African Movies on Netflix', *African Vibes*, 13 November. Available online: https://www.africanvibes.com/our-top-10-african-movies-on-netflix-in-2020/ (accessed 3 February 2021).

Haynes, J. (2016), *Nollywood: The Creation of Nigerian Film Genres*, Chicago: University of Chicago Press.

Ibrahim, S. (2020), 'Netflix's "Strong Black Lead" Marketing Team Shows the Power (and Business Benefit) of Amplifying Black Voices', *Hollywood Reporter*, 6 August. Available online: https://www.hollywoodreporter.com/tv/tv-news/netflixs-strong-black-lead-marketing-team-shows-power-business-benefit-amplifying-black-voices-1305775/ (accessed 7 September 2020).

Kazeem, Y. (2016), 'No Matter Where Netflix Goes in Africa It Will Run into These Two Problems', *Quartz Africa*, 14 January. Available online: https://qz.com/africa/589907/no-matter-where-netflix-goes-in-africa-it-will-run-into-these-two-problems/ (accessed 19 July 2020).

Lobato, R. (2009), 'The Politics of Digital Distribution: Exclusionary Structures in Online Cinema', *Studies in Australasian Cinema*, 3 (2): 167–78.

Lobato, R. (2010), 'Creative Industries and Informal Economies: Lesson from Nollywood', *International Journal of Cultural Studies*, 13 (4): 337–54.

Lotz, A. D. (2021), 'In Between the Global and the Local: Mapping the Geographies of Netflix as a Multinational Service', *International Journal of Cultural Studies*, 24 (2): 195–215.

'Made by Africans, Watched by the World' (2020), *The Media Online*, 24 June. Available online: https://themediaonline.co.za/2020/06/made-by-africans-watched-by-the-world/ (accessed 19 January 2021).

McDonald, K., and D. Smith-Rowsey (2016), 'Introduction', in K. McDonald. and D. Smith-Rowsey (eds), *The Netflix Effect: Technology and Entertainment in the 21st Century*, New York: Bloomsbury Academic, 1–12.

Magombe, V. (2006), ' "Africa Lives on the BBC" – Watershed or Blip?', *Global Media and Communication*, 2 (1): 119–23.

Mwansa, K. (2016), 'Netflix in Africa: Why Video-On-Demand Startups Will Still Flourish', *AFK Insider*, 8 January. Available online: http://afkinsider.com/109585/netflix-in-africa-why-video-on-demand-startups-will-still-flourish/ (accessed 19 July 2020).

Onyango, F. (2020), 'Why Netflix Is a Lifeline for African Film-makers', *The Guardian*, 7 October. Available online: https://www.theguardian.com/film/2020/oct/07/netflix-lifeline-for-african-film-makers-fred-onyango (accessed 1 December 2020).

Renouf, M. (2021), '10 Best African Films Streaming on Netflix', *New African*, 6 April. Available online: https://newafricanmagazine.com/25663/ (accessed 14 July 2021).

Ritman, A. (2020), 'John Boyega Inks Netflix Deal for Slate of African Films', *Hollywood Reporter*, 10 March. Available online: https://www.hollywoodreporter.com/tv/tv-news/netflix-inks-deal-john-boyegas-upperroom-productions-1283371/ (accessed 3 July 2021).

Sawadogo, B. (2017), 'African Film Distribution in the United States: Assessment and Prospective Analysis', *Sanaa Journal*, 2 (1): 21–6.

Seabi, M. (2020), 'Netflix Celebrates Africa Month with Made in Africa Collection', *Netflix.com*, 7 May. Available online: https://about.netflix.com/en/news/netflix-celebrates-africa-month-with-made-in-africa-collection (accessed 8 June 2021).

Sharma, S. (2016), 'Netflix and the Documentary Boom', in K. McDonald and D. Smith-Rowsey (eds), *The Netflix Effect: Technology and Entertainment in the 21st Century*, New York: Bloomsbury Academic, 143–54.

Vickers, S. (2020), 'Zimbabwe's *Cook Off*: How an $8,000 Romcom Made It to Netflix', *BBC*, 24 June. Available online: https://www.bbc.co.uk/news/world-africa-52983564 (accessed 7 February 2021).

Index

Note: Figures are indicated by page number followed by "f". Endnotes are indicated by the page number followed by "n" and the endnote number e.g., 20 n.1 refers to endnote 1 on page 20.

Abudu, Mo 192
Acar, Asli Irmak 113–14
Acevedo-Muñoz, Ernesto R. 57
AcFun 90
ACG fans 90, 92, 96, 100, 103
action films 6
Adejunmobi, Moradewun 4, 172 n.2, 178, 179
Adetiba, Kemi 199
Afolayan, Kunle 163, 179
AfricaFilms.tv 154, 158
African films 8–10, 153 n.1, 197
    cinema online 157–163
    digital democracy/digital divide 155–7
    digital revolution 151
    economic condition and film making 171–2
    as extended cinema 171
    formal circulation of 4
    Ghallywood video scene 179–183
    international distribution of 9
    Netflix effect 163–5
    Nollywood phenomenon 173–9
    online, precarity of 193–5
    storytellers in 171
    technology in 155–7
    video film auteurs 183–5
African Vibes (website) 199
AfricanMovieChannel.com (AMC) 178
Afrinolly 162–3
Ahalya (Ghosh, Sujoy 2015) 140
Akar, Serdar 114
Akhtar, Zoya 134, 137
Akser, Murat 8
Alea, Tomás Gutiérrez 53, 54, 55
Alfonso Cuarón 1, 48
Almeida, R. 33
Almodovar, Pedro 48

Alper, Emin 117
Amazon Prime Video 1–2, 8, 16, 28, 49, 71, 77, 116, 129, 130, 132, 134, 136–7, 140–1
    in Africa 154
    in India 125, 128–44
    in Turkey 116
Amour (Haneke, Michael 2012) 1
Angamaly Dairies (Lijo Jose Pellissery 2017) 140
Angola 160
Ankara 116, 118
Ansah, Kwah 180
anti-Hollywoodian mentality 39
anti-piracy, *see* piracy
App Annie 128
Apple 16, 50
    App Store 160
archive fever 41–2
Argentina 48, 52
'art Cinema' 1, 5
art film 4, 179, 197
artificial intelligence 33, 62
Asian emoticons 95 n.5
Ataman, Kutlug 118
Athique, Adrian 139 n.4
Atkinson, Justine 9
Atlantics (Diop, Mati 2019) 192, 197, 199, 200
Australia 6, 17, 18, 161
Australian Federation Against Copyright Theft (AFACT) 17
the Auteurs 1, 53, 183
'autonomous distributors' 25, 26
Avezzù 77 n.18
AVMS (Audiovisual Media Services) 73, 76
AVMSD (EU's Audiovisual Media Services Directive) 76

Index

AVOD (advertisement-led video on demand) 143–4
Ayagolu, Emma 182

Babel (Iñarritú, Alejandro González 2006) 60
Back to the Future (Zemeckis, Robert 1985) 40
Bakhtin, Mikhail 97, 98
Balaji Telefilms ALT Balaji 126
Banerjee, Dibakar 134
Barefoot in the Park (Simon, Neil 1967) 136
Barlet, Olivier 173, 174, 176, 177, 179
Barra, L. 72 n.9
Barrot, Pierre 181
Barthes, Roland 101
Baschiera, Stefano 7, 69 n.1, 77 n.18, 121
baska cinema 114
Battle of Chile (Guzmán, Patricio 1975) 56
Baxu and the Giants (Schott, Florian 2019) 199
Beast of No Nation (Fukunaga, Cary Joji 2015) 197
Before the Sunrise 182
Bekolo, Jean-Pierre 159
Benim Çocuğum (Candan, Can 2013) 119–120
Benjamin, Walter 42, 43
Benvenuto Presidente! (Milani, Riccardo 2013) 80 n.21
Bernal, Gael García 53, 58
Between Two Hurricanes (Colina, Enrique 2003) 55
Betz, M. 36
Bezos, Jeff 129
BFI Statistical Yearbook 19 n.2
Bharti Airtel 125
Bhatia, Sidharth 133, 144
Bhowmik, Someshwar 133 n.3
Bianca come il latte, rossa come il sangue (Campiotti, Giacomo 2013) 80 n.21
The Big Bang Theory (sitcom 2007–19) 139
Big Bazaar 129
Bilibili 90, 91, 99, 100, 102
Birri, Fernando 53, 56
Bisschoff, Lizelle 9
BitTorrent 16, 18, 22, 25, 33, 41
BKM 109, 110, 113, 114

BL (Boy's Love) 97 n.10, 99
Black Butler (Ōtani, Kentarō and Satō, Keiichi 2014) 103
Blackberry smartphones 159, 163
Blood & Water (drama series) 189, 192
Blue Wave (Dalga, Mavi 2013) 118, 119
BluTV 110, 116, 117, 121
Bodó, B. 22, 23, 31, 32, 33
Bollywood 5, 40, 127, 132, 134, 136, 137, 182–3
Bombay Talkies (anthology film) 134
Bongowood (Tanzania) 156, 160, 172, 182
Bose, Nandana 8
Bourdieu, P. 42
Boyega, John 192
Boyut Film Movie 113
Brazil 52
  group MKO 36
  pornochanchada films 41
Brill publishers 47–8
broadcast streaming 2, 4
broadcasters 2, 71, 80, 117–19, 125 n.1, 128, 160, 196
Brotherhood of Blades (Yang, Lu 2014) 91
bullet screen 89, 92
Bungo Stray Dogs Dead Apple (Igarashi, Takuya 2018) 96–9, 102, 103f, 104f, 105
Buni.tv 158–9
The Burial of Kojo (Bazawule, Blitz) 192, 199
Burke, Graham 17
Burkina Faso 9, 173, 183–5
Butterflies (Karaçelik, Tolga 2018) 116

Caffe sospeso (Iannucci, Fulvio and Santos, Roly 2017) 80 n.21
Çakarel, Efe 1, 50–1, 55
Çamaşırhane Film 113
Cameroon (Collywood) 159, 172, 181–2
Canada 111, 161
Cannes Film Festival 58, 71 n.6
Cardoso, G. 33
carnivalesque experience 97–8
Cartel Land (Heineman, Mathew 2015) 59
Castro, Fidel 53
censorship 3, 8, 18, 38, 99, 109
  ideological/religious 38

in India 133, 135–6, 138
of streaming content 136
in Turkey 111, 117, 120, 121
Ceylan, Nuri Bilge 116, 118
Chan, Jackie 91
Chandra, Vikram 131
The Charcoal Worker (Alea, Tomás Gutiérrez 1954) 53
Chef (Menon, Raja Krishna 2017) 136
Chen, Xiyuan 99
Chen, Yuanyuan 8
Chhabra, Aseem 132, 134, 137, 142
Chico and Rita (Errando, Tono, Mariscal, Javier and Trueba, Fernando 2010) 54
China 3, 95, 99 n.11, 100 n.13, 130
   danmaku commenting 8, 89–91 (*see also* danmaku)
   digital space 127
   internet culture 92
   netizens 96 n.8
   video streaming platforms 89–91, 100
   virtual interactive viewing environment 91–4
   VoD sites 8
Chinaphiles 25, 26
Chopsticks (Yardi, Sachin 2019) 136
Chronic (Franco, Michel 2015) 59
Cidade de Deus (Meirelles, Fernando and Lund, Katia 2002) 40
Ciliv, Serra 118
Cinema Escapist (US website) 199
Cinema Law 113, 117
cinema, *see also* world cinema
   in Africa 152
   in Cuba 53–4
   cultural impact of 5
   global flow of 6
   in global SVOD services 8
   in India 125
   in Italy 79–82
   in Latin America 51
   in non-domestic online markets 3
   non-official circulation of 31
   public and plural 39
   and social media 8
   transformations in face of streaming distribution 6
   in Turkey 109

western cultural production domination 6
cinematographic niches 37
cinephile
   features of 38–9
   file-sharing 31
   formalities of 35–6
   indexing and categorization 41
   Torrent groups 41
Cissé, Souleymane 152
CMYLMZ production company 113
Code Phoenix (Phoenix Code) (2005) 183–4
Coffee for All (Iannucci, Fulvio and Santos, Roly 2017) 80 n.21
Collywood 181–182
comedy films 6, 54, 60, 112, 114, 135, 136, 193, 200
The Comfort of Strangers (Schrader, Paul 1990) 80–1
The Comidark Films 110
Confessions of a Dog 27
content 16, 132
   African audiovisual 151–155, 160
   circulation of 18
   distribution 32
   film cultures and 126
   global and local 6
Cook Off (Brickhill, Tomas 2017) 192, 193, 197
copyright 18, 24, 33, 42
   protection 17–18, 41, 90, 181
Cortesie per gli ospiti (Schrader, Paul 1990) 80 n.21, 80–1
Crawford, Rebecca 8
creators 42, 105, 158, 196
Crisp, Virginia 7, 33
critics 38, 41, 42, 59, 118, 182, 198
crowdfunding 109, 110, 118–122
Cuarón, Alfonso 48, 53
Cuba 52–4, 58, 60
   Curzon Home Cinema 57
   films 55–6
   Mexico and 57
   MUBI 57
Cucco, M. 69 n.4
Cunningham, Stuart 4, 16, 33, 39, 121
curator 42

Index

MKO Curatorship 39–41
  process and cyber-cinephilia 36–9
The Curious Case of Benjamin Button
  (Fincher, David 2008) 40
Curzon Home Cinema 49–51, 54–9,
  60, 62
  carefully curated content 54–9
  flat payment subscription model 49
  pay-per-view options 49
cyber-cinephilia, curatorial process
  and 36–9
'cybertopia' 2, 48, 190–1, 194

Dadak, Zeynep 118
Danaher, B. 18
danmaku 89–90, 95 n.5, 96–7, 102, 105
  carnivalesque experience 97–8
  celebration of postmodern and internet
    culture 94
  'commenting' 8
  in China 89–91
  internet slang 95–6
  otaku subculture and
    nationalism 98–100
  recreation of meanings 101–4
Dao, Abdoulaye 183
Das, Vir 135, 136
'data-driven algorithmic culture' 77
Days of Grace (Grout, Everardo Valerio
  2011) 60
De Kosnik, A. T. 33
Dearham, Mike 161
Delhi Crime (web series 2019) 135, 136
Demirkubuz, Zeki 116, 117
Denmark 57
Dennison, Stephanie 51
di Donatello, David 80
Diallo, Boubakar 183, 184
Diamonds in the Sky (Afolayan, Kunle
  2018) 199
diasporic markets 6, 52, 174, 178
Diawara, Manthia 174, 180
DiCaprio, Leonardo 189
digital
  access and distribution 48
  film archives 31
  legislation 33
  native 92, 95 n.4

technology 38, 48, 52, 95 n.4, 143,
  152, 162
digital piracy, *see* piracy
Dijital Sanatlar 113
Direct Download Link (DDL) sites 22, 25
disintermediation 3, 4, 6, 7, 153, 190
  process of 2, 16
distributors 16, 18, 23, 25–6, 91, 110, 113,
  117, 177, 181
  informal 27
  in UK 20–2
District 9 (Blomkamp, Neill 2009) 200
dittoTV 125, 127
Dixon, Wheeler Winston 4, 194
Dominican Republic 52
Dongmo, Stéphanie 181–182
drama 6
D'Souza, Frank 126, 130, 132, 143, 144
DStv Catch-Up 160
DStv 157, 160, 161

East Asian cinema 26
Eastern Africa Submarine Cable System
  (EASSy) 156
Eastern Legends forum 25, 26
Ebot, Agbor Gilbert 182
Ecumenopolis: City without Limits (Azem,
  Imre 2012) 120
The Elder Scrolls V: Skyrim (video
  game) 96 n.8
El Fani, Nadia 184
Elwes, Cassian 17
Erdogan, Tayyip 111
Erdogan, Yilmaz 109, 110, 113, 114
Eros International Plc 127 n.2
Eros Now 127, 131
Escalante, Amat 53, 58
Eskiya (*The Bandit* 1997) 112
Espinosa, Julio García 53
EU
  audiovisual sector 71
  AVMS (Audiovisual Media Services) 73
  cultural policies and protective
    measures 72
  DSM (Digital Single Market) policies 73
  membership 112
  non-national content 75
  SVOD revenue growth 71

Europe 111, 156, 163
    Indie filmmakers 118
    Netflix in 69
    screen industry sector 72
European Audiovisual Observatory (EAO) 73 n.11, n.12, 74 n.14, 75
European cinema 8
Ezra, Elizabeth 48
Ez Firiyam Tu Mayî Li Ci (Arslan, Müjde 2012) 120

Farr, Brittany 196
Farrell, James 131
Federation of Indian Chambers of Commerce and Industry (FICCI) 2018 report 128, 143
Fespaco festival 184
For a Few Dollars More (Leone, Sergio 1965) 80 n.21, 81
Fida Film 112
Fifty (Bandele, Biyi 2014) 163
56.com 90
The Figurine (Afolayan, Kunle 2009) 179
Fikir Sanat 113
film budgets in UK 19
film clubs 38, 115
film distribution
    economic consequences of 18
    ecosystem 22, 27
    existing power structures, challenge to 18
    informal 15
    media distribution 31
    traditional methods 16
film piracy, *see also* informal online film distribution; piracy
    effects on international box office 18
    from mid-2000s 32
    in 1980s 31–2
    official scenario, impact on 32
    transitional period 2010–14 32–3, 34
    years after 2015 33
FilmStruck 4
Fiore (Giovannesi, Claudio 2016) 80 n.21
The First Princess in the World (music album 2014) 99 n.11
Fisher, Alexander 4, 9

A Five Star Life (Tognazzi, Maria Sole 2013) 80 n.21
Flipkart 128, 129
Forgive Us Our Debts (Morabito, Antonio 2018) 80 n.21
Fongogo 119
formal distribution 4, 7, 15, 21, 23, 27, 31, 33, 190
    systems 15, 33
formal film industry 15
formal gatekeepers 7, 27
    within informal networks 15
Franca: Chaos and Recreation (Carrozzini, Francesco 2016) 80 n.21
France 72, 75, 159, 197
Francophone TV 158, 175
Frida (Taymor, Julia 2002) 58
Friends (sitcom 1994–2004) 139

Galloway 77 n.18
Games of Thrones (TV series 2011–19) 128
Gandhi, Gaurav 130
Garritano, Carmela 179, 181
Garrone, Matteo 80
gatekeeping
    and censorship 3
    informal online 22, 26
    and tastemaking 7
generation X 91 n.2
generation Y 91 n.2, 92
Germany 72, 75, 129
Geronimo Stilton (children animation) 79 n.20
Ghana (Ghallywood) 3, 9, 156, 172–4, 176–8, 183, 197
    video scene 179–183
Ghoul (miniseries) 135
Giallo films 41
Glamour Girls (TV series) 177
Glance, David 51, 62
global content and local content 6
global screens, western cultural production domination on 6
glocalization 198
The Golden Dream (Quemada-Díez, Diego 2013) 59
Goldsmith, Kenneth 43
Gómez, Guillermo del Toro 48, 53

Gómez, Sara 54
Gomez-Uribe, C. 78
Google 17, 28
Google Play 151
The Goonies (Donner, Richard 1985) 40
Gopalan, Lalitha 133 n.3
GORA (Sorak, Ömer Faruk 2004) 112
Gray, Herman 196
The Great Beauty (Sorrentino, Paolo 2013) 80 n.21, 81 n.22, n.23
Grece, C. 72 n.10, 75 n.17
Greek alphabet 95 n.5
Grove, Elliot 20
Guantanamera (Tabío, Juan Carlos and Alea, Gutiérrez 1995) 54
Güeros (Ruizpalacios, Alonso 2015) 59
Gunay, Gaye 120
Gunjan Saxena: The Kargil Girl (Sharma, Sharan 2020) 134
Gupta, Sanjay 127
Guzmán, Chilean Patricio 56

Habana Blues (Zambrano, Benito 2005) 54
Haneke, Michael 1
Hangzhou Saga 91
Hastings, Reed 128, 130–1, 139
Hatfield, Jackie 172
Hausa films 174
Havana Motor Club (Perlmutt, Brent-Jorgen 2014) 55
Havana-set film 56
Hayek, Salma 53
Haynes, Jonathan 172, 200
Heli (Escalante, Amat 2013) 58
Hennebelle, Guy 39
Herbert, Daniel 4
Here Comes the Devil (Bogliano, Adrián García 2012) 60
Heritage Africa (Ansah, Kwaw 1988) 180
Hessler, Jennifer 4
Higbee, W. 69 n.3
Hill, John 69 n.4
Hjort, M. 69 n.3
Hollywood 6, 22, 40, 53, 83–4, 112, 139, 162, 181, 182, 193
  in postcolonial times 39
  vs 'the rest' 5
home video

emergence in informal circulation 32
viewing art film 4
Honda, Toru 98
Hong Kong films 183
horror films 6, 40
Hosanagar, Kartik 130–1, 139, 142
Hotstar 125, 126, 127, 131, 135, 139, 142
House for Swap (1983) 54
House of Cards (TV show 2013–18) 131
humour 96 n.7, 97, 98
Hunt, N. 78

I am Cuba (Kalatozov, Mikhail 1964) 55
I Flew You Stayed (Arslan, Müjde 2012) 120
ibakatv 178
IBERMEDIA 54
Igbo 174
Il giovane favoloso (Martone, Mario 2014) 80 n.21
Il racconto dei racconti (Garrone, Matteo 2015) 80 n.21, 81 n.22
Iñarritú, Alejandro González 48, 53, 60
independent film sector
  in the United States 17
independent filmmaker, in UK 21, 55, 117, 182
India 3
  Amazon Prime Video 125, 128–44
  app-based services 129
  barriers and challenges of OTT 141–2
  cinephilia and film spectatorship 132–141
  as disruptive innovators 130–2
  e-commerce market 128
  Netflix 125, 128–44
  online streaming revolution 125
  OTTs, rise and growth of 8, 126–9
  streaming wars 129–130
Indie films in Turkey 111, 114, 115, 118, 121
IndieGoGo 119
IndieWire (website) 19
indigenous African language 182
Inflame (Ozcelik, Ceylan 2017) 118, 119
Influx (Vullu, Luca 2016) 80 n.21
'informal distribution ecosystem' 22, 27
informal distribution 15, 19, 24, 27, 31, 42, 193–194

economic consequences of 18
existing power structures,
    challenge to 18
informal online
    circulation 16
    film distribution 15, 22
    formal influence in 19–22
    gatekeepers 22–7
    informal online gatekeepers 22–7
    media distribution 31
    power and influence in 15
informal sharing 31, 32, 39
Inside Edge (TV series 2017) 130, 134
*Instituto Cubano del Arte e Industria
    Cinematográficos* (ICAIC) 53, 54
Instructions Not Included (Derbez, Eugenio
    2013) 60
intellectual property rights 33
'intermediary distributors' 25, 26
intermediation
    new forms of 3, 7
    process of 16
internet 1, 2, 8, 33, 35, 41, 43, 94–5
    in Africa 151, 156–7, 165, 198
    culture 8
    digital technologies and 32
    in India 125
    slang 95–6
    in Turkey 116
Iordanova, Dina 4, 16, 33, 121
iQiyi 90 n.1, 91, 100, 127
Ireland 7, 62
    Amazon Prime Video in 49
    Netflix in 49–51
iROKO.tv 162–4, 165, 178, 179
Issakaba (Imasuen, Lancelot Oduwa) 177
Istanbul 116
    Indie Film Festival 118
Italian cinema 8
Italian Films 79, 80 n.21
Italy 69, 72, 75
    cinema in Netflix UK catalogue 79
    Netflix catalogue 72 n.9, 75
    SVOD service 72
The Ivory Game (Davidson, Kief
    and Ladkani, Richard
    2016) 189
Izmir 116

Jabangwe, Godwin 165
Jabong.com 129
Jacobs, Olu 182
Japan 95 n.5, 96 n.7, 99 n.12, 100, 129
    ACG (animation, comic and game)
        websites 89
    manga (comics) 97 n.10
    video streaming website 90
Jauja (Alonso, Lisandro 2014) 57
Jedlowski, Alessandro 164, 175
Jerusalema (Ziman, Ralph 2008) 159, 189
Joji (Pothan, Dileesh 2021) 140
The Journey of Flower (TV series
    2015) 96 n.9
Julie et Roméo (Julie and Romeo)
    (2011) 182

Kaboré, Gaston 183
Kalushi (Dube, Mandla 2016) 192, 199
Kaomoji 95 n.5
Karaçelik, Tolga 114, 116, 117
Kashyap, Anurag 131, 134, 135, 136
Kayan, Merve 118
Kelani, Tunde 172, 179
Kenya 155, 156, 160, 172, 197
'Keyki incident' 99 n.11
Kiley, Dan 93 n.3
King of Boys (Adetiba, Kemi 2018) 192
Kiswahili language 162
Koçer 119
Kouyaté, Dani 183
Kripalani, Nitesh 129, 132
Ku6 90
Kumbalangi Nights (Narayanan, Madhu
    C. 2019) 140
Kurdish filmmakers 109, 115, 119, 120, 121
kykNet 162

La Bamba (Valdez, Luis 1987) 40
La coppia dei campioni (Base, Giulio
    2016) 80 n.21
La grande bellezza (*The Great Beauty*,
    Sorrentino, Paolo 2013) 80 n.21, 81
    n.22, n.23
Lakatos, Z. 22, 23, 32
Landrián, Nicolás Guillén 55
Last Week Tonight with John Oliver (TV
    show 2014–) 135

Latin American cinema 7, 47, 51, 78
  Argentina 52
  Cuba 53–4
  in film festivals 48
  in Ireland and UK 7
  Mexico 52–3
Laxmmi Bomb (Lawrence, Raghava 2020) 134
Le Journal du Jeudi 183
L'estate addosso (Muccino, Gabriele 2016) 80 n.21
legal media distribution 31
legal vs illegal dualism 33
The Legend of Qin (Shen, Robin 2014) 91
Leopardi (Martone, Mario 2014) 80 n.21
Lequeret, Elisabeth 184
LETV 90
Like Water for Chocolate (Arau, Alfonso 1994) 53
Lim, S. H. 69 n.3
Lionheart (Nnaji, Genevieve 2018) 164, 199
Living in Bondage (Rapu, Chris Obi) 174, 177
Lobato, Ramon 4, 6, 15, 70 n.5, 73 n.11, 153 n.1, 190
local content 130–2, 155, 159
  and global content 6
local/global dialectics 6
L'Or des Youngas (The Youngas Gold) (2006) 183–4
Lora-Mungai, Marie 159
Los Bastardos (Escalante, Amat 2008) 58
Lotz 83 n.24, 189 n.1
Love Brewed in the African Pot (Ansah, Kwah 1980) 180
low-budget films 21
  challenges faced by 20–1
  in UK 20
Lucia (Solas, Humberto 1968) 55
Luna, Diego 58
'lurkers' 25, 26
Lust Stories (anthology film 2018) 134, 137

Mad Max (Miller, George 1979) 40
Madd Entertainment 113
Major, Anne 4
Malhotra, Vikram 136
'malltiplex' 139 n.4

Mambéty, Djibril Diop 152, 194
Manovich, Lev 62
manga comics 97 n.10
marginal cinemas 3, 4, 190–1
Marker, Chris 56
Marquez, Gabriel García 56
Martian language 95
Martone, Mario 80
Mattelart, Tristan 18, 42
Maughan, Philip 50
Mauritius 160
Mawela, Calvo 163
McCulloch, Gretchen 95
McDonald, Kevin 3, 191
McKenzie, J. 18
McLelland, Mark 97 n.10
Mehta, Monika 133 n.3
Meilli, Angela 7
Même pas mal/No Harm Done (Martin 2013) 184
Memories of Underdevelopment (Alea, Tomás Gutiérrez 1968) 55
Mendes Moreira De Sa, V. 31
Meng, B. 18
Mexico 3, 47, 52–3, 56, 60, 63
  film industry 52
  high-profile Mexican cinema 53
  melodramas and rural-based musicals 52
Meyer, Birgit 180
Miku, Hatsune 99 n.11, n12
Minhaj, Hasan 135
Mirzapur (web series 2018) 135
Miss Bala (Naranjo, Gerardo 2011) 60
Miyano, Mamoru 96
MKO 36, 38
  curatorship 39–41
M-Mobile 160
M-Net 160–1, 194, 198 n.2
  African Film Library 4
mobile phones 128, 135, 156, 157, 160, 163, 175, 177
Mohd, Fitri Mansor 91 n.2
Moi, Zaphira/I, Zaphira (2012) 184
Money Heist (web series) 63
Money Trap 110
In the Mood for Love (Karwai, Wong 2000) 1, 55

MOP (mop.com) 95 n.6
Morocco 173 n.3
Morris, Wade 77
MUBI 1, 4, 7, 49–51, 60, 63, 116, 154, 157
  carefully curated content 54–9
  flat payment subscription model 49
  pay-per-view options 49
Muccino, Gabriele 80
multinational streaming services 5
Mungoshi, Jesesi 193
My Child (Candan, Can 2013) 119–120
My Way (Panizzi, Antongiulio 2016) 80 n.21
Myntra 129

Nacro, Fanta Régina 183
Nagib, Lúcia 84
Naijapals.com 177, 178
Naijarules.com 177, 178
Nairobi Half Life (Gitonga, David "Tosh") 159
Nan, Cao 95 n.5
Nandy, Pritish 135
Nandy, Rangita 137–8
Narco Cultura (Schwarz, Shaul 2013) 60
Narcos (TV series 2015–17) 63, 131
Narcos: Mexico (TV series 2018–) 63
Naspers 160, 161, 163
national cinema 3, 8, 38, 39, 69–70
Neria (Dangarembga, Tsitsi 1991) 193
Netflix 1, 6, 7, 8, 10, 16, 28, 49–51, 109, 116
  in Africa 151, 162–5
  and Africa business model 189 n.1, 195–7
  algorithms 6, 59–60
  average share of EU 75
  brand image on global tastemaking in African films 197–201
  in British and Italian audiovisual markets 70–2
  business model 195–7
  Cannes Film Festival and 71
  in European market 8, 73–5
  geo-blocking 60–1
  homepage organization 78
  in India 125, 128–44
  Italian cinema for 79–82
  Long Tail business model 195

'national' and SVOD catalogues 76–9
non-domestic African film markets 189
'portal-as-brand' strategy 83
'socio-technical assemblages' 77–8
In Turkey 116, 121
UK catalogue 79
UK, Italian films in 8, 79–80, 197
The Netflix Effect (McDonald, Kevin and Smith-Rowsey, Daniel 2016) 3, 163–6, 191
'Netflix Quantum Theory' 78 n.19
New African (Music album) 199
New Statesman (magazine) 50
niche markets 6
Niconico 90, 99 n.12, 99–100
Nigeria 3, 9, 151, 153, 156, 159, 160, 164, 166, 174, 175, 176, 177, 182, 184 n.4, 192, 197
Njoku, Jason 164
Nnaji, Genevieve 164, 196
Nollywood 5, 9, 151, 152, 153, 162 n.2, 163, 164, 172, 173–9, 181, 182, 193–194, 197, 200, 201
non-domestic online markets, world cinema in 3
North American Free Trade Agreement 52
Novi Digital Entertainment 127
nuke rules 24 n.4
Numero Zero: The Roots of Italian Rap (Bini, Enrico 2015) 80 n 21
Nykaa 129

Obiaya, Ikechukwu 173, 176
October 1 (Afolayan, Kunle 2014) 163
Ogunde, Hubert 173
Okome, Onookome 172 n.2, 175
Oladunjoye, Tunde 184 n.4
Olgac, Bilge 109
online cinema 8
  communities and offline cinephilia groups 38
  in co-national and transnational contexts 6
  distribution formats 3
  of Indie films Turkey 118
  on international box office 18
  and offline cinephilia groups 38
  publishing 48

rhetoric of disintermediation 6
technology 1
online distribution
  in co-national and transnational contexts 6
  distribution formats 3
online technology 1
Onur Saylak 114
Onyango, Fred 189, 198, 201
Orange Is the New Black (web series) 196
Orji, Zack 182
Oscar winning film 55
Otaku subculture and nationalism 98–100
'Ouagawood' 183
Ouédraogo, Idrissa 183, 194
Ouoro, Justin 183
Our Souls at Night (Batra, Ritesh) 136
Out 1: noli me tangere (Rivette, Jacques 1971) 37
Out 1: Specter (Rivette, Jacques 1974) 38
Overbergh, Ann 182
over-the-top (OTT) platforms 8, 125 n.1
  app-based services 129
  barriers and challenges of 141–2
  cinephilia and film spectatorship 132–41
  as disruptive innovators 130–2
  e-commerce market 128
  in India 125
  rapid expansion of 8
  rise and growth, in India 126–9
  streaming wars 129–130
Oya, Berkun 114
Ozbatur, Zeynep 118
Ozcelik, Ceylan 118, 119
Ozen Film 112

Park, Gezi 116, 119, 121
Patagonia 57
Patriot Act (TV show 2018–) 135
Peace Offering (2010) 180
peer-to-peer (P2P) concept 5, 7, 21, 23, 32, 34–5
  in African countries 151
  sharing 5, 7
  technologies 34–5
Per qualche dollaro in pi u (Leone, Sergio 1965) 80 n.21, 81
Peter Pan syndrome 93 n.3

Petty, Sheila 9
Phi (web series) 117
Pinochet, Augusto 56
piracy 15, 32, 38, 153 n.1, *see also* film piracy; informal online film distribution
  anti-piracy 17
  effects of 17–18
  spectre of 17–19
Pitt, Brad 40
polycentrism 84
post-internet cinephilia 37
Potato Potahto (Frimpong-Manso, Shirley 2017) 192
Powers, D. 77
PPStream 90
PPTV 90
The President (Bekolo, Jean-Pierre 2015) 159
PricewaterhouseCoopers (PwC) 126
Priego, Ernesto 48
Pritish Nandy Communications (PNC) 135, 137
producers 9, 17, 31, 42, 118, 120, 184, 190
prosumption 9, 151, 156
public and plural cinemas 39
PuhuTV 110, 116, 117, 121

Queen of Katwe (Nair, Mira 2016) 199
Queen Sono (Lediga, Kagiso 2020–present) 189, 190, 192, 199

Radio and Television Supreme Council (RTÜK) 115
Rancheras (music of Mexico) 52
Ranker (website) 200, 201
Re, Valentina 7, 69 n.1
Recep Ivedik (series of comedy films) 112
reintermediation 7, 16, 190
  process of 2
Reliance Industries, Jio 125, 128
Renouf, Michael 199
Resgate (Fonseca, Mickey 2019) 192
Reygadas, Carlos 53
Rimetti a noi i nostri debiti (Morabito, Antonio 2018) 80 n.21
Riverwood (Kenya) 172

Rivette, Jacques 37
Roberto Saviano: uno scrittore sotto scorta (Diliberto, Pierfrancesco 2016) 80 n.21
Rock, Holy 174
Roma (Cuaron, Alfonso 2018) 1
Rosen, P. 69 n.2
Roth, Tim 59
Rowden, Terry 48
Russian alphabet 95 n.5
Ryan, M. D. 6

Sacred Games (web series) 131, 134–5, 137, 138f
Sairat (Manjule, Nagraj 2016) 140
Salvador Allende (Guzmán, Patricio 2004) 56
Sangaré, Ibrahim 175
Sanogo, Aboubakar 182
Scarlata, A. 73 n.11
'the Scene' 7, 23, 94, 98, 112
  release groups 23, 24, 25
Schwarz, Shaul 60
Sea Cable System (Seacom) 156
Sembene, Ousmane 152, 161, 194, 198 n.2
Senegal 156
Sense8 137
Shadow (web series) 164
Shakuntala Devi: The Human Computer (Menon, Anu 2020) 134
Sharf, Zack 100 n.13
Sharma, Sudeep 195, 196
Shaw, Deborah 51
Showmax 157, 163, 164
  in Africa 161–162
ShowTV 117
Silver, Jon 4
6.cn 90
Slam (Molaioli, Andrea 2017) 80 n.21
Slashdot.org 34
smartphones 128, 156, 162–3
Smith, Michael D. 3
Smith-Rowsey, Daniel 3, 191
Snapdeal 129
social networking sites 47
Sofia 183
Solás, Humberto 54

Son of Pink Panther (Edwards, Blake 1993) 80 n.21, 80–1
Soni (Ayr, Ivan 2018) 135
Sontag, Susan 37, 41
Sony Liv 131, 126
Sorrentino, Paolo 80
South Africa 153, 156, 159–61, 163–4, 166, 192, 197, 199
Spain 63, 72
Spanish-based fund IBERMEDIA 54
Spirited Away (Miyazaki, Hayao 2001) 100 n.13
Spuul streaming service 126
Srinivas, Lakshmi 139 n.5
Star India 127
Stone, Rob 61
Strawberry and Chocolate (Alea, Tomás Gutiérrez 1993) 54, 55
streaming media technologies 5
Subramaniam, Vijay 132
subscription video on demand (SVOD) 1–3, 5, 8, 69–73, 75–7, 81–3, 121, 141, 143, 191, 196
  in African countries 151
  in Europe 70
  global services 8
  revenue in 2020 71
  subscription revenues 71
Suburra (Sollima, Stefano 2015) 80 n.21, 81 n.23
Sugar Rush (Kasum, Kayode 2019) 200
supranational cinema 69–70
supranational institutions 2
surveillance tools market 33
Summer Time (Muccino, Gabriele 2016) 80 n.21
Swahili 182
Swiggy 129

Tabío, Juan Carlos 54
Taff Pictures 113
Tale of Tales (Garrone, Matteo 2015) 81 n.22
Tamaki, Saito 93
Tandaav (web series 2021) 136
Tango TV 159
Tanzania 156, 159, 160, 172, 182

Taratabong (Migliazzi and Bondi 2009) 80 n.21
Tartan Films 26–7
'tastemaking' and 'cultural perception' 7, 31–2, 189, 197, 199
Telang, Rahul 3
TeleGeography 156
Television and Cinema Movie Producers Association (TESİYAP) 110
television streaming 4, 32
Thakkar, Jenil 131, 142, 144
Third Window 27
Thornton, Niamh 7
Thugs of Hindustan (2018) 132
Tiny Times 3 (2014) 91
Tolga Karacelik 114, 117
Too Much Stress for My Heart (Lirosi, Ludovica 2015)
Torrent group databases 32–5, 38, 39, 41, 43
Toy Story 4 (2019) 100 n.13
TRACE TV 159
transactional video on demand (TVOD) 1, 70, 143
transnational cinema 69–70
Traoré, Apolline 184
Traoré, Issa 183
Traque à Ouaga?/Pursuit in Ouaga 183
Treffry-Goatley 156
Trevor Noah: Son of Patricia (2018) 135
'The True Cinema' 39–41
Tryon, Chuck 70
Tsotsi (Hood, Gavin 2005) 189
Tudou 90 n.1
Tumbbad (Barve, Rahi Anil 2018) 140
Tunga (musical animation) 165, 192
Turgut, Pelin 118
Turkey 110
  cinema deal with sensitive issues 109
  Cinema Law 117
  crowdfunding to online release 118–19
  film industry and distribution, history of 111–14
  Indie films in 111, 114, 115, 118, 121
  location based to online viewing 111–14
  online distribution 8, 109, 114–16
  social documentaries, platform for 119–121

The Turkish Cinema Exhibitors Association (SİSAY) 110
Turkish online distribution 8
Twitter 47, 59, 113, 116, 117
  open data research on 48

Uber 129
Uganda (Ugawood) 160, 172
UK (United Kingdom) 7, 8, 49, 60, 62, 129, 159, 164, 178, 189 n.1
  Amazon Prime Video in 49
  distribution 20
  film budgets in 19
  Italian cinema for 72, 79–82
  low/micro-budget film 20
  marketing of film 21
  median budget for 19 n.1
  Netflix catalogue 49–51, 72 n.9, 75
  production activity in 20
  SVOD service 72
Un fantôme dans la ville (Phantom in the City) (2009) 185
Una noche (2012) 56
A United Kingdom (Asante, Amma 2016) 197, 199
United States 17, 59, 60, 75, 90 n.1, 111, 129, 137–8, 141–2, 144, 159, 161, 163–4, 197, 199
Utku, Menderes 112

van Dijk, Arjan 47–8
Vatansever, Ali 117
Viacom18 129
Voot 126
Viaggio da sola (Tognazzi, Maria Sole 2013) 80 n.21
video film auteurs 183–5
video on demand (VoD) 70, 117, 151, 160, 194
  Chinese sites 8
  platform, in India 5, 125
  services 1, 194
Vimeo 116, 151, 157
Vitali, V. 69 n.3
Vizontele (Erdoğan, Yılmaz 2001) 112
Vocaloid (V-singer) 99 n.11, n.12
Voot 129, 131, 143

Waldfogel, J. 18
Walls, W. D. 18
Walt Disney Company 127
The Waiting List (Tabío, Juan Carlos 2000) 54
Warez Scene 23
Wayne, Michael L. 83
The Wedding Party (Adetiba, Kemi) 199
Welcome Mr. President! (Milani, Riccardo 2013) 80 n.21
Wenders, Wim 58
West Africa Cable System (WACS) 156
Western cultural production domination on global screens 6
Western emoticons 95 n.5
White, J. 80
Wikipedia 116
Willemen, P. 69 n.3
Winx (animation) 79 n.20
The Wire (TV series) 133
world cinema, *see also* cinema
  and art cinema 5–6
  global circulation of 5
  mainstream and non-mainstream media 39
  in non-domestic online markets 3
  transformations in face of streaming distribution 6
World Wide Web 34
Wu, Keyki 99 n.11

The XYZ Show (TV show) 159

Yamac Okur 119
Yellin, Todd 78
Yesilcam 111, 114, 115
Yildirim, Muzaffer 112
Yilmaz, Cem 110, 113
Yoruba 173, 174, 175
Youku 90 n.1, 100, 101–2
Your Name (animation film 2016) 95, 96 n.7, 98, 100–102, 105
YouTube 5, 9, 58, 63, 93, 105, 116, 117, 127, 140, 151, 153, 155, 157, 161, 176–8

Zee Entertainment Enterprises Ltd (ZEEL) 127
  dittoTV 125, 126
Zida, Boubacar Sidnaba 183
Zimbabwe 160, 165, 192–3, 197

www.ingramcontent.com/pod-product-compliance
Lightning Source LLC
Chambersburg PA
CBHW062221300426
44115CB00012BA/2161